THE HISTORY 0F DARK CORNER

Campbell County,Georgia

John B. Bailey

THE HISTORY OF DARK CORNER

Campbell County, Georgia

John B. Bailey

Lillium Press

The History of Dark Corner
Campbell County, Georgia

Cover: Fred Finch Graphics.
www.fredricfinch.com

Editorial assistance: Richard F. Argo

ISBN: 978-0-692-24056-4

⚜ Lillium Press

Front Cover: The Kennedy House, built 1905.
Photo 2014 by John Bailey, author.
Back Cover: 1847 Campbell County Map. Federal Department of Archives, Morrow, Georgia

This book is dedicated to

those who value history:

to the historians who

left research for others -

and to those in the future

who will build upon it.

Contents

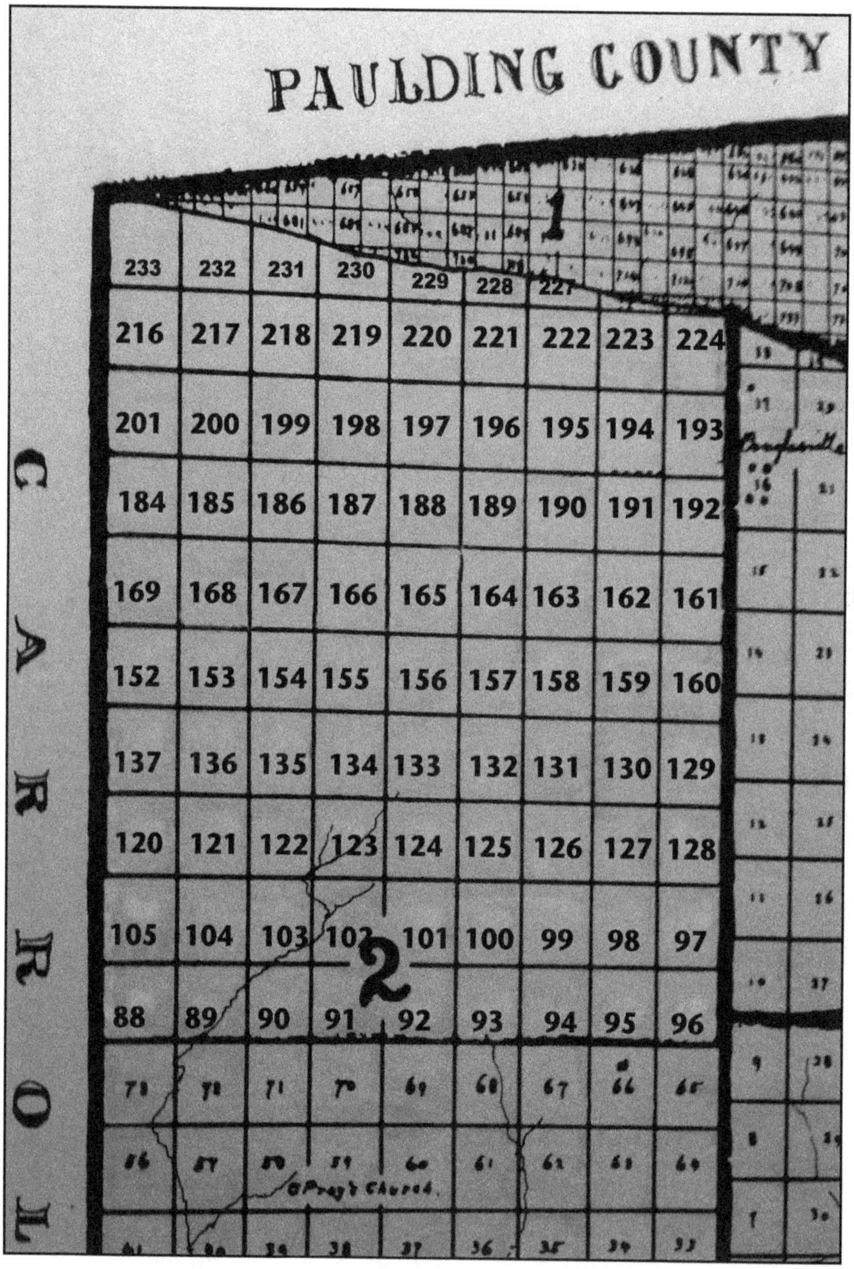

Dark Corner was a Georgia Militia District # 730 located in Section 2, District 5 of Campbell Co. which was formed in 1828. Dark Corner was also an early settlement centered around LL # 222. After 1870, the county name became Douglas and the GMD became #1259, Conners District. After 1870, lines between Carroll and Douglas changed and Dark Corner became a community extended into what *was* Carroll County to land lot # 206 which is in the edges of Villa Rica but still in Douglas County. Courtesy: Campbell County Courthouse, Fairburn, Georgia.

Acknowledgments

History fades as time travels into the future. Dark Corner was one of those places that has faded into the past.

This book is a documentation of an early town and her people who have faded into history. Now unveiled, 186 years later, you can be a witness of what it was like—in earlier times at the start of Dark Corner, Campbell County, later, Douglas County, Georgia.

When I first got the idea of writing a book about Dark Corner, Carl Lewis, a friend and historian, was working on a project about another lost town. The question kept coming up, "Where was the town of Dark Corner? Why was it called by that name?" While Carl worked on Pine Mt. Town, I started working on Dark Corner. When we came upon documents the other needed, we would exchange the information. Carl was not only the one to start me on this book, but he propelled me forward with his great interest and support.

Undertaking a project of writing a book of history, mounds of material must be gathered. First you needed to know the people who were part of that time period, and where they lived. I looked at deeds, land plats, family histories, cemeteries, census records, tax digests, Civil War records, and field reports. I searched court records, went to state and federal archives; searched postal records from the Library of Congress, conducted personal interviews with descendants of the early pioneers. Then all this information and material had to be put together, typed, checked, and rechecked. I tried the best I could to avoid errors and some probably slipped through. So if you find an error, make a note of it, or let me know, so I can fix it in the next edition.

I would like, foremost, to thank my wife, Elaine, for being my research partner. She made calls and set up appointments then accompanied me on many interviews and trips to the achieves, courthouses, and libraries, did all the typing and then set up the publishing of this book.

Thanks to those who gave great help: Carl Lewis, Sandy Whittington, Suzanne Sammons, Fred Finch, Richard Argo, Ray Henderson, Elaine Steere, Myra Wade, Carolyn Bell, Steve Mullinax, Johnny Camp, Harold Parr, Ed Thompson, Mildred Thompson, Alyce Dodson King, Charlie Dodson, Earl Albertson, Tommy Brookshire, Linda Willoughby Leatherman, Greg Dansby, Bertie Lee, Billie Lee, Martha Cole, Joe Bailey, Harry "Glen" Hay, Shiela Wallace at the Douglas County School System, Lisa Cooper - Every Now and Then, and Jeff Champion - Memories of Old Campbell/Douglas County.

A special thanks to: Jake Smith who helped with the monumental task of indexing and for his computer support and to Genna Smith for "bottling," the Dark Corner soil. Thanks to those at the Department of Federal and State Archives at Morrow, Georgia and to Nancy Connell at the Old Campbell County Courthouse and the Campbell County Historical Society and to the Douglas County Genealogical Society.

There are many others who gave tidbits of information that led me in the right direction to some fabulous find. Thanks to all for your help and support.

1

Early Roads Led to Dark Corner

There was a line between the Creek and Cherokee Nations from Buzzards Roost, running along the Tallapoosa Ridge, all the way to Alabama. Twenty-five miles on each side of that line these two tribes were to hunt together peacefully—a fifty mile neutral zone, later changed to five miles.

Sandtown Trail/Old Alabama Road:

Sandtown Trail —one of the earliest roads in the southeastern United States was originally an early path made by animals, then a trail used by the Native Americans when hunting or traveling. This main trail led from Sandtown and Buzzard's Roost Island. After crossing the Chattahoochee, it split, one trail going to Marietta and the other trail ran in a northwesterly direction to Skint Chestnut. Then this path ran north to Cedar Mt. Road where Dark Corner later sprang up, then West to Hixtown (later known as Villa Rica). This well-traveled thoroughfare continued on to Alabama to another intersecting trail also called the Sandtown Trail.

The early settlers coming into Georgia from the eastern part of the United States had few roads leading into and through this wilderness. This road then became the Old Alabama Road over which early white settlers traveled. It was, at one time, a stage coach route through this sections.

The draw of northwest Georgia was much enhanced when the secret of gold was discovered in the early 1800s. Then immigrants flooded the area. So many came that the Native Americans complained to the Governor. Years of dissension continued; finally the United States Government got involved. The solution was to just remove all Native Americans from their soil.

On January 8, 1821, at Indian Springs, the Creek Indians under Chief William McIntosh made a treaty ceeding the remainder of their Creek lands in Georgia. Some tribes volunteered to move to the reservations that the Government had set up. The Cherokees—who decided to stay and protest the removal, lost their right to their land in Georgia and were forcibly removed.

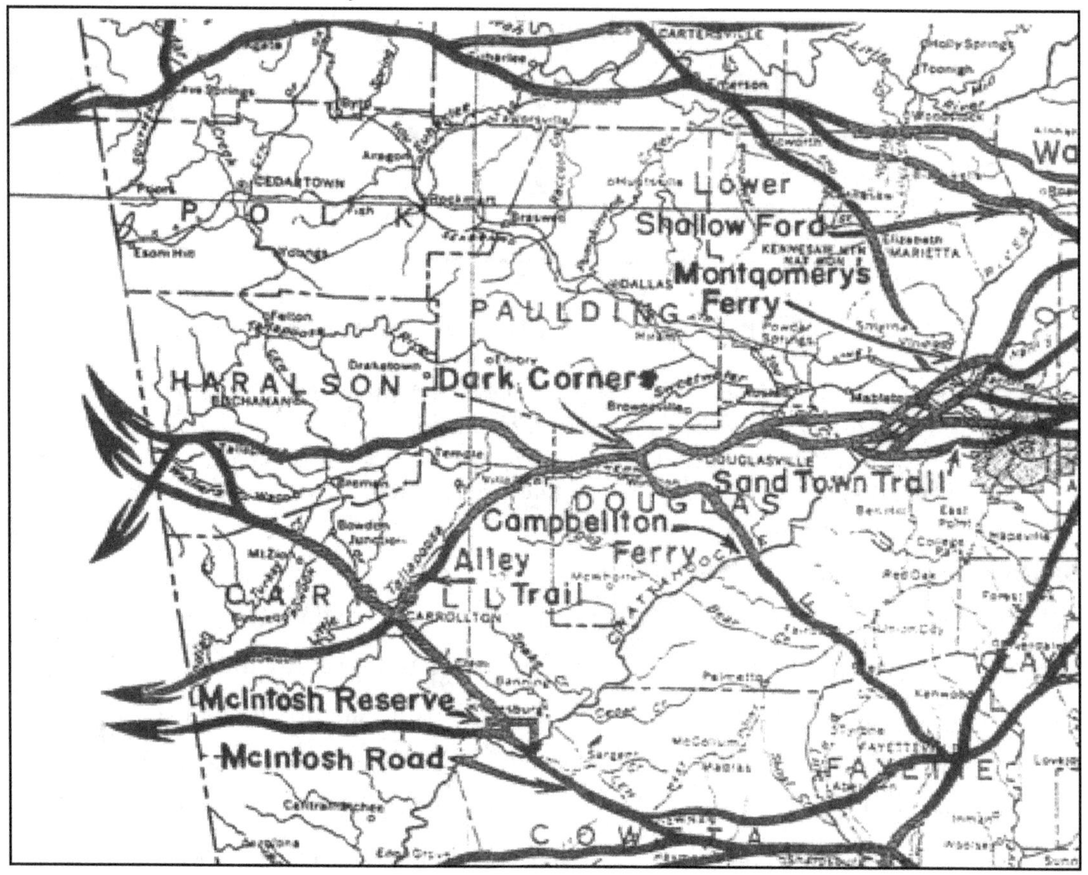

Georgia Early Roads & Trails, Circa 1730-1850

By a series of acts of the legislature, this land was organized into counties. By the act of February 12, 1825, the counties of Lee, Muscogee, Troup, Coweta and Carroll were created. Some of the land of these counties was distributed by George M. Troup, then governor of Georgia, in part by granting it to officers of the Army and State Militia.

This land was owned by the state. A Land Lottery System was set up. To distribute land through a Land Lot drawing, for a small fee, a qualified person could draw a lot consisting of 202 1/2 acres known as "farm lots." Later there was a drawing for "gold lots" consisting of 40 acres. This became a dream come true to the lucky people who drew a land lot in Georgia. The migration began; families came from North and South Carolina, Tennessee, Kentucky, and Virginia. Families traveled, many times, in groups, through Georgia on the Old Alabama Road.

Early pioneer families wanting a new and better life or an adventure began to prepare for the journey south. What to bring, what do we leave behind? Animals had to be fattened, wagons needed to be repaired, tools, supplies, and seeds were packed.

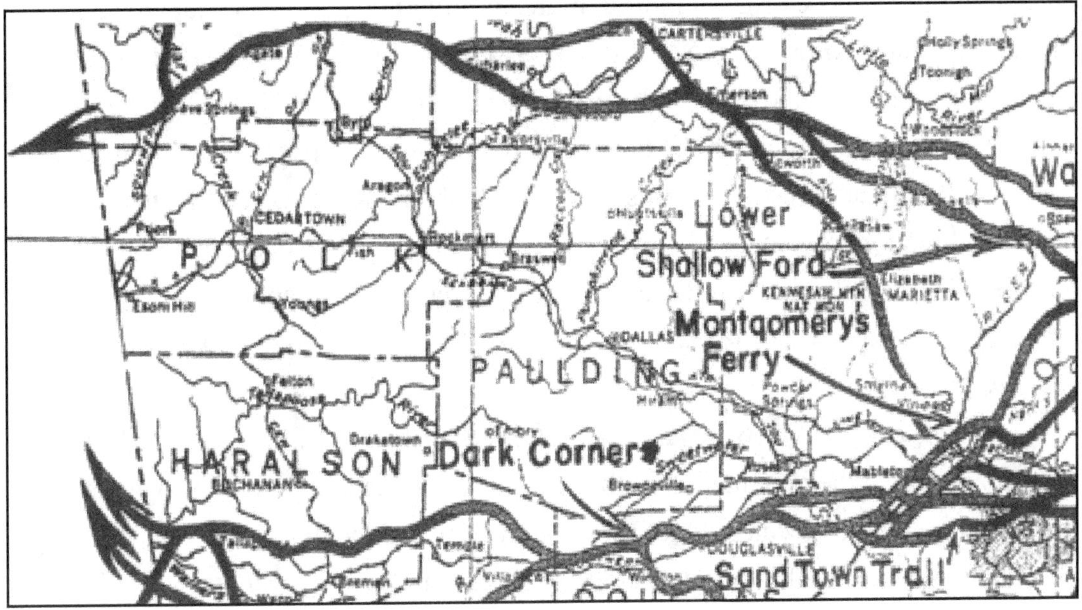

The Middle Alabama Road via Villa Rica sometimes known as the "Tallapoosa Road" and the "Sandtown Road" was a main thoroughfare of its day. This is the main route that brought new settlers into West Georgia and Eastern Alabama during the early 1800s.

Pots and pans and household goods were boxed. Everything was packed that they could not do without. The family piled into the wagon, sitting on top of all the supplies. The unnecessary things they wanted to bring must be left behind or they would have to walk. The wagons were pulled by oxen, mules, or horses. The journey began; a good day's travel was about fifteen to twenty miles a day.

Travel was slowed when crossing rivers, steep hills or when fallen trees blocked the wagon paths; sometimes travel slowed to only a few miles per day. Stopping for meals or to rest the animals slowed progress even more. At night campfires were kept burning to ward off wild animals. Some days there was no travel at all because of: needed repairs to the wagon or the animals needed rest; sickness, childbirth, or the family might be running low on food. If so, a search began: foraging for edible plants and/or berries; hunting for game or fishing in a nearby stream could bring in enough to sustain a family for a few days or a week.

There were some Native Americans still living in the wilderness; most were friendly and willing to help or trade. Day after day, week after week, the settlers moved on; then *Georgia at last*!

Beyond the Chattahoochee River, several roads converged from three main ferries at a ford on Sweetwater Creek about one mile southeast of today's Austell. A portion of one of those original thoroughfares is still known as "Old Alabama Road." The united routes continued westward over Sweetwater Creek, passing below Austell and following closely the present-day route of U. S. Highway 78.

The road continued on through what is today Lithia Springs and Douglasville where it turned northwest. From this point, the Alabama Road turned in a more westerly direction traveling west on what is today, Cedar Mt. Road. About half way between Cedar Mt. and Mann Road lies a strip of dark red soil approximately *six miles wide and twenty-two miles long. This was the future site of the Dark Corner settlement.*

These early pioneers began to search for their land lots. Many times there were no roads, so they cut their way through—literally hacking out their way until their property was located. Once they found their assigned land, they cut trees, cleared stumps and built homesteads. Many slept in the wagon or tents until a log cabin could be built. Farm animals, mules, horses, cows, pigs, and chickens ran free; gardens were fenced. Then came the plowing and planting. Everything depended on the crop they would harvest at year's end.

The earliest pioneers came in the late 1820s—even before the Land Lottery of 1832. Then those who drew from the land lotteries lots or purchased this land—were some of the original settlers— the Bensons, Weddingtons, Winns, Maxwells, McElwreaths, Stewarts, Hartsfields, Kennedys, Bates, and McLarty and many others.

Dark Corner Settlement on Old Alabama Road

Extensive research of the earliest records shows that Dark Corner was a community that sprang up around the early Post Office, located in Mathias Bates home, at the intersection of what was then Alabama Road (now Cedar Mountain Road) and (what is now) South Flat Rock Road at Land Lots # 222 and 221. A United States postal document names Dark Corner's first Postmaster as Mathias Bates, appointed from August 18, 1837 to July 13, 1841.

The evidence of Dark Corner existing at this intersection is strongly presented by the succession of postmasters who were members of the same family living on these same land lots. In a letter dated April 25, 1859, from Dr. E. W. **Maxwell** to

George W. Lowry, Esqr., there is a quote: *"M. H. Woodall has a store at widow Watson's."* Widow Watson is Louanna Watson whose father, Mathias Bates, was the first postmaster, whose husband, Samuel H. Watson, served the next two sessions, then her brother-in-law, George W. McLarty, served as postmaster then Louanna herself.

The first mention of a school in Dark Corner, that was found, was on John Mason Huey's 1854 & 1855 class roll for the school. John M. Huey, teacher at Dark Corner School, lists the parents along with each student on this class roll. Looking up the land lots of the parents of these children shows the parameter of the community of Dark Corner in 1854 & 1855. These land lots, found on the 1855 Georgia, Property Tax Digest for District #730, Dark Corner, showed the extended area of the community whose children attended this school. The circumference of about one-and-a-half mile puts the intersection of Cedar Mt. Road and South Flat Rock Road in the approximate center of the area. This area of the community extends south down South Flat Rock Road, north to Dorris Road; west to what is now Wortham Road and east about one-and a-half miles.

The families who had school children in Dark Corner School in 1855 were: Rev. F. Winn - LL # 223; Mahala Winn, LL #223; James Stewart, LL# 223; Dr. E. W. Maxwell LL #191; E. J. Mattox LL #196; Ann Freeman and M. Freeman LL # 489 (north over Paulding County line); R. H. Weddington LL # 198; Louanna Watson LL # 222; Asia (Asa ?) Sewell LL #161; Wm. P. Grigs LL # 194; Reuben Vansant LL # 190; and Young Vansant LL # 192. Other head-of-households having students in Dark Corner School in 1855, but without a LL shown were: William, David, Mrs. Elizabeth Brown and Mrs. Eliza Brown, J. F. Cochran; G. Lee; H. Norton; Mrs. Whitlow; W. McClung, Jon W. McClung; J. F. Cochran, D. W. Trenthem and Thomas Hicks - all shown on the 1860 Census as neighbors of those listed above.

As settlers inhabited the area, about 1828 this Alabama Road was known as the Alabama via Villa Rica Road. It came north from the Chattahoochee River, through Campbell County, over what is today Campbellton Road, through Dark Corner, through Hixtown, known later as Villa Rica and on westward into Alabama. Later this main thorough-fare, was used by the stagecoach and express mail carriers.

The 1870 Federal Census is the first census to list occupations. For the 1870 Census for Dark Corner, Militia District #730, is twenty pages of residents whose occupation is shown as: farm laborer, domestic servant or keeping house with the exception of a few entries: Pendleton Watson, who lives with his mother, Louanna Watson, on LL # 222, has the occupation of Retail Dry Goods Merchant; Madison Pounds, a blacksmith; Ezekiel McLarty (living with Stephen McLarty) whose occupation is listed as school teacher; Pleasant Davis, another blacksmith; K. B. Mobbs, a house carpenter; Joseph Thomason, a house carpenter and V. (?) P. Phillips another Retail Dry Goods Merchant who lives next door to Nancy Eargle. Nancy Eargle, widow of John Eargle, lived on LL # 189 which is down South Flat Rock Road. Land Lots within this parameter covers approximately a mile-and-a-half circumference matching the area around the intersection.

After the Civil War, more and more settlers inhabited the land around the town of Dark Corner which by then extended westward down that main well-worn road toward what is today's Mann Road. There is evidence found on John Mason Huey's 1873 land survey of Militia District #730, Dark Corner, that the Post Office was then located on Land Lot # 199. His survey shows J. W. Anderson, the next to last post master in Dark Corner listed, owning LL #199. Then a deed was found where J. W. Anderson paid $1,610 in 1869 to W. P. Strickland for 202 1/2 acres of LL # 199, a goodly sum for land bought after the Civil War.

Not only did the parameters of Dark Corner change over the years, but so did the county lines: Campbell County, which was created in 1828, became Douglas County in 1870. Dark Corner not only grew, but spread to the surrounding areas. It gradually grew in Campbell County, extending over the line into Carroll County and was located, in the corner, where the Campbell, Paulding, and Carroll Counties came together.

Early pioneer family genealogy was discovered for families living on Land Lots 202, 203, 204 and 205 claiming to be part of Dark Corner, in Carroll County before 1870. After 1870 their land was part of Douglas County. These early pioneer families are part of the Dark Corner history. Early families, who lived in Dark Corner, with children who married other pioneer families' children, then moved to Paulding, Carroll or even Cobb— just over the line —are also included in the history of Dark Corner.

This northern Paulding-Campbell County line was called the boundary line or Purchase Line as it was the original line between the Native Americans and Campbell County at its formation in 1828. Locals told stories of finding "enough arrowheads to fill buckets" when they were young—further evidence of the native Americans who inhabited this land in earlier times.

To add another interesting touch, there were gold mines sprinkled all in these parts. A present-day resident of Dark Corner told the story of a great-great grandmother who carried “a gold nugget in her apron pocket.”

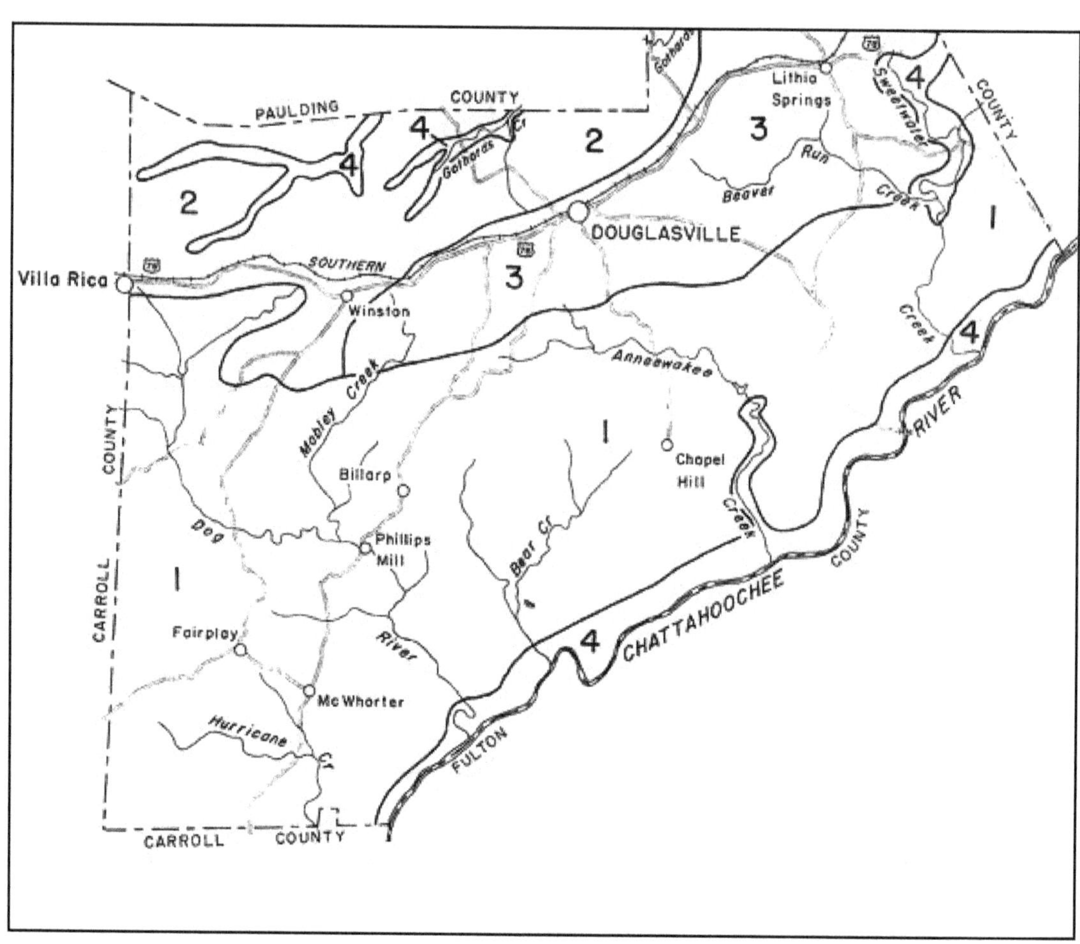

There are basically four types of soil in Campbell, now Douglas, County. Note: from the numbers 1-4, it is concluded that Dark Corner soil, shown at the top of the map next to Gothard's Creek, has the same rating as the rich bottom land soil shown along the bottom of the map, running adjacent to the Chattahoochee River.

2

Why the name Dark Corner?

It was dark. I could not see my hand in front of my face. After walking for a while, careful to stay on the path—to feel hard dirt under my feet and not stumble over into the brush and woods—I heard the mule coming toward me.

From oral history, newspaper articles and history books there exists at least four or more reasons or explanations to how Dark Corner got its name. But the absolute proof has not been found. Here are the most common beliefs on the explanations for the name:

Was Dark Corner named for a Native American?

Before the American Revolution, the French controlled the land west of the Proclamation Line of 1763. Many of the Cherokee and French intermarried and there was a heavy French influence on given names. For example, the name "Dark" is an Anglicized version of the French surname D'arc. There was a mixed blood Cherokee who called himself "The Dark" who set up the first ford, a creek crossing, into Cherokee land. He charged the settlers a fee for crossing the creek. "The Dark" lived a few miles from present day Douglasville and gave his name to the area of Dark Corner. This information is listed in Georgia Place Names but with no reference as to where this information was found. No proof found.

Was Dark Corner named for the color of its soil?

A strip of unusually rich, dark reddish soil running 6-8 miles wide and 22 to 28 miles long in the north west section of Douglas (once Campbell County) is said to be the reason for the name. History books tell that early settlers paid the $1.00 more per acre for this soil than for land in the other parts of the county. The claim was that trees grew taller and crop-yields were greater. One document has been found where Native Americans sold land. Most Native Americans had been escorted out of the North Georgia area by the late 1830s as Revolutionary War veterans and veterans of the War of 1812 drew land lotteries and settled the land that the Native Americans had occupied. The soil here is definitely dark red and seems to be different than what pioneers had seen. It proved to be fertile for growing crops. Farmers in the Dark Corner area, for generations, have had rich harvests and even claimed they could get a bale of cotton from one acre of land without fertilizing the land.

There are basically four types of soil in Campbell, now Douglas, County. Note picture on the previous page: from the numbers 1-4 it is concluded that Dark Corner soil, shown at the top of the map next to Gothard's Creek, has the same rating as the rich bottom land soil shown along the bottom of the map, running adjacent to the Chattahoochee River.

Was Dark Corner named for its remoteness from the county seat?

Was Dark Corner named for its remoteness from the county seat at the time Campbell County was created in 1828?

It's easy to visualize the remoteness of the early pioneer life through analogy. Think of a dark room with a single lit candle on a single table in the middle of an otherwise dark room. The lighted candle, on the table, represents the courthouse, the dark corners of the room represent the furthermost reaches of the county.

The name Dark Corner may have originated from the fact that, for the settlers of Dark Corner, the county seat of Campbellton was about two days walk—twenty-five miles—one way. The settlement of Campbellton was the hub of activity for many years, beginning in 1828: this is where early pioneers went to the county courthouse to record deeds or to serve on the jury; early settlers depended on the various stores for supplies; and here they could visit the various mercantile stores. In the earliest times they picked up from the post office's once-a-month mail delivery. The county seat was also the only center of social activity and news when all other parts of the county were being carved from the wilderness.

There is one other Dark Corner Community in Georgia and one in South Carolina. Both are countryside on state lines and originated very early and were very remote.

Dark Corner, Greenville County, South Carolina is located in a remote mountainous countryside located on the state line between North Carolina and South Carolina that is known back in time for moonshining.

A stranger passing through, asked, "Where is Dark Corner?" The South Carolinian, thinking he might be a revenuer says, "It starts just across the road there." The stranger goes a little further and asks the same question and gets the same answer, "Oh, it starts just past the creek there." After a while the stranger gets a different answer, "It's just a little farther up the road."

Dark Corner, Lincoln County, Georgia is located on the state boundary-line of the Georgia and South Carolina and is shown on an 1864 map of the area almost on the edge of McCormick County, South Carolina.

Did Dark Corner get its name because the area was literally "dark"?

In the late 1820s and the 1830s, an area of vast original pristine trees growing for a hundred years or so—that had never been cut, was called The Big Woods. No one but the Native Americans had ever lived on this pristine land. Early pioneers had to literally "hack" their way when they left the traveled dusty trail made first by game and buffalo then by Native Americans, then by white settlers in the oxen-drawn carts then by horse or mule-drawn wagons. The nights were especially dark. There were no street lights in existence, no lights coming from settlements— the nearest of which was four miles to the south, and even then the light could only be an oil lamp or a few candles burning in the window. The moon was the only illumination. A story told by a farmer in Dark Corner brings us into the appreciation of just how dark the woods at night can be when you have to rely on only the moonlight.

"One night our mule got out of the pen. Dad and I took off to find it. Dad took the new Mann Road —where it had been rerouted; I took the old—original Mann Road. It was dark. I could not see my hand in front of my face. After walking for a while, careful to stay on the path—to feel hard dirt under my feet and not stumble over into the brush and woods, I heard the mule ahead of me. I could not see it, I just heard it stirring around. I called out. Then I could hear the sound of its hooves; I knew the mule was coming toward me. I put my hand out in front of me in the dark and waited. The mule found me. I felt for it and managed to get a rope around its neck. I led the mule home, never really seeing it until we got back into the barnyard and had the lights shining from the windows of the house."

Did the early settlers bring the name with them?

Quite a few of the Dark Corner early pioneers, came from Carrabus County and Mecklenburg County, North Carolina. To get to Campbell County, they had to pass through Greenville County, South Carolina—where there was a community named, Dark Corner. Maybe that's just a coincident!

3

Early Settlers in Dark Corner

". . . an old squaw who was friendly with one of the little girls told her that the tribe was planning a massacre that night but not to worry; she would kill the child "right easy.". . .

John Kennedy (Canady)

The removal of the Creek and Cherokee in Georgia, opened up new land. With this free or almost free land came the promise of a new beginning—a better life. "Let's move to Georgia" was a topic on the mind and lips of many.

On August 9, 1827, land Lot # 201 (in section 2 of Carroll County) consisting of 202 1/2 acres was granted to Solomon Schrimpshire of Paschell's District of Upson County. However Schrimpshire had no interest in the land himself, so he sold the lot for $200 to John Kennedy (Canady) of Hall County. Campbell County was formed in December of 1828 and included LL #201 which formed the western boundary between Carroll and Campbell.

The following is the written history taken from oral history of the John Harrison Kennedy family of six generations - all of whom began in Dark Corner, Campbell County, Georgia.

"In the spring of 1828, John and Elizabeth Kennedy (Canady) and their family which in time numbered eight children, four sons and four daughters, came in a covered wagon to take possession of their new land. The entire lot was in woods, and Indians were still living in the area - an old Indian named Walking Stick lived on "Walking Stick Farm." That spring the Kennedys built a small log cabin near a spring with a shed behind it for their horses. Having cleared a plot of less than an acre, they planted corn and went back to Hall County for the summer.

In the fall they returned to settle permanently. Elizabeth Kennedy often told her grandchildren and great grandchildren of the fearful experience of the return after dark. The woods seemed full of Indians, and the cabin was almost impossible to find because the corn had grown higher than its roof.

The Kennedy family came to Land Lot #201 in 1828 and some of the family have lived on this land for six generations. This is the third dwelling - built in 1905. Photo, John Bailey, 2014.

They were the first settlers in that part of the county, there being no other people between there and Campbellton on the other side of the Chattahoochee River. Neighboring lots were not settled until the next year. However, the Indians did not leave the area for several years. Apparently, the Kennedys had no serious trouble with their Indian neighbors. They saw them quite frequently though. Whenever the Kennedys slaughtered fresh meat, the Indians would line up on the rail fence at the edge of the yard and look on screaming and hollering like it was some sort of celebration. On one occasion, an old squaw who was friendly with one of the little girls told her that the tribe was planning a massacre that night but not to worry; she would kill the child "right easy." However, the massacre never took place.

At first they cleared only three or four acres of the rich, red soil and planted corn. About 500 yards from the first home site, they built a two story log house and dug a well. At first they had to go all the way back to Augusta to trade, consequently, they didn't go very often. In a 1920/21 Carrollton Newspaper, interview, Georgia Ann Canady Alexander, age 84, told 'My father kept a Tavern (Inn), and people going to market at Augusta - the only cotton market in Georgia - would stop with us. I remember that the travelers sat in front of our roaring, log fire and drank peach brandy as mellow as honey, and told tales far into the night.'

In Carrollton, Kennedy probably bought his first slaves, for he brought none with him when he came. The exact number that he owned is not among the family records, but this number was small. The records do include, however, two bills of sale for slaves John Kennedy bought, one a forty-year-old Negro woman purchased for $300 in 1829, and another for an eleven-year-old Negro girl purchased in 1837 for $100. Also, the family cemetery contains the grave of a baby girl, a slave, dated August, 1847. With slave labor the Kennedys were able to clear more land, although not more than fifty acres prior to the Civil War, and plant it in corn and cotton. Part of it was fenced with rail fences for twelve to fifteen head of cattle, sheep, and hogs.

The trip to Campbellton was twenty-five miles and involved crossing the Chattahoochee River on a ferry. Since Campbellton was the county seat, they had to make the trip often to serve on juries for sixty cents a day or to go to court themselves.

John Kennedy died on October 28, 1848. Since there was no will, the estate, consisting largely of the 202 1/2 acres of northwest Campbell County land, was divided into nine equal portions among Elizabeth, his widow, and her eight children.

On August 11, 1849, three of her sons and her four sons-in-law signed a deed, returning their land to Elizabeth Kennedy until her death. She kept the land of her youngest son, John J. Kennedy, who was only twelve at the time of his father's death.

With the labor of her slaves Mrs. Kennedy was able to continue running the farm until her son was old enough to take over."

Sarah Keaton

In 1827, Sarah Peacock Keaten (Keaton) who was born September 2, 1776 in Johnston, N. C. and died August 24, 1867 Carroll County, Georgia drew land lot 78, in the Georgia Land Lottery, consisting of 202 1/2 acres close to the Campbell County - Carroll County border (later Douglas County). Sarah had married Keader (Kadar) Keaton about 1795. Keader Keaton was born February 9, 1769 in North Carolina and died 1830 in Twiggs County, Georgia. Sarah, then a widow, lived with her four children near relatives in Liberty County, near Macon, Georgia. From the Keaton Family

Keaton-Hembree family in 1907. They met to clean off the family cemetery: L - R: bottom row: George Hembree, Claude Keaton, Irby Keaton, Mrs. George Hembree, Mrs. Margaret Keaton, Henry Hendon Keaton, Lule Gilland, Harbey Gilland, Flora Gilland. 2nd row: Mahaley Keaton, Lorra Keaton & baby, Ose Saylors, Mary Saylor, Alice Saylors, Lula Hembree, Marilla Boyd Keaton, Herman Keaton, Jacob Z. Keaton, Marion Gilland. 3rd row: Keader Keaton, baby George Keaton, Lela Keaton, Alonzo Keaton. Fourth row: Dude Saylor, Walter Saylors, unknown, Burnette Keaton, Allen Keaton, unknown, Don Kimble, John Kimble, Witman Kyte. Photo: Courtesy, Herman "Billy" Keaton.

History: "*On learning that this land lot was in the Villa Rica gold mining area and in order to claim the land (it had to be occupied within a limited time), Sarah Keaton with one son and two daughters, taking food and a few clothes, began their journey in a one-horse wagon. Somewhere in Coweta County the horse died. This brave little family pushed on—literally. They pulled and pushed the wagon on for several miles, after which the mother and daughters waited with the wagon until the son returned to Liberty County and obtained an animal from an uncle, then rejoined his family and continued the trip.*

A letter from Mrs. Keaton to her mother, written after she had investigated her surroundings (their new home), was brief and without complaint.

'Dear Mama: No gold, but life is easy up here—lots of wild turkey and a creek teaming with fish.'

"Mrs. Keaton named the creek for her son, John KenKater Keaton. Although she found no glittering gold on her land, this brave lady and her children, through years of hard work and sacrifices, developed it into one of the best farms in the area. The Keaton family cemetery is located on the old Keaton farm.

"William, her son, was a man of great energy and soon had a cabin built from the logs in the forest and land cleared, fenced and in cultivation. The rich bottom land on the place produced corn in abundance. The rich virgin hillsides yielded splendid crops of wheat. They at first raised very little, if any cotton. There was wild game such as deer and turkey in great numbers and wild pigeons by the thousands. The creeks teemed with fish so we can readily see that their living environments were not so bad." See Chapter 14 for more on the Keaton family.

Clinton

William Clinton, born in Virginia in 1749, lived in Kershaw County, South Carolina and fought with the South Carolina troops in the Revolutionary War enlisting the second year of the war, 1776, first as Private, then as Sergeant, and toward the end of the war as lieutenant. He fought under Henderson and then Commander Kershaw. He fought seven years—to the end in 1783, in the struggle of freedom and peace. He was wounded in the thigh and the bullet was never extracted and bothered him until his death on February 17, 1847 in Campbell County, Georgia.

William Clinton married Violet Perry about 1783 or 1784 in South Carolina. She was born 1790 in South Carolina and died February 12, 1852 in Campbell County. William and Violet with their family came to Georgia in 1834 where he had drawn Land Lot # 166 in the Dark Corner District of Campbell County. Listed on the 1840 Federal Census of Campbell County—William Clinton, and his grown sons who were also heads-of-household: David Clinton, John P. Clinton and William P. Clinton. William P. is also listed on the 1830 Federal Census for Campbell County. William and Violet Clinton's children:

1) Elizabeth Clinton; **2)** David, born 1785 in S. C., lived in Dark Corner, then moved to Louisiana. **3)** John Paschell Clinton, born, September 20, 1795 in York County, S. C. and died August 22, 1848, in Campbell County. On July 10, 1816, he married Mary Patton Ingram, who was born November 3, 1793 and died on June 12, 1830. After she died, he married Mary Kelly (January 1, 1799 - June 10, 1856) on January 25, 1831. John is listed on the Campbell County, Georgia Military Indian

War 1st Mounted Militia Volunteers, 1838. Their children: John P. Clinton, Jr; Samuel R; James M.; David; Lydia Ann; Charlotte; Elizabeth S., and Christopher Columbus.

Christopher Columbus "Lum" Clinton, born June 27, 1832, died May 25, 1911, married Mary Ann **Carnes** on February 13, 1856 in Fulton County, Georgia. She was born May 3, 1833 in Carroll County, Georgia and died July 1, 1878 in Villa Rica, Georgia. She was the daughter of John Thomas and Mary "Polly" Carnes.

Christopher Columbus Clinton enlisted as Private in Co. A, 56th Regiment, Georgia Volunteer Infantry, CSA, on April 25, 1862 in Campbellton, was captured at Vicksburg, Mississippi, July 4, 1863, then paroled July 8, 1863. Pension records show his feet were frozen while he was at Knoxville, Tennessee, December 1864. He developed blood poison, which resulted in permanent disability. He surrendered at Greensboro, North Carolina on April 26, 1865.

Christopher C. and Mary Ann Clinton's children are: Mary E. born 1860; Charles M., 1862 - 1923 who married Harriet Sayer; Thomas J, born 1866; John T. 1966-1878; and Julia A. born 1866-1909;

4) William P. born in South Carolina about 1804, died 1860, married Elizabeth, born 1810. Their children: Wiley, Amanda, Jane, Clementine and Wyatt.

5) Susan Violett (Hollis), born in South Carolina about 1807.

6) George P. born in South Carolina in 1810, died 1870.

Carnes

Joseph Carnes was born 1753 and died 1838. He is buried in the New Hope Primitive Baptist Church Cemetery in Villa Rica. He served as Private in the Virginia Militia in the Revolutionary War. On November 12, 1783, he married Comfort Ann Cash in Granville, North Carolina where several of their children were born. Comfort Ann was born 1753 in Virginia and died 1861 in Paulding County, Georgia at age of 108; she is buried at Harmony Grove Cemetery in Dallas, Ga. This pioneer family, came to Georgia about 1828 and bought LL# 109 and # 116 in Carroll County. About 1828, they built a log cabin that still stands today, on the land that after 1870 was annexed into Douglas County, and later became Clinton Nature Reserve. The log house was placed on the National Register of Historic Homes.

Joseph and Comfort Ann's son, John Thomas Carnes, born in N. C. in 1787; died November 1860 and is buried at New Hope Primitive Baptist Church in Villa Rica. John Thomas married Mary Magdalene Anne "Polly" Smallwood in 1807 in

Franklin County, Georgia. She was born 1790 in South Carolina and died 1869 in Villa Rica. Their Children: **1)** Comfort Anne, 1815 - 1880, married Bill Hunt; **2)** John Peter "Jack," born 1816 in Habersham Co.

Carnes cabin built 1828, photo taken 2014 by author, John Bailey

married Hannah Nalley. Children: **a)** Nancy Caroline, born about 1841 who married Brooks Harper on September 8, 1863. **b)** Lucetta, born 1843 who married William Waldrop on June 13, 1869; **c)** Thomas, born 1845 who married Hannah Nalley on November 1, 1868; **d)** Mary Ann, born about 1838 who married James K. Bivins in 1870; **e)** Miles D. Carnes, born about 1850 who married Nancy E. Waldrop; and **f)** John Peter Carnes born 1855 who married Martha Sarah Keaton;

3) Joseph Carnes, March 4, 1818 - Feb 1899, married 1) Nancy Davis in 1850 and 2) Roxanne Cansler on April 10, 1881;

4) Aceneth "Cenia Ann," born January 18, 1823; died November 3, 1896; married Terrell Harper on February 1, 1838;

5) Emily Ann, January 1, 1824 - October 16, 1891, married Miles Hensley; on December 12, 1839;

6) Elizabeth Ann "Betsy," born about 1826, married Henry Morris;

7) Richard Carnes, born September 15, 1828 - August 4, 1908; married Nancy Ruff;

8) Mary Anne, born May 3,1833 - July 1, 1896, married Christopher Columbus "Lum" Clinton on February 14, 1856 in Campbell County;

9) Thomas Anderson Carnes, 1837 - 1862, married Nancy Monk; died in the Civil War;

10) Ritha Caroline "Mittie" Carnes, January 29, 1841 - July 6, 1918, married 1) Charlie Polk, on September 15, 1857 and 2) John Bradley Sheffield, September 14, 1866: **11)** Frederick Carnes, 1832-1875.

The Case of Settlers' Gold Fraud:

State vs. George _____, Joel _____and Thomas _____ in Fraud Charges:

This is a copy of a warrant.
Trial executed July 27, 1830.
(Some surnames omitted; story true.)

Georgia
Campbell County
To John M. Morgan constable and to all lawful officers within the said county.

*Whereas complaint hath been made before me, James M. Smith, one of the Justice of the Peace in and for the said County. On the Oath of Davis Owen, that on the twenty-fifth day of June, in the year Eighteen hundred and thirty, George _____, a certain Joel ______ and Thomas______ of the county aforesaid, did, then and there, combine together, and cheat and swindle the said Davis Owen, John G. Roberts, and David C. Daniel by false representation of and concerning a certain lot of land (to wit) Number two hundred and X (*number omitted*), in the second District of Originally Carroll, now Campbell County, then the property of the said James_____ and that the said George ____, Joel______ and Thomas______ did then and there by digging pits and depositing gold therein, and by diggin up, and showing the same to the said Davis Owen, and the said Roberts and Daniel and by making many false statements and representations of and concerning said lot of land and the minerals therein contained, impose the same on said Deponent (?) and the said Roberts and Daniel at the price or sum of three thousand Dollars, when there was little if any gold on said lot except what had been then and there deposited by the said George ______, Joel _____ and Thomas _____ deceitfully and fraudulently as aforesaid; These are therefore to command you forth with to bring the said George _____, Joel _____ and Thomas _____ before me.*

The State vs Mr. George _____, Mr. Joel _____ and Mr. Thomas _____ (Trial) Executed July 27, 1830.
Returned by John M. Morgan
____cent in full July the 27th 1830.
James M. Smith

4

Early Land Lots Acquired in Dark Corner

Early settlers who drew LLs of 202 1/2 acre, which was 1/2 mile square; the nearest neighbor was a half mile away. That meant the 2nd nearest neighbor was 1 mile away. But there was no chance to be lonely—each family had an average of 10-12 kids— some had 15.

Campbell County was formed by an act of the Georgia Legislature on December 20, 1828 by taking land from Carroll, Coweta, Dekalb and Fayette Counties. In 1832, land from the Cherokee Land Lottery was added, for a total to about 192 square miles. On October 17, 1870 the land lying north of the river was taken along with some of eastern Carroll to form what is now Douglas County. The rest merged with Fulton on January 1, 1932.

Campbell County was named in honor of Colonel Duncan G. Campbell. He and James Meriwether negotiated the Indian Springs Treaty in which the Creek Indian land was ceded on February 12, 1825. The county seat was in Campbellton until 1870. It was then moved to Fairburn where it remained for the life of the county. The county existed from 1828 to 1931 when it was finally merged into Fulton County.

On the 1840 and 1860 United States Federal Census for Campbell County the Dark Corner District is listed in Section 2, District 5, of Georgia Militia District #730. Below are some of the earliest settlers to the Dark Corner District: The following Land Lots were acquired from 1827 - 1851.

Under the 1832 Land Lottery a person was required to live in Georgia for three years and pay a fee of $18. He was not required to live on or cultivate the land.

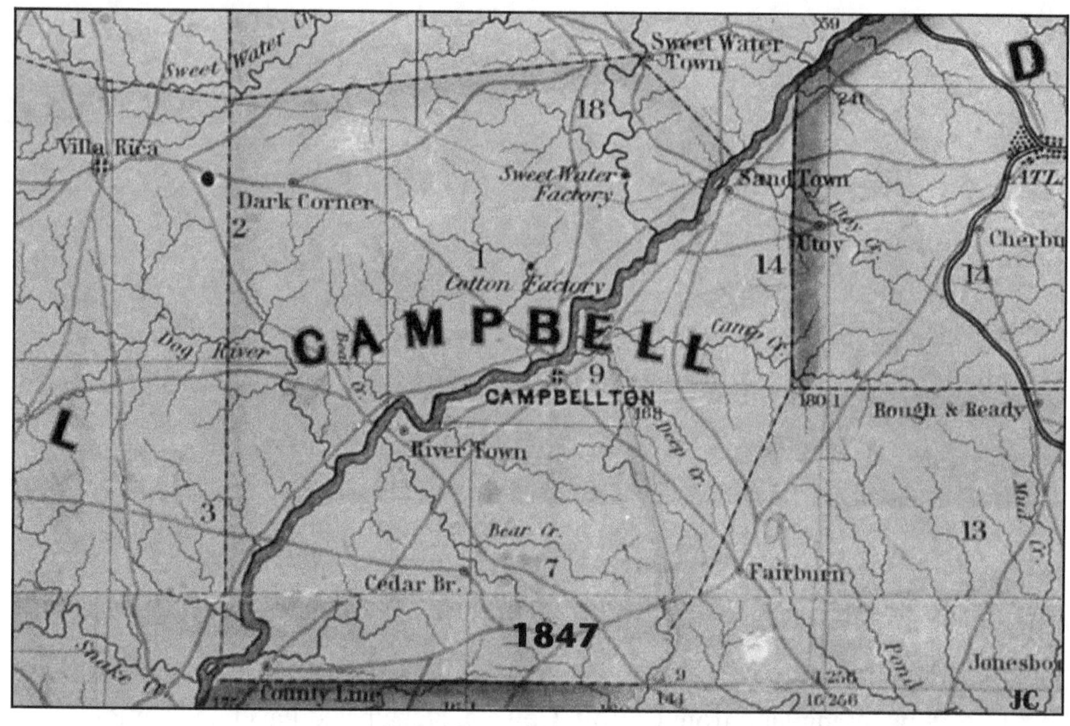

1847 Map of the State of Georgia. Compiled under the direction of His Excellency, George W. Crawford.

Deed Book A, C, D & E, Dist. 2, originally Carroll County, now Campbell Co., Ga.

Lot # Bk/Pg Date Description Purchase Price

136 A/170 12/15/1830 Gwinnett Co. - Benjamin Rhodes of DeKalb Co. to Pleasant R. Lyle of Gwinnett Co. Wit.: William H. Jenkins, William Holland, J. P.
202 1/2 acs. $100.

136 A/184 2/21/1832 Gwinnett Co.- Pleasant R. Lyle of Gwinnett Co. to John Boyle of Campbell Co.
202 1/2 acs. $125.

137 E/198 2/17/1834 Gwinnett Co. - Hardy Heart, Jonathan McLendon & Wm McLendon of Gwinnett to Stephen McLarty. Wit.: John M. Pendergrass, Simon Strickland. Recorded 3/6/1851.
202 1/2 acs. $ 100.

138 E/66 5/18/1850 Ezekiel Pike (Polk) to Cheadle Cochran, both of Campbell County. Land lying on the waters of Crawfish (Creek). Wit.: Thomas Bullard, H. F. Moates,
202 1/2 acs. $150.

152 A/424 1/16/1833 Clayton Williams of Carroll Co. to Stephen H. McLarty of Campbell Co. Wit.: Charles Hulsey, J. P. 202 1/2 acs. $200.

153 1827 Land Lottery Drawn by Joel H. Stubbs of Espy's District Clark Co.

153 A/70 2/20/1830 Clarke Co. - Joel H. Stubbs of Clarke Co. to James Nisbitt, Jr., of Spartanburg Co., S. C. 202 1/2 acs. $87.

153 A/73 7/16/1830 Campbell - James Nelson of Spartanburg Co., S. C. to Michael McClarath of Campbell. 202 1/2 acs. $200.

154 D/56 2/11/1839 Forsyth Co. - Isaac Busby to Benjamin Adams of Carroll Co. 202 1/2 acs. $200.

154 E/174 2/27/1850 Paulding C. - Benjamin Adair of Paulding to Stephen H. McLarty of Campbell Co. S/half, 101 1/4 acs. $ 50.

154 E/229 2/17/1850 Paulding Co. - Bozeman Adair to Mark McElreath, both of Campbell Co. Originally granted to Isaac Busby of Madison Co. Wit.: John B. Blair, James L. Blair. Recorded 4/23/1851. N/half 101 1/4 acs. $ 50.

155 E/162 5/2/1848 Fi Fa from Paulding, Co. Stephen R. McLarty vs. Charles Garner, Sheriff Wm. M. Brtlett sold to highest bidders, James M. Campbell & M. M. Smith. Wit.: H. F. Moates, John James. 202 1/2 acs. $ 5.

155 E/248 4/23/1851 Moses M. Smith & James M. Cantrell of Campbell County to John Baggett of Campbell County. Wit.: R. C. Beavers, William Butt, JIC. Recorded May 7, 1851. 202 1/2 acs. $100.

156 A/73 7/16/1830 Campbell Co. - James Nelson of Spartanburg, SC to Michael McClarath of Campbell Co., granted to Joel H. Stubbs on 12/8/1829, by His Excellency George R. Gilmer. Wit.: Gambriel White, John A. Hopkins, JIC. 202 1/2 acs. $110.

156 E/401 3/22/1852 Wm. C. Wright to George Vansant, both of Campbell Co. 202 1/2 acs., except 1 ac. whereupon Protestant Methodist Church stands and the spring for water. Wit.: E. W. Maxwell, L. H. Watson, J. P. Recorded October 22, 1852. $680.

156 E/402 10/1/1852 Young Vansant of Campbell County to Christian Holman of Coweta, 202 1/2 acs., except 1 ac. whereupon Protestant Methodist Church stands. Wit.: L. H. Watson, Reuben Vansant. Recorded October 22, 1852. $837.

157 E/165 5/5/1849 Isaac W. McKilvey to John Entrekin, both of Campbell County. Land lying on the waters of Crawfish (Creek) S/half 101 1/4 acs. $200.

158 1827 Land Lottery Drawn by the orphans of Nathaniel Wofford of Bakers Dist., Habersham Co.

158 D/509 5/6/1848 Campbell Co. - Stephen H. McLarty to David Entrekin; of Campbell County. Wit.: H. R. Maxwell, J. P. 102 3/4 acs. $250.

160 E/4-1 10/5/1852 Campbell Co. - Samuel Lewis to Samuel M. McLarty, of Campbell County. 202 1/2 ac. $200.

162 E/29 2/26/1849 John McLarty Sr. to A. N. McLarty, Wit.: John Vaughn, S. H. Watson. 115 acs. W/end $2,000.

,

163 E/498 3/16/1850 Thomas Entrekin of Campbell Co. to David Entrekin, Samuel W. McLarty, Alexander McKelvy, Mack McElwreath, George W. McLarty, William C. White, and Francis Winn, Trustees of the Methodist Episcopal Church South 10 acs. Consideration: love and affection. Wit.: Wylie Scogins, S. H. Watson, J. P. Recorded May 12, 1853. $ 0.

163 E/232 1/ 6/1851. Thomas Entrekin of Campbell Co to Tommy Vansant of Campbell Co.; Wit.: Alexander McKelvy, S. H. Watson, J. P. Recorded April 28, 1851. 192 acs. not shown

165 E/433 12/16/1852 Campbell Co., Promissory note from William B. Martin of Campbell Co. to Thomas A. Latham of Campbell Co. Security: Wit.: William P. Clinton, Thomas Thomas, J.P. Recorded January 27, 1853. 202 1/2 acs. $150.64

165 E/622 1/30/1854 Cobb Co - Wm B. Martin of Cobb to Andrew G. Endsley of Campbell County. 202 1/2 acs. $450.

167 E/229 10/14/1830 Emanuel Co. - Alexander Lam to Benjamin Sherard of Emanual Co. Recorded April 23, 1851. 202 1/2 acs. $250

167 E/ 230 6/18/1841 Emanuel Co. - William G. Sherrod, John Sherrod, Benjamin Sherrod, and James Oglesby (who intermarried with Caroline Sherrod), all legatees of Benjamin Sherrod, Dec'd., late of Emanuel Co., to John McElwreath of Campbell Co. Recorded April 25, 1851. 202 1/2 acs. $250.

168 A/205 12/2/1831 Campbell Co.- Enoch Roughton of Washington Co. to Michael ___, of Campbell Co. granted to Enoch Roughton by His Excellency Wilson Lumpkin. Wit.: William Morgan, Burrel Mathews, J. P. 202 1/2 acs.$300.

168 D/371 2/27/1846 Campbell County - Michael McElreath to Martin McElreath of Campbell County. Wit: Anderson Smith, Samuel R. Hartsfield, J. P.

40 acs. $100.

168 E/227 2/27/1846 Campbell Co, - Michael McElreath to Mark McElreath of Campbell Co. Wit: Anderson Smith, Samuel R. Hartsfield. 202 1/2 acs. $100.

168 D/372 10/12/1847 Campbell Co. - Martin McElreath to Stephen H. McLarty of Campbell Co.; Wit.: George W. McLarty, S. H. Watson. J. P. 40 acs. $250.

169 A/60 1/2/1829 William M _____ (unreadable) to Allen Lawhon of Harris Co. Witness: unreadable. Land. $300.

169 A/ 245 7/13/1831 Carroll Co. - Allen Lawhorn of Muscogee Co. to Alexander McLarty of DeKalb Co. Wit.: Bennet Bell, James Dickson. 202 1/2 acs.$300.

169 A/261 12/17/1832 DeKalb Co. - Benjamin Lewis to Alexander McLarty of Campbell Co. 202 1/2 acs. $825.

184 A/254 3/1/1832 Fayette Co.-- Roland B. Cook to Thomas H. Cliatt of Fayette Co. 202 1/2 acs.$450.

184 A/304 12/3/1833 Campbell County - Fi. Fa. out of the Superior Court of Fayette Co., in favor of Morris & Lyle v. Roland Cook, Sheriff Benjamin Easley sold property of said Roland Cook to Thomas H. Cliett as highest bidder at public outcry. Wit: Nathaniel Nicholson, George Lawrence, J. P. 202 1/2 acs. $10.

185 A/212 12/26/1831 Campbell - Fi Fa out of Putnam Co. in favor of Peter Barr vs. James Mulryne & wife - sold by Campbell Sheriff Nathaniel Nicholson advertised for public outcry; sold to highest bidder - Stephen H. McLarty. Wit.: Stephen W. McLarty, C. W. McLarty. 202 1/2 acs.$185.

186 A/ 215 10/16/1830 Campbell Co. - Mark Lot to George W. McLarty of Mecklinbugh Co., NC; drawn by Samuel Walker February 24, 1829. Wit.: Burrell Mathews, J.P., Joel D. Compton, A. McLarty. 202 1/2 acs. $450.

186 A/193 2/8/1832 Campbell Co. - George W. McLarty of Mecklenburg Co., NC, to Samuel W. McLarty of Campbell Co. Wit.: Wade White, J.P., L. H. McLarty, A. W. McLarty. 202 1/2 acs $500.

187 A/484 2/6/1834 Washington Co. Hepsy Goodman to Thomas W. Garmon of Carroll Co. Wit.: Edward Moore, William Joyce, JIC. 68 acs. $66.68

187 A/ 484 1/16/1836 Campbell Co., Ga - Chasmick Tharp of Wilkinson Co. to Thomas W. Garner of Campbell Co.; drawn by James Goodman. Wit.: C. R. Duncan, B. Mathews. 202 1/2 acs. $60.

187 E/370 & 371 5/4/1852 Campbell Co. - Fi Fa's issuing from the Justice Court in the matters of:

William F. Taylor v. William B. Martin and A. G. Weddington;
James Rabon v. William B. Martin & A. G. Weddington;
William M. Butt v. William B. Martin;
Henry Baker v. William B. Martin;
Daskin H. Witcher v. William B. Martin (6 fi fa's);
Samuel C. Chandler v. William B. Martin (4 fi. Fa's.)

Indebtedness: $700. William N. Magouirk, Constable, seized LL #187 - 202 1/2 acs. being the property of William B. Martin and the place on which he now resides, and same was sold by Sheriff William M. Bartell at public outcry to Thomas Latham as highest bidder for $510. Wit.: Thomas Camp, J. M. Wood. Recorded August 4, 1852.

188 E/339 2/3/1851 Campbell Co - M. W. Ford of Cherokee Co. to W. B. Martin & Thomas Entrekin. Wit.: Charity McLarty, G. W. McLarty. Recorded 4/3/1852 202 1/2 acs. $200.

188 E/340 2/7/1852 Campbell Co. - Wm. B. Martin to Thos. Entrekin, of Campbell Co. Wit.: Hugh Baker, S. H. Watson, J. P. Recorded 4/3/1852. 101 1/4 acs.$25.

190 E/232 1/28/1851 Campbell Co. - Anderson Smith to Tommy Vansant of Campbell Co. Wit.: John C. Whitley, L. H. Watson. Recorded April 28, 1851. 202 1/2 acs. $350.

191 A/276 12/5/1832 DeKalb Co. - Aaron Clifton of DeKalb to Royal Clay of Campbell Co. Wit: John P. Word, George Clifton, JIC. 202 1/2 acs. $100.

192 E/576 3/26/1853 Meriwether Co. - Robt. S. Parham to Thomas A. Entrekin of Meriwether. 202 1/2 acs. $250.

193 C/ 9 7/10/1834 Campbell Co.- William Champion of Muscogee Co. to John Wynn of Campbell Co. Wit.: J. D. Compton, J. P., Francis Wynn, T. H. Wynn. 202 1/2 acs. $25.

195 E/427 12/11/1850 Campbell Co. - Anthony Chapell to Wm. P. Griggs of Campbell Co. Wit.: S. H. Watson, Hugh Grigs (sic). Recorded 1/18/1853. 202 1/2 $100.

196 E/113 5/2/1848 Campbell Co. Fi. Fa. from the Superior Court of Paulding Co. in the matter of Stephen H. McLarty v. Charles Garner. Sheriff Thomas Bullard sold to Stephen H. McLarty as highest bidder at public outcry. Wit.: L. H. Cochran, H. F. Moates, J.P. 202 1/2 acs. $20.

196 E/114 10/28/1850 Campbell Co. - Stephen H. McLarty to Earley J. Mattox. Wit.: Samuel W. McLarty, G. M. McLarty. 202 1/2 acs. $250.

197 A/ 387 8/5/1834 Campbell Co. - Fi. Fa. out of the Superior Court of Cobb Co., Patrick B. Conally v. Livingston Skinner, Campbell Co. Sheriff Wesley Camp sold to John J. Jones of Carroll Co., as highest bidder at public outcry property of said Livingston Skinner. Wit.; George Lawrance, Joel Yates, J. P. . 202 1/2 acs. $176.

197 E/466 3/25/1851 Campbell Co.- A. Chappell, Benton Co., Al. to Madison Furman of Campbell Co. Wit.; J. B. R. Hopkins, Thomas Bullard, Clerk. 202 1/2 acs. $400.

197 E/467 2/14/1853. Campbell Co - Madison Furman to Moses Hartsfield of Campbell Co. Wit. James H. Cudley (sic), G. W. McLarty, J.P. 202 1/2 acs. $700.

198 A/154 11/2/1830 Habersham Co. - William Synard of Habersham Co. to James Stewart of Campbell Co. granted to William Synard in the land lottery. Wit.: John Woody, J. P. $100.

198 A/192 9/14/1831 Campbell Co. - James Stewart to Reuben Benson of Campbell County. Wit. George Harris, Jesse Humprey. 202 1/2 acs. $500.

198 A/ 485 10/22/1831 Jasper Co. - Reuben Benson of Campbell Co. to Study (sic) Garner of Franklin Co. drawn by William Synnard. Wit.: James Garner, Felix G. Denman, C. R. Dunkin. 202 1/2 acs. $500.

198 A/297 11/6/1833 Campbell Co. - Reuben Benson to Sturdy (sic) Garner of Franklin Co. drawn by William Synnard. Wit.: James Garner, Felix G. Denman, C. R. Dunkin. 202 1/2 acs. $500.

199 1827 Land Lottery Drawn by Nathan Maples of Douglass District, Decatur County in 1827.

199 A/77 10/1828 DeKalb Co.- Pursuant to a Fi. Fa. out of the Justice Court of DeKalb Co. in the case of R. M. Cleveland & Co. vs. Joseph Bass. Sheriff Neil Stone of Carroll Co. sold to R. M. Cleveland & Co. as highest bidder at public outcry. Wit.: Allen G. Fambrough, M. McWhorter, JIC. Land lying in LL 199 - $25.

199 A/231 7/24/1830 Carroll Co. - R. M. Cleveland & Co. of Campbell Co. to James Bell of Campbell Co., drawn by Nathan Maples. Wit.: A. Horton, J.P., A. C. McDowell, John S. Welch. 202 1/2 acs. $25.

199 A/173 4/3/1832 Decatur Co. - Nathan Maples to William Morgan of Campbell Co. 202 1/2 acs. $400.

200 A/ 214 4/5/1831 Campbell Co. - Alexander H. McCarty of Campbell Co., Guardian of the orphans of John McCarty, Dec'd., and Jerimiah McLarty of Campbell Co., to Samuel McLarty of Campbell Co, drawn by the orphans of John McCarty in the late land lottery. Wit. Joseph Speer, O. H. Kenan. 202 1/2 acs. $1,000.

200 A/ 296 12/4/1832 Campbell Co.- George Harris to F. G. Denman of Franklin Co. Wit.: B. Mathews, J. P., James R. Smith, Reuben Benson. 202 1/2 acs. $1,000.

201 A/ 80 8/9/1827 Butts Co.- Solomon Serimshire of Upson Co. to John Kennedy (Kenady, Canady) of Hall Co. Wit., Dolphen Lindsey, Samuel Bellah, J. P. 202 1/2 acs. $200.

216 A/9 1/28/1828 Carroll Co.- John Dickens to James Cox, both of Carroll Co, lying between the N'rn/half of lands drawn by B. Chalpecto of Newton Co. Wit: Sampson B. Kimball, James ---JIC. 101 1/4 acs. $300.

216 D/225 10/3/1845 Carroll Co.- L. C. Huff to L. B. Hawkins. Wit.: M. C. Awtry. J. C. Williams, J.P. 202 1/2 $200.

217 1827 Land Lottery Drawn by Nimrod Ray of Rhodes District, Oglethorpe Co.

217 A/ 121 8/21/1827 Walton Co.- Nimrod Ray of Walton Co. to Elemander Washington of Gwinnett Co. Wit.: Thomas Camp, Britton Smith. 202 1/2 acs. $300.

217 A/178 9/24/1827 Gwinnett Co. - Ellimander Warbington (sic) of Gwinnett Co. to Robert B. Haynes. Wit.: Henry Curlip, J. P., James Carson, Evan Howell. 202 1/2 acs. $1,000.

217 A/ 421 10/31/1834 Campbell Co. - Robert B. Haynes to Little B. Hawkins of Campbell Co. drawn by Nimrod Ray. Wit.: Jacob Autrey, Samuel B. Cobb. 202 1/2 acs. $1,500.

217 D/147 1/25/1844 Campbell Co. - Lewis Solomon to Charles Gorman of Campbell Co. Drawn by Joseph Tarpley. Wit.: John Hindman, J. P., Rob Buffington. 202 1/2 acs. $1,812.

216, 217 & 130
E/ 464 8/19/1847 Campbell Co. - L. B. Hawkins to Charles L. Polk of Campbell Co. Wit.: Ezekiel Polk, G. W. Blair. 202 1/2 acs. in LL 216 & 217 plus 100 acs. in LL 130. $1,400. Recorded February 23, 1853.

218 A/228 11/17/1831 Campbell Co. - James Fields of Carroll Co. to George W. McLarty of Campbell Co. (Drawn by Thomas Orps of Chatham Co.) Wit.: Samuel McLarty, George Harris. 202 1/2 $550.

218 A/ 228 4/6/1832 Effingham Co.- William Phillips of Effingham Co. to James

Fields of Carroll Co. Wit.: James Crow, David Felmly, J. P. 202 1/2 $40.

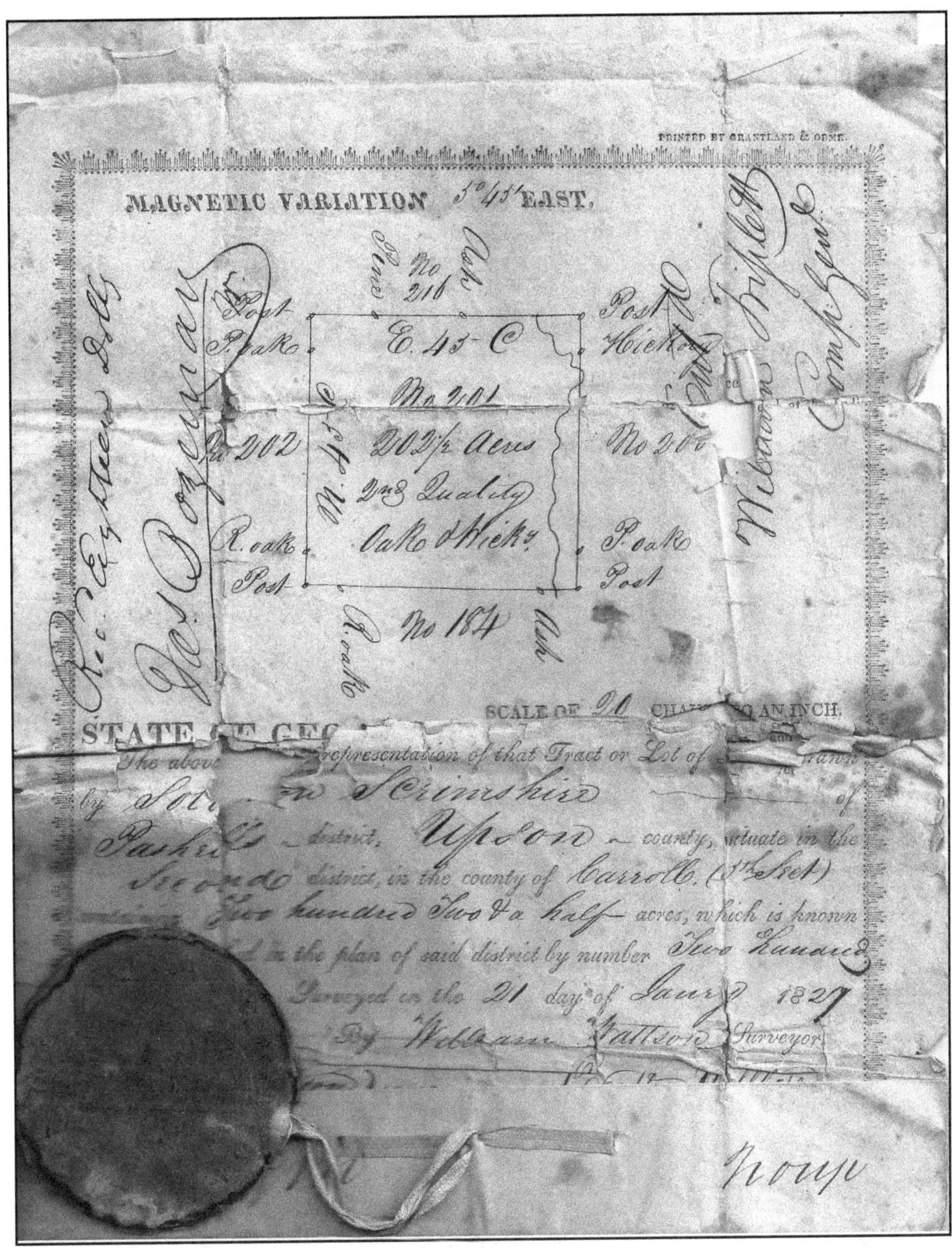

PRINTED BY GRANTLAND & ORME.

MAGNETIC VARIATION 5°45' EAST.

No 216

Post P. oak — Post Hickory

E. 45 C

No 201

No 202 — 202½ Acres — No 200

2nd Quality

Oak & Hick'y

R. oak Post — P. oak Post

No 184

SCALE OF 20 CHAINS TO AN INCH.

STATE OF GEO...

The above ... representation of that Tract or Lot of ... drawn by Solomon Scrimshire of Parker's district, Upson county, situate in the Second district, in the county of Carroll, (5th Sect) containing Two hundred Two & a half acres, which is known ... in the plan of said district by number Two hundred ...

Surveyed on the 21 day of Jany 1827

By William Mattson Surveyor

Original land grant for LL # 201; 202 1/2 acres - $200 bought by John Kennedy; 21st day of January 1827, date of survey; can be read in the bottom right hand corner. Seal, attached with a ribbon, magnified, shows the seal for the State of Georgia dated 1790. Courtesy Sam Henley.

218 A/252 4/7/1832 Chatham Co. - William Thrower, John Thrower, Sarah Ann Thrower, and Elias Bullard, orphans of C. Thrower, all of Chatham Co., to James Fields of Carroll Co. Wit: John J. Dews, James Cleland, J. P. 202 1/2 acs $200.

219 E/38 7/28/1845 Campbell Co. - Claiborn Gorman of Campbell Co. to William H. Gorman of Campbell Co. Wit.: Thomas Black, Charles D. Black, JIC. 202 1/2 acs. $712.

219 E/460 1/31/1851 Campbell Co. - Wm. H. Gorman to Hanson Kennedy of Cass Co. Wit.: W. P. Clinton. Recorded 2/22/1853. 202 1/2 acs. $1200.

219 E/460 2/4/1851 Carroll Co. - Hanson Kennedy of Cass Co. to Samuel R. Hartsfield of Campbell Co. Wit.: Samuel C. Candler, Joseph C. Williams, J. P. Recorded February 22, 1853. 202 1/2 acs. $1,400.

220 C/238 1/15/1838 Campbell Co. - Thomas Worthington of Campbell Co. to Samuel H. Watson of Campbell Co. Wit.: Richard Potter, Jacob Y. Worthington. 202 1/2 acs. $600.

220 C/ 278 4/3/1840 Campbell Co. - S. H. Watson of Campbell Co. to Nathan Camp of Campbell Co. Wit.: Riley Shirley, A. J. Camp, JIC. 202 1/2 acs. $600.

221 Land Lottery Drawn by Bennett Reeves of Ragsdale Dist. Wilkes Co. in 1827.

221 A/69 First Tuesday in March 1830.- Nathaniel Nicholson, Sheriff of Campbell Co., on an execution order from a Wilkes Co. court, to E. Daggett and Tarleton Sheets (sic) of Campbell Co. as highest bidder. Wit.: Gilbert Coffee, Samuel Wilkerson. 202 1/2 acs. $70.

221 A/117 12/22/1830 Baldwin Co.- Ezra Daggett of Baldwin Co. relinquishes all rights in 101 1/4. Said land originally drawn by Bennet Reaves in the land lottery and sold to Lewis S. Brown of Wilkes Co. at the Sheriff's sale for the sum of $2.

221 A/ 116 3/1/1831 Campbell Co. - Tarlton Sheats (sic) of Campbell Co. to Lewis L. Brown of Wilkes Co. Wit.: Isaac N. Mathews, Thomas Anderson, JIC. 101 1/4 acs. $50.

221 D/392 4/3/1838 Wilkes Co. - Lewis S. Brown of Wilkes Co. to George W. McLarty of Campbell Co. Wit.: Jacob Y. Worthanton, Watkins Bates. 202 1/2 acs. $450.

221 D/392 2/13/1845 Campbell Co. - George W. McLarty of Campbell Co. to Edward Drumond of Cobb Co. Wit.: L. Watson, S. H. Watson, J. P. 101 1/4 acs. $83.87 1/2.

221 D/125 10/31/1843 Cass County. - Geo. W. McLarty to Francis Irwin. 100 acs. $180.

221 D/393 3/10/1846 Cobb Co. - Edward Drummond to George Allen of Campbell County. 101 1/4 acs.. $100.

221 E/429 12/1/1852 Floyd Co. - Francis Irwin of Floyd Co., for the "legend" I have for my namesake, John Irwin Feely (a minor) of Campbell Co., "I give unto Mrs. Nancy Ferris, his grandmother, and her legal representative for my namesake," 100 acs. $50. Wit.: (None shown). Recorded January 18, 1853.

222 Land Lottery 1827 Drawn by James Jones of Lingo Dist, Baldwin Co. in 1827.

222 A/105 6/9/1827 Baldwin Co. In the 51st year of the Independence of the United States of America. Deed from James Jones of Baldwin Co. to Thomas B. Stubbs and Benjamin A. White of Baldwin Co. (Drawn by said James Jones in the late land lottery and granted April 20, 1829.) Wit.: John B. Gorman, B. P. Stubbs, J.P. 202 1/2 acs. $500.

222 A/104 7/23/1829 Baldwin Co. - Thomas B. Stubbs and Benjamin A. White of Baldwin Co. to James McConnell of Hall Co. (Granted April 10, 1828, to James Jones by His Excellency George M. Troup, Governor of Georgia.) 202 1/2 acs. $300.

222 A/158 12/13/1830 Hall Co. - James McConnell of Hall Co. to Eli Tanner of Hall Co. Wit.: Moses M. Cantrell, V. Dorsey, J.P. 202 1/2 acs. $225.

222 A/186 1/24/1831 Hall Co. - Eli Tanner of Hall Co. to Simeon Strickland of Gwinnett Co. Wit: Asahel R. Smith, J. P., John Strickland, Mathias Bates. 202 1/2 acs. -$150.

222 A/220 1/4/1832 Gwinnett Co. - Junior Strickland of Gwinnett Co. to Mathew Bates of Gwinnett Co. Wit: James Austin, John Miller, J. P. Land - with mines and mineral excepted. 202 1/2 acs. $375.

223 A/ 78 A 7/26/1830 Hancock Co. - Thomas Norwood of Hancock Co. to Francis Wynn of Campbell Co. Wit.: 202 1/2 acs. $200.

224 A/ 89 A 9/7/1830 Campbell Co. - Fi. Fa. in favor of W. Neal v. John Barro out of the Justice Court of Fayette Co. Nathaniel Nicholson, Sheriff, Campbell Co., seized property belonging to John Barro, and upon duly advertising same, sold to John Turner as highest bidder. Wit.: William R. Turner, George Lawrance, J. P. 202 1/2 acs. $110.

224 A/243 10/13/1832 Campbell Co. - Silas Lawrence of Gwinnett Co. to John Wynn of Campbell Co. Wit.: George Harris, J. P., Francis Wynn, Mathias Bates.

202 1/2 acs.$500.

226 E/497 10/3/1848 Campbell County - Upon due advertisement in the Cherokee Advocate at Marietta, Ga, Simon Strickland, Admr. of estate of Mathias Bates, dec'd, late of Cobb Co. Ga. sold to highest bidder, Francis Mims. Wit.: James A. Strickland, Wingfield Davis, J. P. Recorded 5/12/1853. 49 acs. $50.

231 E/321 2/7/1851 Campbell County - Willie B. Hinton to John A. Clinton. Wit.: Charity G. McLarty, G. W. McLarty. 168 acs. $500.

231 E/321 2/17/1851 Campbell County - John A. Clinton to Leroy Hartsfield of Carroll. (Granted to John P. Clinton on 9/2/1848.) Wit.: Samuel R. Hartsfield, G. W. McLarty, J. P. 168 acs. $1000.

232 E/463 10/2/1849 Campbell County - Property of John P. Clinton, dec'd, sold at auction to highest bidder, Charles L. Polk. Wit.: Ezekiel Polk, G. W. McLarty. Recorded 2/23/1853. 189 acs. $302.

233 E/609 4/24/1846 David J. Bothwell of Dooly Co to James H. Dudley of Campbell County. Wit: L. H. Watson, J. P., Samuel E. Bothwell, Samuel W. McLarty. Recorded 4/3/1854. 101 1/4 acs. $300.

5

1830 & 1840 Campbell County Federal Census

Dark Corner, Ga. 1841:
. . . Times are dull in this section of the country. Money is scarce. Property is low of all kinds. There are good bargins to be got in land in this country. Corn is selling at $1.50 per barrel. Bacon ten dollars per hundred . . .
Michael McElwreath

Dark Corner pioneers listed on the 1830 Federal Census for Campbell County:

Bates, John
Bates, Mathew
Clinton, William P.
Hartsfield, Moses,
Holloway, Levi,
Humpreys, (Umpreys) Jesse
Kennedy, (Canady), John
Strickland, Simon
Wynn, Francis

1840 Federal Campbell County Census for Militia District #730, Dark Corner:

Total for Head of the household - 65.

Males: Under age 5 - **51**; Ages 5 to 10 - **44**; 10 to 15 - **22**; 15 to 20 - **18**; 20 to 30 - **25**; 30 to 40 - **30**; 40 to 50 - **11**; 50 to 60 - **6**; 60 to 70 - **3**.

Females: Under age 5 - **55**; Ages 5 to 10 - 39; 10 to 15 - **20**; 15 to 20 - **11**; 20 to 30 - **36**; 30 to 40 - **17**; 40 to 50 - **6**; 50 to 60 - **7**; 60 to 70 - **3**; 70 to 80 - **2**.

Allen, George
Austin, Etheldrid

Brooks, Isaac
Brown, William H.
Clinton, David
Clinton, John P.
Clinton, William
Clinton, William P.

Endsley, James
*Farrish, (Farriah) John
Finch, James K.
Freemon, James
Garner, Thomas W.
Garrer, Benjamin
**Godfrey, Thomas P.

Harden, Asa C.
Harris, Drury L.
Hartsfield, Moses
Hartsfield, LeRoy
Hartsfield, Samuel R.
Hawkins, L. Berry
Hogan, Thomas M.
Hollis, Morrison
Holloway, Levi
Humphrey, William

Jones, Watson
Kennady, (Canady) John

Mathews, Jeremiah
Mathez, Gilbert L.

McClung, Reuben
McClung, William W.
McElwreath, James.
McElwreath, Michael
McLarty, George W.
McLarty, Samuel W.
McLarty, Stephen H.
McMim, Robert
McWhorter, Arthur
McWhorter, Moses
Miller, James M.
Miller, Robert
Mitchell, Henry
Morgan, John M.
Morgan, William H.
Norton, Carney
Norton, Curnilas (Cornelius)

Polk, Ezekiel
Poss, John
Reeves, Jonathan

Sewell, James
Stewart, James
Taylor, Aquilla

Watson, Samuel H.
Wedington, Alexander G.
Wheeler, Benjamin
Whitney, John
Williford, Stephen
Winter, Jeremiah
Wynn, Francis
Wynn, John

Wynn, John J. H.

Wynn, Lorenzo D.

This census compiled by Martin H. Cochran.

House located near the corner of Cedar Mt. and Mann Roads - LL #200; Referred to for generations as "The Civil War House," photo by author, John Bailey, 2014.

Letter from Michael McElwreath

April the 6, 1841
Georgia, Campbell County

Dear Son and Daughter,

I take the opportunity of writing to you to inform you that we are all well at present. Hoping these few lines may find you and family enjoying the same blessing. I received a letter from Joel and Mary Jane some time past that stated they are well and also stated that James and Rachel were living in the Missouri State and doing well also. The part of your connection living in this region are in good health and sends best wishes to you and your family.

John and Mark are married since I saw you. John was married last December to wife Elizabeth Mcclung. Mark was married a few days ago to wife Jane McLarty. They are well and send their love to you.

I have been looking for some of you out here for some time but I have not got you out coming yet. I would like very well to see you all again but the distance is to far that I do not feel able to undertake it again. Whitaker and family are well and send their respect to you. I have nothing of importance to write you at this time.

Times are dull in this section of the country. Money is scarce. Property is low of all kinds. There are good bargins to be got in land in this country. Corn is selling at $1.50 per barrel. Bacon ten dollars per hundred.

I inform you that since the date of my letter and before the sending of it, I got a letter from my brother James McElwreath and also one from Nathaniel Smith. Nathaniel stated that you and family were well a few days before the date of his letter. He also stated that your son, Edley was married but did not state the girl he married. I would like for you to write to me as soon as you get this how you all are and the girl's name he married as we are all anxious to know her name. His uncles and aunts all wish him great joy on his marryiable occasion and we hope that you were all well pleased with the choice he made.

Nothing more at present but still remain your affectionate father until death.
Michael McElwreath
You will send your letters to Villarier Post Office, Carroll County, Ga.

*John Farrish is listed as having 2 schools and 50 scholars (pupils).

** Thomas P. Godfrey is listed as having one school and 18 scholars.

6

The Dark Corner Settlement

The Post Office, the School, the Brush Arbor Church

Louanna Watson was a Postmaster in Dark Corner, 1864-1866.

Post Office 1837—1881

The appointment of postmasters was one of the "spoils" of Presidential politics in the early 1800s; whoever won the Presidency got to fill postmasterships with his political appointees. Since few of these persons were known to the President and the Postmaster General, recommendations were frequently accepted from interested Senators and Congressmen. Experience helped; good judgement and honesty were valued, but the main requirement for a postmastership was party loyalty. Through the 1830s, virtually all new postmasters were Jacksonian Democrats.

A postmastership was certainly a job worth having. Under an 1825 law, postmasters received no salary, but were entitled to a share of their postal revenues at a scale ranging from 30 percent for the first $100 worth of postal business they did each quarter to 8 percent of all above $2,000 until the commission reached its maximum of $2,400. Very few postmasters came close to that maximum (twice the 1836 salary of most state governors). Most kept another business—frequently a store in addition to their postal position.

The work of the postmaster was challenging but not overtaxing. He was usually referred to as postmaster of a town, although his "jurisdiction" extended to the suburbs and into the country, until it met the territory of the next town's postmaster. People from all over the town and surrounding area brought their letters to the postmaster, who listed them in his ledger, making special note if postage was paid in advance. As people came in to pick up their mail, he collected the postage on each letter and noted the charges in his book.

The postmaster sorted the letters from his town for delivery. Letters for each post office along the local post road were bundled and set aside to be sent when the stage or rider for that route stopped by.

Postmasters, as a rule, did not deliver mail to individuals; people picked their letters up at the post office. The post office itself was a government office established to receive and deliver mail. In most towns, it shared quarters with the postmaster's other business, often taking a corner of the store or business office.

Post roads were generally designated along the major roads of the state. By the mid-1830s, most all of the State Roads were also designated as post roads, and many of the smaller roads used by the stage lines.

Mail carried by stage was transported in leather chests or containers which were unlocked by postal officials at each stop. Mail for that stop was removed, and mail received by that office added to the chest. The container was then relocked and the stage sent on to its next post office.

Along the smaller post routes, delivery was often made by a single carrier on horseback sometimes on foot. Mail was carried in his saddlebags and delivered to the postmaster at each stop.

How the Post Offices were established.

Citizens of a community who desired a new post office generally submitted a request to the Post Office Department stating reasons why they thought a post office should be established, the number of patrons who would be served, and the names proposed for the post office. Other factors considered were the nearest existing postal units and the relative cost involved, including the estimated expense of mail transportation to the proposed office.

From 1836 to 1971, postmasters at the larger post offices were appointed by the President, by and with the consent of the Senate. Postmasters earning less than $1,000 per year were appointed by the Postmaster General, generally upon the advice of the local Congressman or Townspeople. Regulations required a valid bond and taking an oath of office. U. S. Citizenship was required for appointment to all but the smallest post offices prior to 1971. It was also required postmasters live in the delivery area of their post office.

Post office names were typically suggested by prospective patrons. There are now postal records that explain their origin. Generally a post office establishment date is the date of appointment of its first postmaster.

The Letter

Letters looked physically different than they do today. Envelopes were not used. The ends of the letter were folded in toward each other, then the bottom folded up and the top folded down over it. The top was then sealed to the bottom by a wafer, a small disc which was moistened and stuck between the top and bottom of the letter (black wafers were sometimes used on letters announcing a death.) If the person opening the letter were not careful, part of the letter could be torn off when the letter was opened by breaking the wafer. He usually noted the name of his post office (usually the town name) and the date mailed.

At left: An 1848 letter showing paper folds, hand-written postage, stamped post office name, and remains of a sealing wafer.

This was sometimes done in manuscript, but often a wooden or metal stamp, similar to our modern ring dater, was used. The letter was then added to the next mail going in the direction of its address.

Other special markings were sometimes added to these letters. If the postage was paid in advance, the work "PAID" was noted next to the postage indicator. If the letter was to be carried on a ship (from towns on waterways), the name of the ship was frequently also noted on the envelope.

It should be noted that postage stamps were not used in the 1830s. The idea of stamps originated with Rowland Hill in England in 1840, and the United States didn't issue its own stamps until 1847. By then postal rates had been standardized at 5 cents under 300 miles, 10 cents over 300 miles for a one-sheet letter.

1836 Postage Rates (single sheet)

0-30 miles	6 cents
30-80 miles	10 cents
80-150 miles	12 1/2 cents
150-400 miles	18 1/2 cents
400+ miles	25 cents

1847, Benjamin Franklin,
1st U. S. Postal Stamp

Dark Corner Post Offices

Dark Corner had a post office from 1837 to 1881. Before the Civil War, the original post office was located at the intersection of South Flat Rock and Cedar Mountain Roads. In 1870 residents got their mail in Powder Springs. In 1873, the last post office was located on LL # 199 on Cedar Mountain Road about one mile east of the intersection at Mann Road.

Dark Corner Postmasters

Mathias Bates	August 18, 1837
Samuel H. Watson	July 13, 1841
Samuel H. Watson	December 29, 1845
George W. McLarty	March 22, 1855
Mrs. Louanna Watson	October 7, 1864 -1866

After the Civil War, the people of the Dark Corner District Post Office were served at the Powder Springs, Post Office, Powder Springs, Georgia.

When Douglas County was created from Campbell County in 1870, the post office was reestablished and there were two more Dark Corner Postmasters:

James W. Anderson	October 13, 1874
Isham A. King	August 31, 1881—January 2, 1883 Discontinued

After Isham A. King's appointment expired, the Dark Corner Post Office was officially discontinued.

An 1873 Land Survey by John Mason Huey showed James W. Anderson listed on Land Lot #199. Then a deed was found showing that James W. Anderson paid $1,610 in 1869 for 202 1/2 acres of LL # 199, a goodly sum for four years after the Civil War ended.

Long-time residents in the area remember this building as being the last Dark Corner Post Office. Photo: *McLarty Family of Kintyre.*

In a 1991 interview for the ***North Georgia Journal of History***, Mrs. Lucy Kate Queen Parr, then age 73, remembers when the old Post Office building stood in Dark Corner. In the interview, Mrs. Parr says, "I can't remember it being an active post office, but I remember hearing people talk about having to get their mail there." Mrs. Parr's grandfather, John R. Benson, worked the farm where Mrs. Parr lived.

About 1928, Jud Benson built and operated a general store in the Dark Corner community. The store, made of field stone with iron bars on the windows, offered farming implements, dry goods, sewing accessories—all the merchandise of a typical Depression-era store. The family lived on this land—LL # 198 & 199—on Cedar Mountain Road for four generations.

Another long time resident of Dark Corner, Mrs. E. C. Ivey, recalls that the old post office building was used for voting. "I don't remember seeing anyone vote there. I just remember hearing older people telling about it."

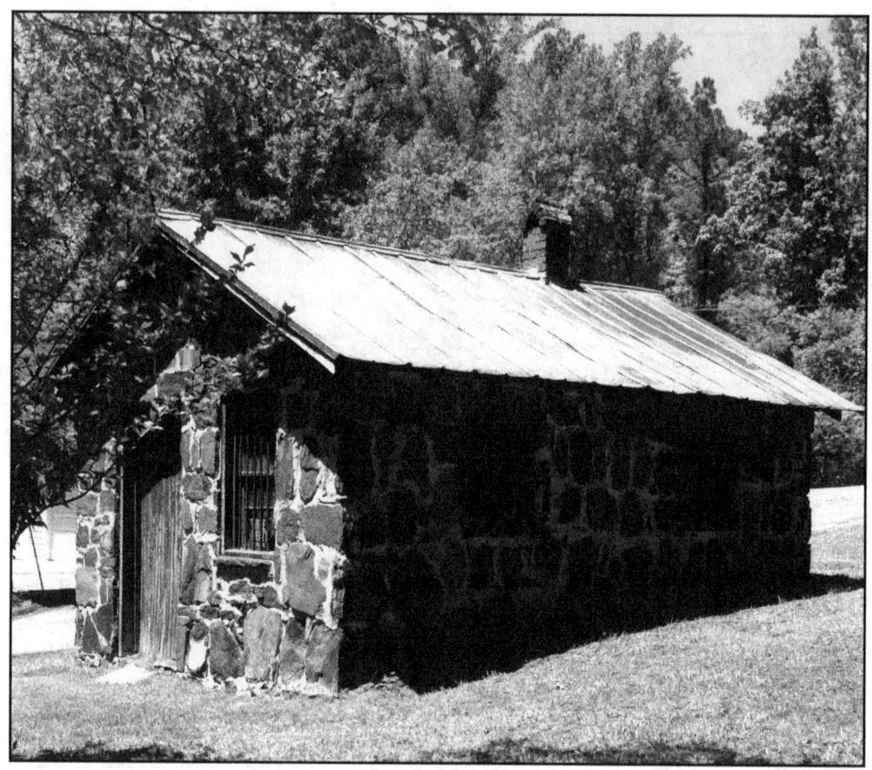

Jud & Verna Benson's general store made of field stones; windows have iron bars. Built 1928 on LL 218 - across from LL 199. Photo John Bailey, 2014.

Family History of Dark Corner Postmasters:

Mathias Bates

Through Mathias Bates' efforts the Dark Corner Post Office was established, and he was the first Postmaster beginning in August 18, 1837 to 1841. The Dark Corner Post Office was located in his home on Land Lot #222 near the intersection of Cedar Mt. Road and South Flat Rock Road near Douglasville, Georgia. Mathias' son-in-law, Samuel H. Watson, succeeded him as postmaster, then G. W. McLarty, then Mathias' daughter, Louanna Watson, was Postmaster from 1864-1866.

Mathias Bates, son of John Bates of North Carolina, was born about 1767 in Wilkesborough, Wilkes County, North Carolina. He is shown on the 1820 and 1830 U. S. Federal Census in Gwinnett County; Mathias Bates is shown on the 1840 census in Cobb County. He died May 17, 1847 in Campbell County, Georgia. His wife was Matilda Fountain: Their children:

1. Millie (1807) who married Lorenzo Dow **Winn** (born 1803) of Gwinnett

County and Campbell County.

2. Anthony Bates who was killed in the Mexican War;

3. William Bates, born 1801, who "died at Dark Corner in his old age";

4. Charity (January 12, 1813 - October 25, 1882) who married George **McLarty**; both are buried at the Old Villa Rica Cemetery;

5. Elizabeth who married John Lowe of Cobb County;

6. Louanna who married Samuel H. **Watson**;

7. Matilda who married Reverend Simeon **Strickland.**

Samuel H. & Louanna Watson

Samuel Hughes Watson, Jr was the son of Samuel Hughes Watson, Sr. who came from England in 1776 to Virginia, and then lived in North Carolina. Samuel Sr. married Martha Motley Watson in 1811.

Samuel H. Watson, Jr. was born December 29, 1812 in Virginia and died March 3, 1855 in Dark Corner, Campbell County, Georgia. He married Louanna Bates on July 29, 1838, in Campbell County, Georgia. She was born October 27, 1817 and died November 25, 1892, the daughter of Mathias and Matilda (Fountain) Bates. Samuel is shown on the 1840 Federal Census for Campbell County, District #730. He and/or his family are listed on the 1850, 1870 and 1880 Federal Census for Campbell County—#730 Militia District of Dark Corner.

Samuel H. Watson, Jr. was appointed Postmaster of Dark Corner beginning on July 13, 1841; the second appointment began December 19, 1845. He was an acting Justice of the Peace at Dark Corner in 1853. Louanna served as Postmasters in Dark Corner beginning October 7, 1864 to 1866. Samuel is buried in Winn-Watson Cemetery on North Flat Rock Road, at Dark Corner, and Louanna is buried at the Douglasville City Cemetery. Samuel H. and Louanna Watson's children:

1) James Anthony Watson, born August 15, 1844 - February 22, 1923; in 1887, he married Anna S. Anderson; 1858-1951; both are buried at the Powder Spring Cemetery, in Powder Springs, Georgia.

2) Samuel H. Watson III born 1846, died in infancy;

3) John Pendleton Watson born 1849 in Georgia; died in 1917; married 1st Savannah Stewart; married a 2nd time - to Reecie Stewart. John Pendleton Watson was also a merchant in the Dark Corner district in 1870 and later in Douglasville. In 1886-87, he was a State Representative for Douglas County.

4) Sarah Elizabeth "Sallie" Watson born August 17, 1849 - February 25, 1928 in Georgia; Sallie Watson remained unmarried. She is buried in the Douglasville City Cemetery.

5) Isaac M. Watson born 1853 in Georgia;

6) Virginia Louanna Watson born 1854 in Georgia; married Charles W. Weddington.

7) "Mathias" Bates Watson was born May 30, 1855 and died March 30, 1932. Mathias Bates Watson married Lillie Jane Vansant in 1881. She was born in 1865 and died in 1883, the daughter of Young Vansant. Mathias B. Watson's second wife was Ella Talulah **Strickland** 1866 - 1901, daughter of Williamson Parks Strickland. M. B. Watson, Lillie Vansant Watson and Ella Talulah Watson are buried at the Douglasville City Cemetery, Douglas County, Georgia.

Mathias Bates Watson and wife Lillie Jane Vansant, abt. 1881.
Photo: Davis: *Indian Trails to I-20*, page 18.

George W. McLarty

George Washington McLarty was the Postmaster at Dark Corner beginning on March 22, 1855. He was born in Mecklenburg County, North Carolina, August 30, 1804 and died in Dallas, Paulding County, Georgia, January 15, 1885. His family came to Campbell County about 1832. On January 24, 1833, he married Charity **Bates** (daughter of Mathias Bates) in Campbell County, Georgia. She was born January 12, 1813 in Georgia and died October 25, 1882; both are buried in the Old Villa Rica Cemetery. G. W. McLarty and Charity's children:

1) Julia A. McLarty born 1833; 2) Harriet J. McLarty 1834; 3) John Newton

McLarty 1836-1858 (Selma, Al).

4) William Wallace McLarty, 1838-1862; Pvt., Co. K 41st Georgia Infantry, enlisted 3/4/62 in Campbell County; Kill in action 10/8/62 at Perryville, KY; **Memorial marker in McLarty Cemetery.**

5) George Washington McLarty Junior 1840-1864; Pvt., Co. C, 30th Georgia Infantry; enlisted 9/25/61 in Campbell County; died 12/1/64, Camp Chase Columbus, Ohio.

6) Mary Elizabeth McLarty, born 1842, married Frank McClung and Thomas A. Owen;

7) Dr. Thomas Anthony McLarty, born 1844, Pvt., Co. C, 30th Georgia Infantry; enlisted 8/10/62; captured near Chattahoochee July 16, 1864 (with his brother); sent to Camp Chase August 5, 1864; sent to City Point for exchange March 4,1865.

George W. & Charity Bates McLarty & Family
Photo: *Who Was Who in Douglas County.*

8) James Madison McLarty, 1846-1871; Pvt., Co. B 4th Georgia Reserves, enlisted in Atlanta; died in Villa Rica, Ga.

9) Josephine Eliza McLarty, born 1848;

10) Jane Matilda McLarty, 1850-1914.

11) Dr. Walter Archibald McLarty, 1852-1881:

12) Emma Catherine McLarty, 1854-1929

Page No. 44

merely by an affirmative mark, as /.

SCHEDULE 1.—Inhabitants in Dark Corner District, in the County of Campbell of Georgia, enumerated by me on the 27 day of June, 1870.

Post Office: Powder Springs

H. Bowden

Dwelling-houses, numbered in the order of visitation.	Families, numbered in the order of visitation.	The name of every person whose place of abode on the first day of June, 1870, was in this family.	Description: Age at last birth-day. If under 1 year, give months in fractions, thus, 3/12.	Sex.—Males (M.), Females (F.)	Color.—White (W.), Black (B.), Mulatto (M.), Chinese (C.), Indian (I.)	Profession, Occupation, or Trade of each person, male or female.	Value of Real Estate Owned: Value of Real Estate.	Value of Personal Estate.	Place of Birth, naming State or Territory of U. S.; or the Country, if of foreign birth.	Parentage: Father of foreign birth.	Mother of foreign birth.	If born within the year, state month (Jan., Feb., &c.)	If married within the year, state month (Jan., Feb., &c.)	Attended school within the year.	Education: Cannot read.	Cannot write.
1	2	3	4	5	6	7	8	9	10	11	12	13	14	15	16	17
536	336	Polk Ezekiel	61	M	W	Farmer	6000	1000	NC							
		" [illegible]	61	F	W	Keeping House			"							
		" Nancy	28	F	W	House Keeper			Ga							
		" Georgia	22	F	W	" "			"							
		Washington Fanny	17	F	W	" "			"							
		McLarty Henry	14	M	W	Farm Lab			"						/	/
337	337	Washington George	35	M	B	" "		100	NC						/	/
		" [illegible]	30	F	B	Keeping Ho[illegible]			Ga							

Dark Corner District, Campbell Co. is shown as Powder Springs Post Office on the 1870 Federal Census Record

James W. Anderson

James W. Anderson was the Postmaster beginning on October 13, 1874. Born June 14, 1838 in Georgia and died June 28, 1881, James W. Anderson was the son of James Freeman Anderson, born July 27, 1814 in North Carolina and died March 4, 1881 in Douglas County, Georgia. James W. Anderson's mother was Sarah Eleanor McLarty (Anderson), July 27, 1814 - March 4, 1881. When her husband—James Freeman Anderson died, she married John **McLarty**, Jr.

James W. served in the Civil War, enlisting in Company C, 30th Georgia Infantry. In 1870, he and his family moved from Paulding County, Georgia to the Conner District near Dark Corner. On the 1880 Conner District Federal Census Record, he is listed as being temporarily disable having an abscess on the lung.

His wife was Martha Elizabeth "Mattie" Benson, daughter of James LaFayette **Benson** and Harriet Caroline **McLarty**. After James Anderson died, Martha married James M. **Dorris**. No children are listed on the 1870 Paulding County Federal Census or the 1880 Conners' District, Douglas County, Georgia Federal Census.

Isham A. King

Isham A. King was the last Dark Corner Postmaster; his appointment began on August 31, 1881. He was born November 5, 1853 in Georgia; he died July 24, 1926 in Paulding County, Georgia. On the 1860 Carroll County Federal Census, Isham A. King (age 7) lived with his parents—William L. King born 1816 in Georgia and Nancy born 1832 in Georgia. On the 1870 Federal Census, Isham is listed, age 17, living with the Turner family and working on their farm. On the 1880 census, he lives in Conners' District of Douglas County. He married Elizabeth Jane Clonts in 1876. She was born October 19, 1849 in Campbell County and died January 15, 1934 in Paulding County, Georgia. They had two children: Wesley J. 1878-1948 and Tommie J. born November 18, 1884 and died January 20, 1956 in Douglas Co., Georgia.

Dark Corner School

1854, John M. Huey, teacher

Names of Students:
E. D. Winn, T. S. Winn, M. C. Winn, A. J. Winn;
C. A. Oliver;
(illegible) Brown, Dana? Brown;
G. W. Stewart;
J. M. Entrikin, M. F. Entrikin;
J. A. Watson, L. A. Watson;
I. M. Reeves;
5, 6, 7, 8, illegible; M. McClung, N. McClung; 1/2 page water damaged.
September 1854:
J. W. Winn, T. S. Winn, M. C. Winn, F. M. Winn;
M. A. Weddington, Wm M. Weddington;
J. M. Reeves;
Jas McClung;
G. W. Stewart;
M. A. Hunter, Wm M. Hunter;
T. Y. or Y. Y. (?) Entrikin;
J. J. Brown, M. E. Brown, N. J. Brown;
S. H. Watson, J. A. Watson;
G. A. McClung;
Calton Oliver;
E. D. Winn; J. M. Brown, N. Brown, Wm H. Brown, P. N. Brown; J. N. Entrikin;
W. J. McClung, J. R. McClung, L. J. McClung;
A. I. Winn, Irena Brown.

Dark Corner School, January - October 1855
John M. Huey, teacher

Parent(s): **Students:**
Rev. F. & D. Winn's Children: F. Newton Winn, Ellen D. Winn, George A. Winn, A. B. Winn, Thomas L.(sic) Winn, M. C. Winn

Mrs. Mahala Winn's children: J. C. Winn, D. C. Winn, F. M. Winn, M. A. Winn, A. H. Winn, A. J. Winn

James and Nancy Stewart's children: G. W. Stewart, N. J. Stewart, R. J. Stewart, J. L. Stewart, M. L. Stewart

William H. Brown's children: J. M. Brown, Narcissa Brown, W. H. Brown, P. N. Brown, Irene Brown

David R. Brown's Children: W. F. Brown, R. J. Brown, N. A. Brown, J. L. Brown

Mrs. Eliza Brown's children: J. J. Brown, N. J. Brown, M. E. Brown

Reuben and Flora Vansant's children: A. M. Vansant,

Dr. E. W. and M. Maxwell's daughter: M. A. E. Maxwell

Young and Nancy Vansant's children: E. Vansant, M. C. Vansant, Dan'l Vansant

E. J. and E. Mattox's children: E. C. Mattox, William Mattox, M. A. Mattox, Elijah Mattox, Lucy J. Mattox

Mrs. Ann Freeman's children: M. J. Freeman, James Freeman,

M. & M. Freeman's son: William Freeman

R. H. Weddington's children: L. E. Weddington, M. A. Weddington, W. M. Weddington,

J. F. Cochran's (illegible): M. T. Cochran

G. Lee's (sic) (blurred) son: James M. Lee

H. Norton's (blurred): M. J. Norton

Mrs. Whitlow's children: L. A. Whitlow, M. F. Whitlow, N. O. Whitlow, W. P. Whitlow:

Wm. W. McClung's children: G. A. McClung, James R. McClung, William J. McClung, L. J.

McClung, M. M. McClung, N. C. McClung,

Jon. W. McClung's son: James McClung

An Orphan Boy: C. A. Oliver

Mrs. Louanna Watson's children: J. A.. Watson, S. H. Watson, J. P. Watson

Thomas and Jane Hicks' children: J. E. Grigs, (sic) M. A. Hicks, J. T. (F.?) Hicks

Wm. P. Griggs' daughter: L __(?) Grigs

A young man, formerly Post Boy: William N. Hicks

Asia (Asa?) Sewel's children: J. H. Sewel, Jno. Sewel, N. O Sewel, M. P. Sewell

William H. Brown's son: Posey Brown

J. F. (blurred): S. E. or L. E. Cochran

Mrs. Elizabeth (blurred): (torn) E. Brown, M. L. Brown

D. W. (blurred): Irene B. Trenthem

Note from 1855: Dark Corner was located northwest of the present location of Douglasville, Ga. near the Paulding County line. The capital letters S and L in the above document are written in a similar fashion.

Brush Arbor Church

The first church in the area began in the homes of the residents. Sometimes before 1850, Rev. Francis Winn, a local preacher, who had come originally from South Carolina, lived in Coweta County before coming to Campbell County, realized a need for a place of worship in the community. He invited the people to open their homes for religious services. They came in large numbers to the various homes to hear him preach from the Word of God.

The community came together late summer and early fall, when the crops were "layed by." They gathered for religious services followed by social and recreational activities. As the congregation out-grew meeting at homes, the discussion came up about building a house of worship. It was decided to build a brush arbor at the large flat rock located about two miles west of Skint Chestnut (later Douglasville).

Here, at the New Brush Arbor on this large flat rock area, the first camp meeting in the area was held. This first church was so popular that a larger structure was needed.

On March 16, 1850, Thomas Entrekin of Campbell County deeded 10 acres of Land Lot #163 to David Entrekin, Samuel W. McLarty, Alexander McKelvey, Mack McElwreath, George W. McLarty, William C. White, and Francis Winn, all Trustees of the new Methodist Episcopal Church South. These 10 acres cost - for the price of consideration, love and affection. The church members cut logs from the nearby forest and erected a log cabin—the first permanent structure—in which to hold services. There was no organ or piano. Later a frame building was erected with benches in the rear for slaves who were members of the church with their masters.

The first pastor to succeed Reverend Winn was Reverend Clayburn Trussell, who lived near Villa Rica. He came on horseback once a month to preach on Saturday and Sunday. "Uncle" Miles Norton was an exhorter and great help to the church. "Uncle" Ike McKelvey was an exhorter and was noted for his uplifting prayers. The family name of some of the charter members were: Winn, Maxwell, Wright, McElreath, McKelvey, McLarty, Entrekin, Weddington, Watson, Polk, and Norton.

Local Landmarks:

Every community has its local landmarks and so does Dark Corner: there is "the big rock" (about 20 acres of granite rock, close to today's Ragan Road), The Big Road, Waterfall Creek (adjacent to today's Old Mt. Top Church), Gothard's (Goddard's) Creek, Mud Creek and Sweetwater Creek, the big swamp, the big wood, arrowhead bottoms, Still House Road and the cane break. Then there is Cracker's Neck Swamp, where Sweetwater Ts into Mud Creek—close to where "High Point Road ends and Brittain Road begins." Historical papers inform that Dark Corner was located two miles south of the headwaters of Gothard's Creek.

With all these landmarks, it was hard to get lost in Dark Corner, except when one man fell asleep in a mining shaft and had the entire community looking for him 'til he woke-up and came out after dark.

7

1855 Property Tax Digest

The total land acreage given includes land of 1st quality, 2nd quality, 3rd quality, and pine (forest) land.

Below is a list of all land owners in 1855 in the Campbell County, Georgia Militia District #730, Section 2 which is Dark Corner. Land Lots (LL) were 202 1/2 acres; half lots, thus, were 101 1/4 acres. When an individual owned land in adjacent counties, these LLs and numbers are shown also. The total land acreage given includes land of 1st quality, 2nd quality, 3rd quality, and pine (forest) land. The actual tax on the land is not shown below, but the Total Aggregate Value of the total acreage is shown here. Agt. stands for Agent meaning a person who does business on behalf of another. Sixty (60) is the symbol given meaning the person is age 60 or more; Dec. stands for deceased. Orph. is orphan; Wid. is widow; this person usually has an agent shown.

Name	Total Acreage	Land Lot #(s)		Total Aggregate Value
Allen, George	101 1/4	1/2 of #221		$1,100
" "	202 1/2	# 211	(Carroll)	
Allen, James (Agt. George Allen)				
Andrews, J. C. (no info.)				
Baggett, John	607 1/2	#s 133, 134, 155		2,000
Black, William G. (no info.)				
Clinton, William P.	202 1/2	#166		860
Couch, John	101 1/4	#70		300

Clinton, Columbus C. (no info.)			
Clinton, Wiley A. (no info.)			
Davidson, James - Agt. John Couch		part #136	
Dempsy, Israel	227 1/2	#135	$ 840
Dudley, James H.	202 1/2	#233	
		#680 (Pauldin)	2,200
Dorris, James M. (no info.)			
Enterkin, David (60)	101 1/4	1/2 of #158	1,000
Enterkin, Samuel K.	202 1/2	#126	700
Endsley, John	607 1/2	#s 72, 73 & 57	
" "	202 1/2	#165	2,200
Endsley, Matthew	101 1/4	#124 (or 127)	600
Enterkin, John (60)	128	#157	1,200
Endsley, Joseph	1,212 1/2	#s 102,103, 123 91, 62	$ 2,000
Endsley, Samuel R. (Agt. J. W. McClung)			
Endsley, James	101 1/4	#26	400
Endsley, Andrew G. (no info,)			
Enterkin, Thomas A.	202 1/2	#192	250
Endsley, James A. (no info)			
Freeman, Madison	202 1/2	#489	500
Farris, Nancy (wid.) (Agt R. M. Hartsfield)			
	101 1/4	#121	600
Freeman, Linsey (no info.)			
Farmer, Joseph R. (no info.)			
Freeman, Hezekiah (no info)			
Goodson, G. W.	202 1/2	#88	
	120	# 200, #223, #645 w/Polk	1,000
Grubbs, John (no additional info)			
Griggs, William P.	303 3/4	1/3 of #s 194, & 195	600
Grubbs, Tatton (no additional info)			

Griffin, Christopher (Agt. C. C. Clinton) (no info)

Holman, Christian	405	#156, (#172 in Carroll)	1,300
Hartsfield, Leroy (no total acreage shown)		#169	1,200
Hammonds, Thomas (no info.)			
Hennon, Thomas (no info)			
Hammonds, Andrew (Agt. J. W. McClung) (no info.)			
Hallman, Samuel	405	#99, #164	975
Huey, John M. (no info.)			
Henderson, James M.	202 1/2	# 105	1,050
Harp, Wiley (no info.)			
Hightower, Isaac F. (no info.)			
Hartsfield, George	23	part of #718	75
Hix, Alford W. (Agt. Samuel Hartsfield) (no info.)			
Hartsfield, Moses (60) (Agt. R. M. Hartsfield) (no info.)			
Hartsfield, R. M.	141 1/4	#197, (# 945 Pauldin)	$575
Hartsfield, Chaffin L.	101 1/4	#197	500
Hartsfield, Samuel R.	225 1/2	#219, part #718 (Pauldin)	1,700
Hicks, Thomas M. (Agt. E. W. Maxwell) (no info.)			
Jones, Isaac (Agt. for Orph.)		part of #718 (Pauldin)	
Killgo, John (Agt. A. G. Wedington) (no info)			
Kanady, Elizabeth (wid.) (Agt. Jas. Stewart)			
	202 1/2	#201	$1,500
Leminack, G. W.	101 1/4	#132	$700
Lee, John	202	#89	1,400
Lee, William A. (no info.)			
Laminack, John (no info.)			
Lee, Green (Agt. J. ___ Cochran) (no info.)			
McLarty, George W.	202 1/2	#218 Campbell	
	20 each for	#948 & #275 Pauldin	
	40	#983 Cobb or Cherokee	
	5	#718 (Pauldin)	Total 2,250
McLarty, William A.			

McLarty. A. N.	242 1/2	#s 162 & 85	$2,100
McLarty, S. H.	890	#s 121, 137, 152,	
"		#s 154, 168, 185	2,800
McClung, John (Agt. William W. McClung) (no info.)			
McClung, Joseph (no info.)			
Moody, B. F. (Agt. James Endsley)			
	101 1/4	#26	414
Miller, Robert	253	#101, 1/4 124,	1,025
Miller, Benjamin G. (Agt. Robert Miller)			
	50	1/4 of #124	200
McKelvey, Alexander	300	#131, 1/2 158,	1,800
Maxwell, Dr. E. W.	202 1/2	#159	1,500
Maxwell, Margaret (Agt. Dr. E. W. Maxwell)			
	202 1/2	#191	1,000
Maxwell, M. C. Maxwell (a minor) (Agt. Dr. E. W. Maxwell as parent) (no info.)			
Moore, George (no info.)			
McElreath, Mark	343	#167, 1/2 #154, part #168	1,500
Matax, E. J. (Agt. James Stewart)			
	303 1/4	#196, 1/2 of 195,	1,500
McLarty, Samuel W.	761	#s 182, 199	
		#s 160, 200	
	40	in Pauldin Co.	Total 4095
McLarty, Mary (wid.) (Agt. Samuel McLarty)			
		1/6 of 718 Pauldin	no value shown
McLarty, John (Agt. Samuel McLarty) (no info.)			
McLarty, Charles B. (Agt. S. McLarty) (no info.)			
Neal, Marion (Agt. George Moore) (no info.)			
New, Nicholas M. (Agt. James H. Dudley) (no info.)			
Norton, Hancil (Agt. James Stewart) (no info.)			
Polk, Charles L.	650	#s 217, 216, 232	
		#s 724, 682, 683	

	2 1/2 acres of	# 718	Total $2,200
Polk, Ezekiel	1990	#s 120, 138, 139,153,	
		#s 154, 168, 169, 184,	
Polk, Ezekiel (as guardian J. P. Clinton orph.)			
		1/2 of #s 106, 414, 183	Total $ 7,250
Presley, Benajah H.	202 1/2	#61	450
Rice, Joel	1/2 of 101 1/4	#132	800
Robbins, Daniel (no info)			
Roggers, James (Agt. Samuel McLarty)			
Sewell, Asa	405	#s 161, 22	1,500
Smith, William A. (no info)			
Shearer, John (no info)			
Smith, James M.	101 1/4	1/2 #122	450
Sellers, John	25	part of #136	(no value shown)
Strickland, Roswell (no info)			
Strickland, William (Agt. R. Strickland)			
Stewart, James	780 + 824	#s 550, 452, 556, 558, 559, 560, 561	
		562, 629, 630, 631, 632, 633, 634, 635,	
		636, 697, 698, 699, 700, 701	
		Campbell & Pauldin	$6855
Stewart, James (As administrator of John Kanady, deceased) (no info.)			
Lowdes, George (Agt. S. McLarty) (no info.)			
Settle O. J., Physician (no info.)			
Teal, John R. (no info)			
Taylor, Aquilla	150	#56	$800
Taylor, David (Agt. Aquilla Taylor) (no info.)			
Umphrey, John (Agt. Jas. Stewart)		NK Dist 1 Sec. 3	1,200
Vansant, Reubin	274	# s 190, 157	1,100
Vansant, Young	192 1/2	#163	1,500
Vansant, Jacob	405	#s 125, 127	1,300
Williams, Westley N. (no info)			

Winn, Francis	387	#s 223, 226, 225,	
Winn, Francis N.		#s 709, 645, 736	2,700
Winn, Francis N. (Agt. Francis Winn) (see above)			
Winn, John W. (Agt. Francis Winn) (no info.)			
Winn, James H. (Agt. Francis Winn)			
	40	#708	200
Winn, Mahalah, widow (Agt. Francis Winn)			
	405	#s 224, 193	1,000
Weddington, William (60)	137	#s 287,288	1,200
Weddington, Robert H. (Agt. W. Weddington) (no info.)			
Weddington, A. G.	607	#s 186, 198, 177	3,300
Woodard, James (no info.)			
Williams, Thomas (Agt J. H. Dudley) (no info.)			
White, James T.	101 1/4	#116	800
Wheeler, Carrington (no info.)			

Defaulters in the #730 Georgia Militia District - Dark Corner

Andrews, John N.			
Clay, Henry			
Ensley, William			
Heath, David	101 1/4 NK Carroll		300
McClung, Wilson			
McLarty, Alexander			
McWater, Arthur			
Smith, Anderson	400	#s 90, 71	1,000
Taylor, Wiley			
Willingham, John			
Willingham, Thomas			
Winn, John C.			
Wallis, T. D.			
Williams, Newton J.			

Tax Statement prepared by J. L. Irwin, July 30, 1855

8

From the Cornfield to the Battlefield

November 24, 1861
. . . when I return home if the yankeys don't get to smart
I expect to live a corn field life.
Hastin Y. Huggins—Jr. 2nd Lt. Co C 34th Reg, Ga Inf. CSA
(Killed at Missionary Ridge - November 25, 1863)

The Willoughby Family During the War Years

Although the Willoughbys had just come from England, when the State of Georgia joined the other Confederate States, they volunteered. Thomas H. Willoughby and all four of his oldest sons enlisted in various units.

The first Willoughby to enlist was the 4th son, Alonzo Oliver, or Ollie, who joined the First Georgia Militia. When he took the dreaded diarrhea, he was sent home from the Army, sick. His mother, Christiana, did not know how to care for him and blamed herself when he died in 1862, around age 18.

Thomas Sr., Thomas, Jr., and William James were all volunteers in Company I, 56th Georgia Regiment, Confederate States Army. They were in battles in Mississippi. Corporal Thomas Willoughby, Sr., was in the siege of Vicksburg, escaping from the surrender of the Army on July 4, 1863. After making his way home, he did not rejoin.

Thomas Willoughby, Jr., then a Corporal, was captured at Champion Hill, Mississippi on May 16, 1863, sent to Ft. Delaware, Delaware, and was subsequently exchanged at City Point, Virginia around July 6, 1863, was released and rejoined his unit. He was captured again in July 1864, was sent to Louisville, Kentucky and took the Oath of Allegiance to remain north of the Ohio River for the duration of the war.

William James Willoughby also joined Company I, 56th Georgia Regiment,

Confederate States Army. He was also in the fighting and the siege of Vicksburg. Conditions were so bad during this siege that the people and soldiers were starving and reduced to eating bugs, rats and anything else they could find. The Army was surrendered on July 4, 1863 and paroled on July 8th, 1863. The Confederate Army, including William James, went right back to fighting. William James was captured again in July 1864, sent to Louisville, Kentucky, where he took the Oath of Allegiance to remain north of the Ohio River for the duration of the war. (He obviously did not do that as he got married in December 1864.)

John, 3rd son of Thomas and Christiana, enlisted June 22, 1861 in Company I, 19th Regiment of the CSA. This unit was called the "Villa Rica Gold Diggers." Unlike the 56th, this regiment was sent to Virginia. John was wounded in June, 1862, transferred to a couple of hospitals, ending up at Chimbarazo Hospital # 4, where he died on August 27, 1862. He is buried somewhere around Richmond, Virginia, exact location unknown.

When Thomas, Jr., and William James returned home, they used their pay to purchase 202 1/2 acres which was to become the line of the separation of Carroll and Douglas Counties.

There were almost unbearable hardships on the family who were at home. Christianna worked hard to have something for the children to eat. The meager corn and other food, kept for survival, was hidden in the "canebrake."

Letter from a Captain about back pay for Pvt. Henry A. Winn, deceased:

Private Henry A. Winn of Capt. J. J. Bowen Co. K 41 Regt Ga Volunteers was enlisted by Capt. J. J. Bowen at Campbellton, State of Georgia on the fourth of March 1862 to serv (sic) for the period of three years or the war—said soldier is 23 years of age 5 feet 10 inches high, fair complexion, Hazel eyes and sandy hair; by occupation when enlisted—A farmer. said soldier has been furnished pay to the First day of March 1863; the government is due him his wages from the 1(st) March to 1863 (to) the 17 August and collation from the 8 October 1862 to the 17 August 1863 after deducting $32.50 for clothing drawn in (illegible) during that period.

Given under my hand in camps near Dalton, Ga this March the 10 1864,

J. J. Bowen, Capt.
Co. K 41st Ga Regiment.

Private Allen Jacob Young, Co. F. 1st Georgia Cavalry
Photo: Courtesy Ed Thompson

Dark Corner Men and Boys Rally to the Call: Many of the men and boys from Dark Corner enlisted in Ga. Regiments, some of which were: Co. F, 1st Georgia Cavalry; Co H, 56th Georgia Regiment; Co. F, 40th Georgia Regiment - Paulding County; Co. G, 30th Regiment Georgia Volunteer Infantry - "Campbell Greys"; Co. F 39th Georgia Regiment; Co. C 35th Regiment Georgia Volunteer Infantry - "Campbell Rangers"; Co. E, 35th Regiment Ga. Volunteer Infantry - "Campbell Volunteers"; Co. I, 56 Ga. Volunteer Infantry and 19th Ga Regiment, the "Villa Rica Gold Diggers."

Co. A., 56 Regiment Georgia Volunteer Infantry, Army of Tennessee: CSA made up of men from Campbell (and Coweta):

Charles M. Polk; Thomas Carnes; Christopher C. Clinton; Wiley A. Clinton; John H. Dalrymple; James M. Darnell; Mathew Endsley; Thomas A. Entrekin; George W. Hartsfield; Richard M. Hartsfield; Thomas C. Holloway; John M. Huey; Carson S. McElreath; John P. McKelvey; Archibald D. McLarty; John H. McLarty; William A. McLarty; Killis B. Mobbs; William H. Polk; Henry Strickland; Levi S. Strickland; Eli Vansant; Emanuel Vansant; John Vansant; Noah Vansant; and Samuel J. White.

Two Hildebrand Brothers:
Memorial marker for Alfred Green Hildebrand, born October 1, 1842; enlisted in Co. I, 56 Regiment Ga. Volunteer Infantry; killed July 3, 1863 at Vicksburg, Mississippi. Isaac Newton Hildebrand, born March 19, 1840; enlisted Co. F later Co. C, 30th Georgia Volunteer Infantry; killed July 20, 1864 in Atlanta Campaign. Photos, John Bailey, 2014.

30th Georgia Regiment Campbell County:

Excerpts from **A Brief History of the Thirtieth Georgia Regiment**, by A. P. Adamson, written in **1912**.

This regiment was raised in what was then the upper part of Campbell, now Douglas County, in the summer of 1861. W. N. McGouirk was elected Captain; C. P. Bowen lst Lieut.; J. C. Danforth, 2nd Lieut.; A. G. Weddington, 3rd Lieut.; and H. H. Williamson, Orderly Sergeant. The other sergeants were: W. R. Selman, J. S. Rutherford, W. R. Harry and J. W. Selman.

This company went to Camp Bailey the latter part of September and became Co. F, Thirtieth Georgia Regiment, but at the re-organization, the position was changed and it was afterwards known as Company C. At the re-organization the position was changed and it was afterwards known as Company C. At the re-organization of the regiment in April, 1862, Capt. McGouirk, and the same Lieutenants were re-elected, but there were some changes in the non-commissioned officers. In the early part of 1863 Capt. McGouirk resigned and 2nd Lieut. Danforth died. Lieutenant Bowen was promoted to Captain and the vacancies for Lieutenants were filled by the election of H. H. Williamson and James W. Selman. In 1862 the company received a number of recruits and was the second largest of the regiment. This company was with the regiment throughout the war and was in all the engagements in which the regiment participated; the casualties in battle and by disease were considerable.

Among those killed of the company was Lieutenant H. H. Williamson, who was killed upon the breastworks near Atlanta in July, 1864. At the battle of Jackson, Mississippi, July 16, 1863, Sergeant A. W. Ballentine was killed in the charge upon the Federal lines; he was a brave soldier and had many friends in the regiment. A singular incident connected with his death was that he dug his own grave. For several days the regiment lay in an old creek run and the men had dug holes in the banks to protect themselves from the enemy's sharp shooters, and on the night after the battle, just before the lines were evacuated, the body of young Ballentine was buried in one of these excavations, which he had assisted in digging.

Another brave soldier of this company, who gave his life to his country, was Sergeant W. R. Selman. He was badly wounded at the battle of Chickamauga, and was afterward captured and taken to Camp Chase, Ohio; while there in prison, gangrene got into his wound. He was offered his release if he would take the oath, which he refused to do, preferring death to the disgrace of forsaking the cause of his country. He died in prison, October 18, 1864, and in his death Company C lost one of its best men, and the South one of its most loyal patriots.

Capt. W. N. McGouirk, the first captain of the company, was somewhat past middle life when he enlisted in 1861. While he was not skilled in military tactics, nor given to ostentation, he was a noble, true-hearted man, possessed with a good amount of common sense, plain, honest and straight-forward. He was so popular with his men that at the re-organization of the company he was re-elected. He remained in the army until August 5, 1863 when he resigned at Morton, Mississippi because of dropsy, resulting from bilious fever. After the war, he was one of the leading citizens of the new county of Douglas, and was elected to represent the county in the Legislature for one term. He was quite popular in his county, and had the reputation of being an honest upright man. He died in Douglas county in 1903.

Captain C. P. Bowen enlisted in the Confederate service in 1861, and was elected 1st Lieutenant of Company C, Thirtieth regiment. There was not a more popular and efficient officer in the regiment. Upon the resignation of Captain McGouirk in 1863, he was made captain of his company. He was with the regiment almost the whole time during its service. He was wounded at Chickamauga, September 1863, and was captured at Nashville, December 16, 1864. Soon after the creation of Douglas County he was elected to represent the new county in the Legislature.

Roll of Company C, Campbell, now Douglas County:
Captain, W. N. McGouirk, resigned 1863. Died, Douglas County in 1903.
Captain C. P. Bowen; enlisted as 1st Lt. Oct. 1861. Promoted to Capt. 1863. Wounded at Chickamauga, Sept 1863; Captured. Died, Douglas County 1907.
2nd Lieut. John C. Danforth; died at Savannah, 1863.
3rd Lt. A. G. Weddington; promoted to 1st Lt. 1863. Died 1903.
3rd Lt. H. H. Williamson; enlisted as Sergeant. Promoted to 3rd Lt. 1863. Killed near Atlanta, July 1864.
1st Serg. W. R. Selman; wounded at Chickamauga, Sept. 19, 1863. Captured and died at Camp Chase, Ohio, Oct. 1864.
2nd Serg. J. S. Rutherford; died in prison, Camp Douglas, 1865.
2nd Serg. S. M. McCarty; wounded at Jackson, Miss., July 16, 1863. Died 1863
3rd Serg. W. W. Harry; died in Douglas County, 1881.
4th Serg. A. W. Ballentine; killed at Jackson, Miss., July 16, 1863.
5th Serg. J. C. Morris; wounded, Jackson, Miss. 1863, and at Calhoun, May 16, 1864.
6th Serg. T. H. Williamson; killed at Chickamauga, Sept. 19, 1863.
Corporal J. P. McEwen; in 1912, lives in Florida.
Corporal W. F. Mosely; lives in Birmingham, Ala.
Corporal G. W. Lane; lives in Powder Springs, Georgia.
Corporal S. W. McGouirk; lives in Tennessee.
Corporal J. H. Walden; wounded, Chickamauga, Sept 19, 1863; died of wounds.
Corporal J. W. Anderson; died in Douglas County, 1881.
Corporal S. H. Worthy; lives in Augusta, Ga.

Privates*

Allen, W. J.; died, Savannah, 1862.
Alexander, W. J.; living in Douglas County.
Argo, L. D.; supposed to be living in Indiana.
Baggett, Allen; died in Mississippi, 1863.
Ballentine, J. W.; lives in Augusta, Georgia.
Black, G. B.; died 1890.
Blair, Allen.

Blair, James; died 1890.
Bishop, John V.; died 1894.
Bone, Manning; killed in Tennessee
Bowen, A. J.; living in Atlanta.
Brown, J. J.; died 1864.
Brown, P. N.; lives in Douglas County.
Bullington, R. P.; wounded Jackson, Miss., 1863. Lives in Douglas County.
Burton, James; no record.
Burton, S. F.; died Savannah, 1862.
Butler, Joe; died since the war.
Cash, Wm. C.; died Mobile, Ala., 1863.
Causey, J. H.; lives in Douglas County.
Causey, W. H.; lives in Paulding County.
Campbell, W. B.
Chapman, A. J.; lives in Talbot County.
Chapman, James; lives in Heard County.
Chapman, John; died 1890.
Clay, G. H.; died Savannah, 1862.
Collins, J. W.; died in Tennessee, 1889.
Dorsey, J. M.; wounded Chickamauga, Sept 19, 1863. Captured Nashville, Dec. 1864. Prisoner at Camp Chase, Ohio. Lives at Powder Springs, Ga.
Eason, J. R.; killed by mule running away, 1889.
Eason, O. R.; dead.
Endsley, George; died Camp Douglas, Ill., 1865.
Endsley, James; died at Savannah, 1882.
Endsley, Berry; lives in Texas.
Endsley, Joseph; wounded Chickamauga Sept. 19, 1863. Went to Texas.
Endsley, Pleasant.
Endsley Manning; died in Savannah, 1862.
Farmer, J. R.; died in Mississippi, 1863.
Gamiel, H. B.; lives in Paulding County.
Gamiel, J. B.; died at Griswaldville, Dec. 1861.
Gamiel, W. F.; died in Douglas County.
Gilbert, W. F.; wounded in battle.
Goodson, A. J.; lives in Arkansas.
Goodson, M. J.; died in Arkansas, 1870.
Gore, Manning A.; lives in Cobb County.
Hall, Asa; lives in Heard County.
Hall, J. M.; living last account.
Hall, J. P.; captured May, 1864. Died at Rock Island Prison, 1864.
Harper, Beverly; lives in Carroll County.
Henderson, Jackson; no record.
Henderson, J. M.; lives in Douglas County.

Hendley, P. L.; died in 1862.
Hendricks, William; lives in Paulding County.
Hightower, Isaac; lives in Tennessee.
Hilderbrand, J. H.; died 1864.
Holloway, L. S.; died 1891.
Holloway, N. J.; lives in Douglas County.
Holloway, S. H.; died since the war.
Holloway, Willis; died 1864.
Holloway, W. P.; died in Mississippi, 1863.
Hurt, J. W.; lives in Texas.
Irwin, A. N.; died in Mississippi, 1863.
James, Charles; died in Mississippi, 1863.
James, Counce (sic); died 1862.
James, Stephen M.; killed at Franklin, Tennessee, Nov 30, 1864.
James, Wm. M.; wounded at Chickamauga, Sept. 19, 1863, died 1863.
Johns, J. J.; lives in Paulding County
Johnson, W. H.; lives in Douglas County.
Johnson, W. J.; lives in Paulding County.
Laminack, J. D.; wounded at Chickamauga, Sept. 19, 1863; lives in Alabama.
Laminack, Toliver; lives in Alabama.
Lane, W. A.; died 1891.
Langston, J. W.; died 1862.
Lipscomb, N. S.; lives in Douglas County.
Lovin, (sic) E. W.; transferred to 1st Battery, Sharpshooters.
Mattox, W. H.; died 1883.
Maney, W. F.; no record.
Maxwell, E. W.; died 1873.
Maxwell, J. G.; died 1909.
McLarty, A. N.; died in Texas, 1867.
McLarty, G. W.; died Camp Chase, Ohio, February 16, 1865.
McLarty, G. W. Jr.; lives in Cullman, Alabama.
McLarty, G. G; ---------Texas.
McLarty, J. J.; died since the war.
McLarty, J. S. H.; died in Texas since the war.
McLarty, S. A; lives in Douglas County.
McLarty, S. M.; promoted to 2nd Serg. Wounded, Jackson, Mississippi, July 16, 1863. Died 1863.
McLarty, S. W.; died since the war.
McLarty. T. A.; died since the war.
McGuire, G. T.; Discharged 1862; died since the war.
Meeks, J. W.; wounded, Chickamauga, September 19, 1863. Lives in Paulding Co.
Moates, G. S.; no record.
Moates, J. M.; died, Griswaldville, 1862.

Moates, J. P.; lives in Marion County, Alabama.
Morgan, J. G.; lives in Alabama.
Nixon, A. F.; lives in Arkansas.
Nixon, John W.; died in Mississippi, 1863.
Nixon, Elijah; lives in Harralson County.
Norton, J. G.; wounded, Chickamauga, Sept. 19, 1863. Lives in Douglasville.
Oxner, Henry; discharged 1862. Died 1870.
Polk, James; died 1888.
Rice, Vincent; dead.
Rogers, Elijah; killed in Texas, 1890 by cowboys.
Selman, T. H.; lives in Douglas County.
Sprayberry, James; no record.
Stewart, G. W.; lives in Paulding County.
Stewart, J. R.; killed, Chickamauga, September 19, 1863.
Stewart, P. G.; died 1885.
Strickland, W. A. died 1862.
Strickland, W. J.; killed, Chickamauga, September 19, 1863.
Strickland, G. N.; lives in Harralson County, Ga.
Stone, A. N.; wounded at Murfreesboro, Tenn, 1864; lives in Douglas County.
Taylor, M. G; died 1888.
Taylor B. F.; lives in Texas.
Tidwell, T. J.; promoted to Corporal; dead.
Tolbert, E. H.; lives in Carroll County.
Vansant, Wilkes; wounded, Chickamauga, September 19, 1863; lives in Alabama.
Walden, W. W.; wounded, Chickamauga, September 19, 1863; lives in Douglas Co.
Wedington, C. W.; lives in Douglas County.
White, A. J.; died 1864.
Wilson, C. F. E.; living.
Winn, A. B.; living in Polk County.
Winn, J. C; died 1863.
Winn, A. H.; living in Cordele, Ga.
***The names of the Privates on the four previous pages are not in the end-of-book index.**

From the Campbell County Tax Digest—1866

List of Civil War Veterans who lost a limb during the war.

John Brooks	1 Arm
Valentine Dale	1 Arm
Saml Long	1 Arm
N. Summers	1 Arm
John James	1 Leg
James Hicks	1 Leg
P. Tatum	1 Leg

Letter from a soldier to his wife:

"Vicksburg, Mississippi
February 14, 1863

Dear Wife:
I seat myself to answer your letter which was dated Jan. 26th. I was exceedingly glad to hear from you, although sorry to hear that Emma had the hooping cough. I have been under the weather for some time, though I am some better today. Our Regiment has gone to Warrington on picket which is ten miles below here on the river, they started yesterday and will come back tomorrow evening, myself and almost one half of the company were not able to go. I am very much dissatisfied with the place, I don't think we can live here during the summer so I am in hopes that we will not have to stay here long. You stated in your letter that you wanted to know whether we were expecting a fight here or not. I believe the most of the officers are looking every day for a fight but I have looked for a fight so often that I have just quit looking. I don't believe the enemy will ever attack us here though they run another of their gunboats by here last knight about midknight (sic). They want to take the place very bad but I think they will eventually give it out as an unhealthy under taking. (Turn over) Tel Margaret and Amanda to come over and bring me a cool drink of water, for this is the worst water that I have ever drank in my life. It is as slick as soap suds. It can almost work a chew of tobacco out of a fellow's mouth. Everything is very high here. We have to pay thirty cents per pound for (?) and thirty cents for flour. Write as soon as you get this mail and write oftener. I believe this is the fifth letter that I have wrote since I left home and have not received but one. I wrote three to you and two to Pa. Write me a long letter give me all the news. I will close by extending to you the best wishes of your affectionate Husband.

C. M. Polk

I am very lonesome today I almost wish I had went on picket though I am almost too week to walk so fare. Tell all of our boys that are able to come that they had better git up and dust for Gen. Stephenson has ordered a detail of five commission officers from each Regt. to go home and bring back every man that they can find. I expect Capt. Cobb will to for his company and ours.

Charles M. Polk"

9

The Civil War Comes to Dark Corner

Dark Corner, April 1865
I camped out in the woods for five or six weeks, thinking the Yankees would be driven back. David Clopton

Georgia's Militia Districts

The state of Georgia was divided into 159 counties, and each county was subdivided into further political divisions known as militia districts. Georgia is the only state to have such a designation, although other states do divide their counties into smaller units, usually called townships. Each militia district was entitled to one justice of the peace, elected by the people, one notary public, recommended by the grand jury, and both commissioned by the governor, two bailiffs, elected by the people, and commissioned by the ordinary, and one justice court, and a voting precinct.

Georgia's militia dates back to colonial days and was authorized by the General Assembly April 16, 1751. The original intention was to provide protection against the Indians. All able-bodied male white citizens, between the ages of 18 and 45 (unless exempt) were at that time enrolled into the militia.

Each militia district was served by a company of approximately 100 men who elected one of their members to be the captain in charge. The districts were at first named for their captains, but confusion arose because of duplications of names and changes in command. It was then decided to use the present system, numbering the districts, beginning with the first organized. Besides using the numbers, some districts have retained the original names for the first captains, others have been named for prominent men, towns or communities, or from other origins.

The militia was under the direct command of the governor, could not be sent out of the state, and could only be used to repel invasion and preserve order. After the

Indians were finally driven from the state, the militia organization gradually took on a sort of social aspect.

During the Civil War, the Conscription Act of the Confederacy in effect wiped out the state militia by forcing its men into the regular Confederate Army.

During the Civil War, the Confederate and Union troops were stationed at Dark Corner. Here is correspondence from the Official Records written while the troops were in this area:

Civil War troops at a Ferry. www.archives.gov

Confederate Reports written in Dark Corner:

Dark Corner, September 30, 1864:

Brigadier-General Govan, Commanding and & c:

General Hood desires that you will give Brigadier General Iverson any aid you can in resisting any cavalry expedition against the West Point railroad, but not to allow yourself to be cut off from Moore's Bridge, as you must cross the Chattahoochee there, whenever you are ordered to join the main army.

A. P. Mason Assistant Adjutant General

Dark Corner, September 30, 1864
Brigadier-General Iverson: Commanding Cavalry:

General Hood desires that you should report daily in future, whether anything important transpires with you or not, he desires you to put on a line of couriers from your headquarters to Moore's Bridge, where we will have a station, or near there, as I am having a line put on to Newnan. Brigadier General Govan has been directed while he remains at Moore's Bridge to cooperate with you in resisting any cavalry movement against the West Point railroad. A. P. Mason, Assistant Adjutant General

Brigadier General Alfred Iverson

Alfred Iverson was born February 14, 1829 and died March 31, 1911. He was a lawyer, an officer in the Mexican-American War, a U. S. Army cavalry officer, and a Confederate General in the American Civil War. He served in the 1862-63 campaigns of the Army of Northern Virginia as a regimental and later brigade commander. His career was fatally damaged by a disastrous infantry assault at the first day of battle of Gettysburg. General Robert E. Lee removed Iverson from his army and sent him to cavalry duty in Georgia. During the Atlanta Campaign, he achieved a notable success in a cavalry action near Macon, Georgia, capturing Union Army Major General George Stoneman and hundreds of his men.

Dark Corner, October 1, 1864, Brigadier-General Iverson, Commanding Cavalry:

General Hood directs me to inform you that he has positive information that Garrard's cavalry command has gone up the railroad and across the Etowah and that Kilpatrick's division is in your front. The General desires you to hold yourself in readiness to meet Kilpatrick should he advance against you. Call upon General Govan should you need assistance. General H. expects you to give him prompt and

reliable information of all movements.
A. P. Mason, Assistant Adjutant General

Dark Corner, October 1, 1864
Brigadier-General Iverson,
Commanding Cavalry
Right Wing:

General Hood desires me to say that he thinks you had better bring Lewis' brigade farther to your left - that is, nearer to the West Point railroad, unless you have some information of the enemy's movements, which makes the present position of that command necessary. Our information here is that Kilpatrick is on this side of the Chattahoochee and Garrard's command has gone up the Chattanooga railroad. Should the enemy leave Atlanta to attack this army you must endeavor to destroy all stores the enemy may leave there.
A. P. Mason, Assistant General.

October 6, 1864
Brigadier-General Iverson Commanding Cavalry:

General Hood directs that should Morgan's brigade not have crossed the Chattahoochee River before the pontoon bridge at Moore's is taken up that he must swim the animals and cross his men, saddles, &c., in the ferry-boat, and get over with all possible dispatch, and instead of taking position from Salt Springs to Campbellton, as previously ordered, he will move his command to Villa Rica, reporting to Brigadier General Jackson by letter at this point.
A. P. Mason Assistant Adjutant-General

Official records: Series 1, Vol 29, Part 1 (Allatoona)— Mason's report:
Numbers 109. Itinerary of the Army of Tennessee:

September 29, 1864. Army of Tennessee left Palmetto and crossed the Chattahoochee River. Lee's and Stewart's corps at Pumpkin Town, and Cheatham's corps at Phillips' Ferry. That night the army bivouacked near Pray's Church, where General Hood's headquarters were. We found General Jackson's cavalry already there.

September 30. Left Pray's Church and encamped near Dark Corner. Remained there the next day.

October 2. Came to Flint Hill.

October 3. Encamped at Carley's, on Dallas and Marietta Road. That evening Stewart struck railroad with his corps, THIRD division, and broke it up from near Harrison's Station to beyond Acworth, which latter place capitulated about 9:30 o'clock on the 4th of October. French went on to Allatoona with his division: attached place (October 5); Lost men and officers; not successful. Stewart captured about 360 men on the expedition; was successful. We lay quiet about Lost Mountain on the 5th of October.

October 6. Moved to Dallas. General Hood's headquarters here. Lee's at Dallas, Cheatham's at Parsons, Stewart's at New Hope Church. All well thus far.

Kept by Colonel Edwin J. Harvie, assistant inspector-general, C. S. Army. OFFICIAL RECORDS: Series 1, Vol 39, Part 1 (Allatoona). Jackson's Calvary and Brigadier General Iverson's detachment of troops followed the same path, 24 - 48 hours later:

September 29. Headquarters left Palmetto at 12 m., and camped at Pray's Church at night, several hours in advance of the army. Crossed Chattahoochee River at 5 p.m.

September 30. Army all crossed the Chattahoochee River. Jackson's cavalry left Pray's Church at 7 a.m. army headquarters moved at 1 p.m.., and halted near Dark Corner, eight miles from Pray's Church.

October 1. The army is in bivouac in front of this place (Dark Corner); Jackson's cavalry are at Powder Springs. He has detached a force and sent them to operate on Atlanta and Chattanooga Railroad in the vicinity of Marietta. Firing has been heard in that direction today. From information received we learn that Kilpatrick's command is on this side of the river. Garrard's (Yankee) cavalry has gone up the Chattanooga railroad in the direction of Rome, Ga.

DARK CORNER, October 2, 1864
Brigadier-General GOVAN,

Moore's Bridge:
General Hood desires me to say that you must keep in constant communication with Brigadier-General Iverson, that you may be thus informed of any movement of the enemy against Moore's Bridge. Should they move on this bridge with a serious force, sufficient to drive your command away, you must destroy the bridge, first allowing our wagon trains to get on this side the river. You must use your own judgment as to any force of the enemy that may move against you, and if (is) only desired to destroy the bridge when you can hold it no longer. You must not rely solely for information on the cavalry, but send some of your good men up the river on both sides as scouts, and keep out a picket up the river on both sides, to see that the enemy don't cross above you.
A. P. Mason,
Assistant Adjutant-General

DARK CORNER, October 2, 1864
Brigadier-General IVERSON,
Commanding Cavalry:
General Hood desires that you will keep in constant communication with our wagon trains hauling supplies to the army from Newnan, so that they may have timely notice of any movement of the enemy which might endanger their safety and have time to get out of harm's way.

October 2. The army moved from Dark Corner at 9. a.m.. Headquarters arrived at Flint Hill Church at 5 p.m. and camped for the night.

Dark Corner Home Guard - 1864

This is a list of men enrolled in Georgia Militia District # 730 as required by the act of December 14, 1863, for reorganizing the militia of the state. The Home Guard was for the protection of the women, the young and the old from marauders and deserters who sometimes roamed the countryside preying on the unprotected population while their men were away from home fighting the war.

36th Senatorial District - #730 Militia District
BAGGETT, John, 46 yrs. 1 mo., Farmer, born NC
BLANCHARD, T. J., 54 yrs. 6 mos., Farmer, born GA

BROWN, W. H., 52 yrs. 11 mos., Farmer, born GA
CABLASS, Timothy, 53 yrs., Farmer, born GA
CLINTON, W. B., 22 yrs. 3 mos., Farmer, born GA
DARNELL, D. Y., 47 yrs. 7 mos., Farmer, born GA; Exempt: Certificate
DARNELL, Joseph Y., 16 yrs. 2 mos., Farmer, born GA
DAVIDSON, James, 36 yrs. 3 mos., Farmer, born GA; Disability
EARGLE, John, 50 yrs., Farmer, born SC
HENDERSON, J. M.., 47 yrs. 6 mos., Farmer, born SC
HENDERSON, John, 46 yrs., Farmer, born GA
HICKS, T. E. 47 YRS., FARMER, born GA
HURT, J. H. 49 yrs., Farmer, born SC
JARMAN, James, 53 yrs. 4 mos., Miller, born SC
JOHNSON, James, 49 yrs. 1 mo., Millwright, born NC
JONES, Isaac, 51 yrs. 2 mos., Farmer, born GA
LAMINACK, George W., 49 yrs. 11 mos., Farmer, born NC
MADDOX., E. S., 54 yrs. 4 mos., Farmer, born GA
McKELVY, Alexander, 59 yrs. 1 mo., Farmer, born GA
McLARTY, A. J., 16 yrs. 3 mos., Farmer, born NC
McLARTY, A. N., 52 yrs., Farmer, born NC
McLARTY, Harvy, 57 yrs., Farmer, born NC
McLARTY, J. W., 18 yrs. 6 mos., Miner, born NC
McLARTY, J. W., 59 yrs. 5 mos., Farmer, born GA
McLARTY, S., 17 yrs. 11 mos., Farmer, born GA
McLARTY, S.M., 17 yrs. 6 mos., Farmer, born GA
McWHORTER, Marion, 45 yrs. 4 mos., Farmer, born NC
MILLER, Robert, 58 yrs. 1 mo., Farmer, born GA
MORROW, J. K., 18 yrs. 4 mos., Farmer, born GA; Exemption: Discharged
MORROW, V. P., no information given
NEWTON, Henry, age not given, School Teacher, born GA
OXINNER, Henry, 46 yrs. 3 mos., Farmer, born SC
POLK, C. S., 49 yrs. 6 mos., Farmer, born NC
POLK, E., 55 yrs. 4 mos., Farmer, born NC
POOL, W. H., 30 yrs. 1 mo., M.D., born SC; Exemption: Disability
POTTS, Roswell, 43 yrs., Farmer, born SC; Exemption: Discharged C. S.
ROBINS, D. W., 18 yrs, Farmer, born GA
SHERER, John, 42 yrs. 4 mos., Farmer, born NC
SPRAYBERRY, J. F., 50 yrs. 9 mos., Farmer, born GA
VANSANT, John 16 yrs. 8 mos., Farmer, born GA
VANSANT, Reuben, 50 yrs., Farmer, born SC
VANSANT, Young, 48 yrs. 3 mos., Farmer, born SC
WATSON, L. H., 16 yrs. 6 mos., Farmer, born GA
WEDDINGTON, A. J., 57 yrs. 4 mos., Farmer, born NC
WEDDINGTON, R. H., 47 yrs. 11 mos., Blacksmith, born NC
WEDDINGTON, William, 17 yrs., Farmer, born GA

WHEELER, Anderson, 54 yrs., Farmer, born GA
WHEELER, Carrington, 48 yrs. 3 mos., Farmer, born GA
WHEELER, W. M., 17 yrs., Farmer. born GA

V. P. Morrow, Enrolling Officer; Henry R. Harris, Aid de Camp

Brotherhood of man

. . . many a soldier asked himself the question:
What is this all about? Why is it that 200,000 men
Of one blood and one tongue, believing as one
Man in the fatherhood of God and the universal
Brotherhood of man, should in the nineteenth century
Of the Christian era be thus armed with all the improved
Appliances of modern warfare and seeking one another's lives?

This quote is from an unnamed soldier who ends his lament by saying, "We could settle our differences by compromising, and all be at home in ten days."

The Union Army Invades

Silas Adams was born in Pulaski County, Kentucky, on February 9, 1839 and moved to Casey County with his parents in 1841. He attended Kentucky University at Harrodsburg, Transylvania University and Lexington Law School. He was a lawyer and politician from Kentucky.

He entered the Union Army during the Civil War as a first lieutenant, First Regiment, Kentucky Volunteer Cavalry and was later promoted to captain, lieutenant colonel and colonel of the regiment. He was mustered out December 31, 1864. He died May 5, 1896.

Colonel Silas Adams, 1st Regiment, Kentucky Volunteer Cavalry

Union Records from Dark Corner:

Thursday, July 7, 1864: From the The Civil War Day by Day, An Almanac, 1861-65 is this entry: Reconnaissance and raids on their lines of communications brought fighting at Adairsville, Dark Corner, Vinings' Station and Summerville, Ga.

General Stoneman

General Stoneman still continued making demonstrations on the right of our lines, while the chief movements for gaining Sherman's objective point, Atlanta, were made from the left. On the 12th, the First Kentucky, with other regiments under Stoneman, marched west in direction of Carrollton, twenty miles, and went into camp. The next day the command moved out early and went to Moore's Bridge, on the Chattahoochee River. The following is taken from General Stoneman's report of the same date:

"By taking a roundabout way, and by unfrequented roads, our parties succeeded in capturing or cutting off every scout the enemy had out. We surprised the guard at the bridge (the First Tennessee Cavalry) and drove them away before they had time to set fire to the straw and pine knots prepared for its conflagration. The Eleventh Kentucky Cavalry had the advance, under Colonel Adams, and did the thing handsomely. The bridge had been partially destroyed by tearing up the sleepers and planks, but we will have it repaired during the night. It is a covered structure, 450 feet long, very well built, on two main spans. One of the couriers we captured came down on this side of the river, bore a message to the commanding officer here that the Yankees were coming in large force, and that he must hold the bridge at all hazards, and that reinforcements were on the way."

After driving away the enemy, the bridge was repaired, and a few men crossed over and captured a few wagons, mules, and prisoners. The command was ready to cross the bridge at daybreak the next morning, but on attempting to cross, the enemy opened with four pieces of Artillery from the edge of the timber on the opposite side, and endeavored to retake their rifle-pits near the water's edge. General Stoneman now deemed it inexpedient to push his endeavors further, ordered the bridge to be burned, and the boats which had been collected there for security, destroyed. It is the recollection of the Author, that Lieut. Wm. P. Bailard, Company E, First Kentucky, performed the dangerous duty of applying the torch to the prepared combustibles to destroy the bridge, as the climate was getting very torrid around that point at the time. Stoneman remained during the morning, sending scouts down the river to within thirteen miles of Franklin, and finding neither fords nor ferryboats, in the evening fell back to Villa Rica, and encamped near that place. On the 15th, the regiment moved to Skin Chestnut, in the neighborhood of Sweetwater.

On the 16th, the regiment marched on the Sandtown road, went one mile to the left and encamped, where it remained until the 19th. On this day the enemy was reported crossing the river, the regiment was formed in line of battle, and in this position it lay during the night. At 4 o'clock, Company J was sent to the picket-post near the river to relieve Company G. On the 20th, the regiment moved to its former camp near Sweetwater factory, where it remained until the 23 of July.

Troops in Dark Corner

A Union Army military map, listed in the Atlas To Accompany the Official Records of the Union and Confederate Armies, depicts troop movement. This map identified the march of the 15th Union Army Corps through Dallas, Georgia, includes Dark Corner. It shows one lone road passing through the town connecting it to Villa Rica to the west, and Salt Springs (known today as Lithia Springs) to the east.

October 1, 1864 - 1 p.m.
General G. H. THOMAS
Chattanooga:

Hood has evidently crossed the Chattahoochee to the west, but has not gone to Blue Mountain. Kilpatrick, on the Sweet Water, reports he could hear drums at reveilee. There is too much ostentation in this move of Hood's, and he may attempt to swing his cavalry on our road. I have ordered General Garrard (**US**) over to Powder Springs. I will watch him close. Make as quick work with Forrest as you can, and get back to co-operate with me.
W. T. SHERMAN,
Major-General

October 1, 1864
General COX:

Let that DIVISION move to Flat Rock and not beyond. Howard has two DIVISIONS down toward Fairburn. I will send all of Kilpatrick's and Garrard's **(US)** cavalry over to Powder Springs, and we will find out if Hood is drawing over to Alabama. I hope he will, for I think he makes a mistake, and I think I see how we can take advantage of it. Keep me advised of all symptoms. Forrest is now threatening Huntsville, and Thomas has sent there Morgan's DIVISION. Road and telegraph to Nashville all right yet—W. T. SHERMAN

"Yankee Occupation of Atlanta." Note: shanty structures, made of wood, for soldiers. Lloyd Street in foreground; Decatur Street in background.

October 3, 1864

HDQRS. MILITARY DIVISION OF THE MISSISSIPPI,

In the Field, Atlanta, Ga.

General VANDEVER,

Marietta:

There is no doubt Hood is over about Powder Springs with a part of his infantry and cavalry, and the balance is intrenched down by Palmetto. I have sent four DIVISIONS to Smyrna, and in case you are threatened join them, or better, take refuge on

Kenesaw. Don't lose your men. Marietta is of no value to us, and it might be well now to move your command to Kenesaw where - could better guard the road. Two hundred men on the mountain and the balance on the ridge next north would be impregnable. If you have reason to believe a heavy force of the enemy is in striking distance of you, you had better move at once. A town is a weakness in military matters.
W. T. SHERMAN,
Major-General, Commanding.

October 3, 1864
HDQRS. MILITARY DIVISION OF THE MISSISSIPPI,
In the Field, Atlanta, Ga.
COMMANDING OFFICER,
Alatoona:
Hood has some infantry and cavalry about Powder Springs. I am watching him close. He might deceive us by his cavalry along Noyes' Creek, and slip up to Acworth and Allatoona. I want the utmost vigilance there. If he goes for Allatoona I want him delayed only long enough for me to reach his rear. Of course his cavalry can only run across the road and bother us, but his infantry would try to capture stores, without which Hood cannot stay where he is. If he moves up toward Allatoona I will surely come in force.
W. T. SHERMAN,
Major-General, Commanding.

October 4, 1864
HDQRS. MILITARY DIVISION OF THE MISSISSIPPI,
In the Field, Atlanta, Ga.
General D. S. STANLEY,
Smyrna Camp:
I heard from General Elliot last night. He was on the Sandtown and Allatoona road, and reported he would push for Dallas to-day. Hood is reported with infantry at Powder Springs and Dallas; his cavalry upon our road above Marietta. I will be up to-day and move to Kenesaw. Cox and Howard moved at dayLight (sic), and will reach Smyrna to-night. Send word to Vandever to move his force to Kenesaw, leaving a picket in Marietta.

W. T. SHERMAN,
Major-General, Commanding.

Colonel Frank Wolford, was born September 2, 1817 in Adair County Kentucky and died August 2, 1895. He fought in the Mexican War and maintained a career as a lawyer and politician in the antebellum years. He served as a member of the State House of Representatives in 1847, 1848, 1865 and 1866. When the war broke out, Wolford was one of the first Kentuckians to fight the rebellion and preserve the union. He was a Colonel in the 1st Kentucky Cavalry. Colonel Wolford and his troops burned Moore's Bridge on the Chattahoochee, then traveled to Villa Rica through Dark Corner.

FROM STANLEY TO SHERMAN
SMYRNA CAMP-GROUND, GA.
Elliot not yet heard from; also "if Hood shows any disposition to turn east I (General Stanley) will move to Lost Mountain in the morning." 11:30 p.m., telegraph working. Received dispatch from General Vandever, at Marietta, who says that one of his scouts just in reports that citizens say that Hood had a large infantry force at Powder Springs this evening and is moving north toward Dallas, and has ten days rations with him.

SMYRNA CAMP-GROUND, GA.
October 4, 1864
6:10 a.m. telegraphed, to General Sherman the report of General Vandever's scout, and that General Elliott has not yet reported, and asking for information on Hood's whereabouts. We will not move from this point until we hear from General Elliott or of the whereabouts of General Hood, or get instructions to that effect from General Sherman.

8:15 a.m. received dispatch from General Sherman stating that he heard from Elliott last night, who was on the Sandtown and Allatoona road, and reported that he would push for Dallas to-day; that Hood is reported with infantry at Powder Springs and Dallas, and his cavalry is on our road above Marietta. He (Sherman) further states that he will be here to-day and move to Kenesaw. Cox and Howard moved at dayLight, and will march to Smyrna to-night, and send word to Vandever to move his force to Kenesaw and leave a picket in Marietta.
8:30 a.m. sent word to General Vandever as above directed; also telegraphed Colonel Vandever as above directed; also telegraphed Colonel Hayes to bring up train from Chattahoochee bridge to this place; also asked General Sherman, "Shall I (General Stanley) move to the WEST of Kenesaw and tell Davis to follow?"
9:00 a.m. General Vandever reports that the signal officer on Kenesaw Mountain says that a large force of the enemy is burning the railroad on both sides of Big Shanty.
9:40 a.m. received dispatch from General Elliott, dated 6.15 this morning, two miles from Powder Springs.

October 3, 1864
SPECIAL FIELD ORDERS, HEADQUARTERS DEPARTMENT AND ARMY OF THE TENNESSEE, Numbers 156. Dallas, Georgia. **(US)**
I. The movements of the army to-morrow, November 4, 1864, will be as follows:

1. Major-General Osterhaus, commanding Fifteenth Corps, will move with his command from his present position by the most direct and practicable road to Powder Springs.

2. Major-General Blair, commanding Seventeenth Corps, will move with his command at 7 a.m., on the Marietta road, via Powell's Mill, to the vicinity of Powder Springs, followed by the supply train of his corps and the cattle under charge of Lieutenant Todd, acting commissary of subsistence.

3. The Fifth Kentucky Cavalry, with the supply train of the Fifteenth Corps, will move to Powder Springs, by the direct Dallas and Powder Springs road.

4. The train of these headquarters will follow the ordinance train of the leading DIVISION of the Seventeenth Corps.

November 3, 1864

By order of Major-General O. O. Howard:
SAML. L. TAGGART,
Assistant Adjutant-General.
SPECIAL ORDERS, HDQRS. FIFTEENTH ARMY CORPS, Number 160,
In the Field, Georgia
I. The command will move forward at 7 o'clock to-morrow morning in the following order:

1. Brigadier-General Hazen, with Second DIVISION, will have the advance. He will assign two sections of artillery, which will report to him for position in his column.

The Second DIVISION will be followed by

1. The DIVISION ambulance train and medical wagons.
2. Ten wagons infantry ammunition.
3. Pioneer corps wagons.
4. Headquarters train, Fifteenth Army Corps.
5. Headquarters train, DIVISION and brigades.
6. Regimental wagons, one to each regiment.

This train will be well guarded and followed by one regiment of infantry.

7. Brigadier-General Woods, with the First DIVISION, will follow in rear of Second DIVISION, with two brigades and one section of artillery, followed by DIVISION ambulance train and medical wagons, pioneer wagons, ten wagons of infantry ammunition, headquarters wagons of DIVISION and brigades, regimental train, one wagon for each regiment; the whole train sufficiently guarded for any emergency and followed by the troops of the remaining brigade of the DIVISION. One army wagon will follow each battery. DIVISION commanders will cause the trains to be kept closed up at all times, and to that end will cause a commissioned officer to be constantly with the trains of their respective DIVISIONS.

By order of Major General P. Joseph Osterhaus:
FRED K. WHITEHEAD,
Assistant Adjutant-General.

A large map prepared to exhibit the Union Army's Army of the Cumberland campaign depicts Dark Corner and marks a trail through the town where General Palmer's Union cavalry thundered past in pursuit of Confederate President Jefferson

Davis, during the final days of the War Between the States.

The women, waiting at home, received dreaded news:

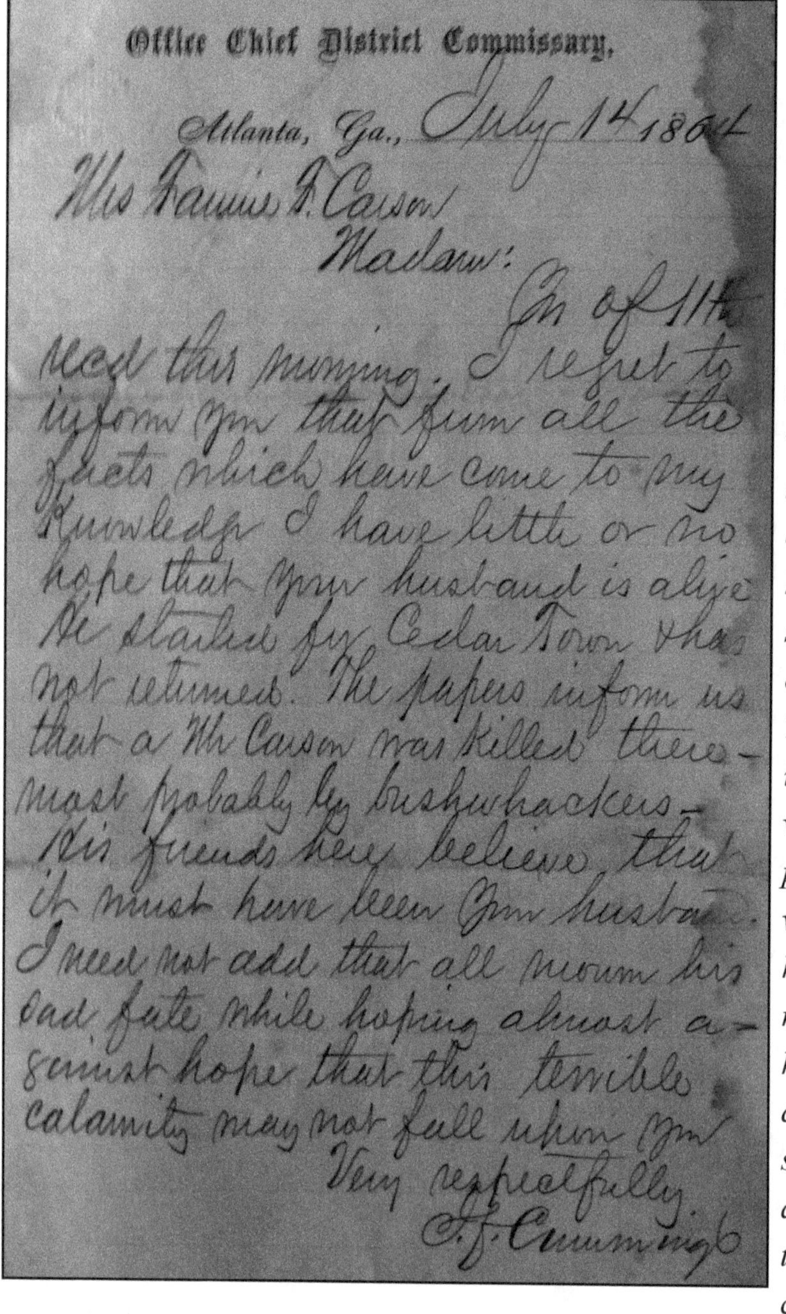

Office Chief District Commissary,
Atlanta, Ga., July 14 1864
Mrs Fannie F. Carson
Madam:
Con of 11th rec'd this morning. I regret to inform you that from all the facts which have come to my knowledge I have little or no hope that your husband is alive He started for Cedar Town & has not returned. The papers inform us that a Mr Carson was killed there - most probably by bushwhackers - His friends here believe that it must have been your husband. I need not add that all mourn his sad fate while hoping almost against hope that this terrible calamity may not fall upon you
Very respectfully
J. F. Cummings

Photo: Annie Belle Weaver Collection

Office Chief District Commissary,
Atl. Ga., July 14, 1864
Mrs. Fannie F. Carson

Madam:

Con of HQ rec'd this morning. I regret to inform you that from all the facts which have come to my knowledge I have little or no hope that your husband is alive. He started for Cedar Town & has not returned. The papers inform us that a Mr. Carson was killed there - most probably by bush-whackers. His friends here believe that it must have been your husband. I need not add that all mourn his sad fate while hoping almost against hope that this terrible calamity may not fall upon you.

Very respectfully,
J. F. Cummings.

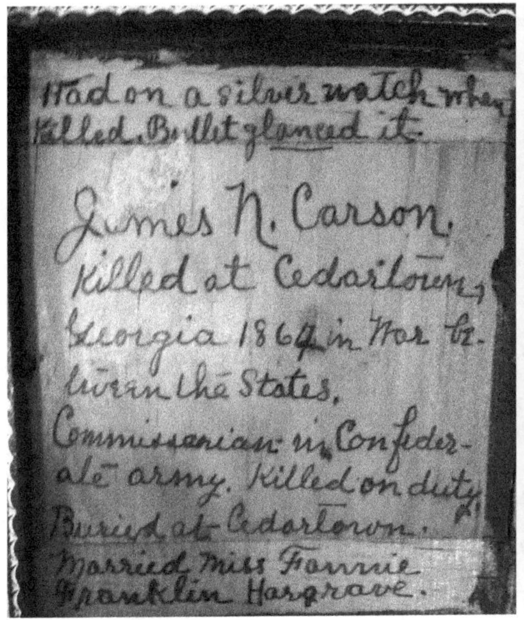

Had on a silver watch when
killed. Bullet glanced it.
James N. Carson.
Killed at Cedartown,
Georgia 1864 in War be-
tween the States.
Commissarian in Confeder-
ate army. Killed on duty.
Buried at Cedartown.
Married Miss Fannie
Franklin Hargrave.

James N. Carson, husband of Fannie G. Hardgrove Carson

Photos: Annie Belle Weaver Collection

Too little credit has been given to the slaves who "carried on" without the plantation owner who was away fighting for the Southern cause. Approximately forty-four percent of the population in the South was made up of slaves who were expected to care for the women and children, the livestock, the farming and the plantation for that matter without guidance. The following is a letter that illustrates that role by, Edy, a slave on the Clopton plantation, located on Land Lot # 194 in Villa Rica, Carroll County—close to Dark Corner, while her master, David Clopton, was away. This letter, written by David Clopton to Fannie Hardgrove (Hardgrave), daughter of Bright W. Hardgrove—a member of the community of Villa Rica in Carroll County. Sherman's troops were in Dark Corner and David Clopton went into hiding. He writes his letter to tell Fannie what has happened since last summer when the Yankees and foragers came through "and left the country almost destitute of anything for the people to live on."

March 21, 1865

Dear Fanny:

Your letter of 12th of last month came to hand a few days back, and as Mr. McClure is with me and will leave in the morning for the low country I will send this by him. If I mail it here it is very uncertain whether you will ever get it. I will not attempt to give you a history of my ups and downs since I saw you; it would take a volume. I will only say I left home Saturday before the Yankees came on Monday. I did expect they would get here on Sunday morning from what I had heard.

They robed my house, took a part of my meat and corn, and broke up things generally. They found the box containing your bedclothes, etc. and took most of your things, scattered your books all over the yeard, robed Edy of her money and the most of her fine clothes and took many things from the rest of the negroes. Your box was under Edy's bed. She thought, and was told that Yankees would not rob negroes. Edy sent Mr. Pentecost's trunk to Patience's house and had it hid, but they found it and took out all his clothes.

I camped out in the woods for five or six weeks, thinking the Yankees would be driven back. I then left the country and landed down in Chambers County, Alabama, where I staid until sometime in September when I thought I would come home and see if I had anything left.

I found the negroes had not worked one week all put together. They did cut a little wheat but let it get spoiled. I had been but a short time at home when the Yankees moved up from Stilesborough and for weeks they were camped on this side of the Van Wert and raiding through here every day. They passed my house many times but paid no attention to me. They stripped my house again of everything they wanted and left me almost without anything to keep house on. I have but two old broken knives and forks and would have been without bedclothes to sleep under had not Edy patched up a comfort or two.

The Yankee army has passed twice through here and our army once. The deserters and stragglers of our army have been in here all the summer and all together they have left this country almost destitute of anything for the people to live on.

They have taken five horses from me, about 80 heard (head) *of hogs, and everything in the shape of a cow I had on the place and fully half of what little corn that was made. I am now without syrup, without milk, and have only corn and meat enough to last me half the summer.*

But I am better off than some of my neighbors. There is poor Kingsbury had every pound of meat, and every bushel of corn, every horse, cow, hog, and chicken taken; the house stripped of everything they could carry off and he and his family left with only the clothes they had on, without one mouthful to eat. And he is not alone.

Dodds and some others here left in the same fix.

The negroes I took off with me, I left in Alabama working for their victuals and clothes. I could not feed them if I had them here. The families of Seaborn Jones and George Rentz have just reached home. I don't know where they will live. I was at Seaborn's a few weeks since and he and Mr. Rentz were living on two scanty meals a day and as for their negroes, they did not taste of meat.

I have lost four negroes since you left. Jesse and Big Joe sickened and died. Adaline took fire with her child in her arms and they both got burnt so badly that she died the second night after.

I am glad to know you have got a good place among kind and friendly people. You have ample means to pay your way and I would advise you to stay there, and not think of coming to this destitute country. It is not the country it was when you left—everything wears a gloomy aspect—everyone stays at home and we see nobody passing unless it is some poor refugee slowly wending his way to his devastated home.

How is it, Fanny, you bear your misfortune with so little fortitude so little patience? There are many who have been equally, or more, unfortunate than you have been whose situation is far worse than yours and they become reconciled after the lapse of time.

It is useless, Fanny, to attempt to resist the degrees of Providence—you can't do it. We all have to submit to fate and it is well for us if we can do it cheerfully.

I have received a letter from Martha—the first I've received in twelve months. They all seem to be getting on well—everything quiet there.

Your friend,
David Clopton

April 1865 Dark Corner:

Once again Dark Corner was part of Civil War history: After the shooting war had ended, Jefferson Davis, President of the Confederacy, with what remained of his Confederate government and treasury were trying to escape. President Lincoln had been assassinated and orders were given to General Palmer Union Cavalry, to pursue Jeff Davis to the ends of the earth. When Davis later heard how Palmer and his men just missed capturing him as he escaped through Greensboro, it prompted Davis to grin and remark, "A miss is as good as a mile." Jeff Davis barely missed being captured several other times as Palmer and his men pursued him through Georgia. This brought Palmer and his men to Dark Corner and Powder Springs, using this area as a staging area sending out scouting parties to look for the elusive Confederate President who was later captured on May 15, 1865 at Irwin, Georgia by another Federal Unit—the 4th Michigan Cavalry.

On April 9, 1865, Lee surrendered to Grant at Appomattox Court House, Virginia. On May 12, 1865, the last Confederate forces in Georgia surrendered at Kingston.

The war ended after four long years. Georgians had rallied when duty called - 130,000 of them. At the end of the war, more then 11,000 Southern soldiers had perished on the battlefields, in prisons, or in hospitals. Some made it home and died from sickness or wounds. The South suffered a devastating loss and their lives lay in shambles. Home and fields had been destroyed. Most livestock were gone, either taken by the Union forgers or were dead—having died from starvation. Many returning soldiers were disabled; the women and children planted the crops and carried on life as best as they could. All involved were glad the war was over.

10

Freedmen

. . . system that required free slaves to work on former plantation land under pay scales fixed by the (Freedmen's) Bureau . . .

Advocate for the Freedmen:

Oliver Otis Howard, November 8, 1830 - October 16, 1909 was a career United States Army officer and a Union general in the American Civil War. As a brigade commander in the Army of the Potomac, Howard lost his right arm while leading his men against Confederate forces at Fair Oaks in June 1862, an action which later earned him the Medal of Honor. As a corps commander, he suffered two humiliating defeats at Chancellorsville and Gettysburg in May and July 1863, but recovered from the setbacks as a successful corps and later army commander in the Western Theater.

Oliver Otis Howard

Known as the "Christian General" because he tried to base his policy decisions on his deep religious piety, he was given charge of the Freedmen's Bureau in mid-1865, with the mission of integrating the freed slaves into Southern society and politics during the second phase of the Reconstruction Era. Howard took charge of labor policy, setting up a system that required free slaves to work on former plantation land under pay scales fixed by the Bureau, terms negotiated by the Bureau with white land owners.

Howard's Bureau was primarily responsible for the legal affairs of the freedmen. He attempted to protect the Negros from hostile conditions, but lacked adequate power, and was repeatedly frustrated by President Andrew Johnson. Howard's allies, the Radical Republicans, won control of Congress in the 1866 elections and imposed Radical Reconstruction, with the result that freedmen were given the vote. With the help and advice of the Bureau, they joined Republican coalitions along with "carpetbaggers" and "scalawags" to take political control of most of the Southern states. Howard was a leader in promoting higher education for freedmen, most notably in founding of Howard University in Washington and serving as its president 1867-73.

From the Georgia, Campbell County Tax Digest, District #730:
Freedmen in 1867:

Employer:	**Freedmen**
Blanchard, J. T.	Ned Parker
Darnell, D. Y.	Clark Endsley
Furr, H.	Jess Vinsant
	Clark McLarty
	Harry McLarty
Garman, Jas.	Bob Farmer
	Peter Farmer
Hughey, J. M.	Mem Stewart
	George Hous
	Bob Holymon
Canady, J. J.	Oliver McLarty
McKelvey, J. W.	Lewis Winn
G. W. McLarty	Lewis Brown
	Lundy Orr
Mattox, E. J.	Squire McKiney
Polk, C. S.	Jesse Jones
Polk, E. Z.	Peter Polk
Vinsant, Young	Mike Vinsant
Vinsant, Reubin	Burgess Vinsant
Wedington, C. W.	Isaac Williams
	William Williams
Winn, J. H.	Bob Clonts
Sum Total of the #730th Dist. G. M	21

Defaulters	Simon McKelvy	
	Daniel Boyd	
	Balus McLarty	Total = 24

Freedmen in 1868:

Employer:	**Freedmen:**
Blanchard, T. J.	Lewis Brown
	Ned Ponfrer (?)
	Bah Clonts
	Cunigan George
	Clark Endsley
	Jackson Tody
	Peter Farmer
	George House
	Jesse Jones
	Van Henry
	Balas McLarty
Wihtto Poke (sic) (Polk)	Squire McKiney
	Peter Polk
	Mimm Stuart
Weddington, C. W.	Bill Williams
	Green Wright
	Lewis Winn
	Isaac Williams
Vansant, R.	James Vansant
	Bery Vansant
	Mike Vansant
	Total 21

Freedmen in 1869:

Cunnigan, George
Bruce, Thomas
Brown, Lewis
Parker, Ned
McLarty, Henry
Midle Brooks, Green
Ensley, Clark
Williams, William
House, George
Bruster, Henry
Jones, Jesse
Vansant, Jesse
Vansant, Bringer

McKiney, Squire
Vansant, Mike

Total 15
Defaulter
Plesant Davis + 1 = 16

Freedmen in 1870 Campbell County GMD #730

Brown, Lewis
Davis, P.
Wilson, George
Bruster, Van
Endsley, Clark
Vansant, Bringer
Weddington, W. R.
House, George
Wedington, George
Elheredge,(?) Green
McLarty, Henry
Blanchard, A
Parker, Nead
McLarty, Henry
Midlebrook, Green
Williams, William
Vansant, Jesse
Slowter, Jo
Vansant, Mike

Total 19

After 1870, this Georgia Militia District divided, and Dark Corner is listed separately from #730 which becomes "Town District."

Freedmen in 1871 Douglas County, Dark Corner

Employer	Freedmen
Polk, Ezekial	Carnes, Peter
	Wedington, G.
	Hawkins, Nat
	Davis, Please
	Hart, Neill
McLarty, G. W.	Barnes, George
Anderson, W. P.	Carns, Robert
McLarty, Ann wid(ow)	McLarty, Clark

Enterkin, Conally	Wilson, George
Chamblis, A. (illegible)	McLarty, Joseph
Anderson, J. W.	Bruster, Van
Parrish, John M.	Parker, Ned
Stone, W. P.	Thrasher, Perry
Howell, H. P.	Gammon, Randole
	Tate, James Sr.
	Tate, James Jr.
	Holmon, Charles
	Heard, Robert
	Endsley, Clark
	Total 19

Freedmen in GM District #730 - Town District (Douglasville)

Employer	**Freedmen**
James, Stephen	Brown, Seaborn
McLarty, G. W.	Middlebrooks, Green
Winn, T. S.	Cole, Henry
	Winn, Thomas
	Slater, Joseph
McKinney. A. G.	Vansant, Jesse
Winn, A. Y.	Winn, Lewis
McKelvey, Alexander	Etherge, Green
	Hanner, Andrew
Brown, W. H.	Vansant, M.
	Goodday, Jackson
Vansant, Rubin	Vansant, William
Stewart, G. W.	Cunnagin, George
Wedington, C. W.	Williams, William
	McDoo, Munson
Watson, J. P.	Houser, David
Winn, (illegible) C.	Williams, Isom
Selmon, William	Price, Essops
Morris, E. A.	Smith, Rubin
	Total 19

11

Voters & Reconstruction Oaths

... given that African-Americans are over-represented compared to their percentage of the population, it's obvious that some whites did not register.

After the Civil War, The Reconstruction of 1867 required Southern states to ratify the 14th amendment, draft new state constitutions and register voters, both black and white. In order to vote, men had to swear an Oath of Allegiance to the United States, and some were disqualified for their participation in Confederate government posts.

The registers were intended to list all eligible voters, but don't assume that because your ancestor is not listed that he was not in the country. He may have been ineligible (if he had been a Confederate official, etc.), he may have refused to sign, and so on. We don't have good data on how many people are not on the registers, but given that African-Americans are over-represented compared to their percentage of the population, it's obvious that some whites did not register.

Below is a reproduction of a document that had to be completed and each person had to sign.

STATE OF GEORGIA NO. . . ***214*** . .
COUNTY OF . . . ***.Campbell. . .***
PERSONALLY APPEARED before me this . .***15th***. . .day of.. . . .***August*** 1867
. . . . ***James Endsley***. . . . . who states that he resides in the . . . . . ***736th***. . . . . . . Election Precinct of. . . ***Campbell***. . . . COUNTY, GEORGIA, and who makes oath as follows:

"I . ***James Endsley*** . . .do solemnly swear in the presence of Almighty God, that I am a citizen of the STATE of GEORGIA. I have resided in the State . . .***12*** . . . months next preceeding the date, and now reside in the County of . . .***Campbell*** . . . . . . in the said state; that I am 21 years old; that I have not been disenfranchised for participation in any rebellion or Civil

War against the United States, nor for felony committed against the laws of any State or the United States; that I have never been a member of any State Legislature, nor held any executive or judicial office in any State, and afterwards engaged in insurrections or rebellion against the United States, or given aid or comfort to the enemies thereof; that I will faithfully support the Constitution and obey the laws of the United States, and will to the best of my ability, encourage others so to do. So help me, God."

The said . . ***James Endsley*** . . . . . . further swears that he has not been previously registered under the provisions of "An act supplementary to 'an act to provide for the more efficient government of the rebel States'— past March 2, 1867—and to facilitate restoration," under this or any other nation, in this or any other Election District; and further, that he was born in . . . . .and naturalized by . . . .
on the . . . . . day of . . . . . . 18***67*** in the . . . ***James Endsley.*** . . . .
SWORN TO AND SUBSCRIBED before me . . ***date, precinct, heretofore said*** . . . . .
Register of the 36th Registration District

The following 126 names are from the Georgia, Returns of Qualified Voters and Reconstruction Oath Books, 1867 - 1869. They were registered in precinct #730, Dark Corner, County of Campbell, State of Georgia, by the Board of Registration for the 36th Electorial District.

Date of Registry:

August 16th 1867 - Page 19

Name of Voter	Book, Page Number	Color
Black, William E.	A/275	White
Vansant, Reubin	A/276	White
Griggs, Robt. C.	A/276	White
Polk, Charles S.	A/277	White
Parris, Nathan	A/277	White
Howell, Lewis W.	A/278	White
Hightower, Berry	A/ 278	White
Lindly, Wm. T.	A/279	White
Rice, Jay	A/280	White
Vansant, Wilks	A/280	White
Parker, Edward	A/280	Colored
Orr, London	A/281	Colored
Vansant, Bringer	A/281	Colored
Boyd, David	A/282	Colored

Brown, Lewis	A/282	Colored
Bowles, Jno. L.	A/283	White
Weddington, Robt. H.	A/283	White
Wynn James H.	A/284	White
Mattax, William H.	A/284	White
Smith, Jasper S.	A/285	White
Stewart, James C.	A/285	White
Darnell, James M.	A/286	White
Wood, Saul A.	A/286	White
Rogers, Alex	A/287	White
McClarty, Geo W.	A/287	White
Taylor, Aquilla	A/288	White
Brown, Parker N.	A/288	White
Brown, William H.	A/289	White
Huey, John M.	A/289	White
Vansant, Jacob	A/290	White
Laminack, Geo. W.	A/290	White
Black, William G.	A/291	White
McKelvy, Simon	A/291	Colored
Vansant, Joseph	A/292	Colored
Wynn, Lewis	A/292	Colored
Vansant, Jesse	A/293	Colored
Steward, Memory (sic)	A/293	Colored
Johnson, William H.	A/294	White
Grifin, Christopher	A/295	White
Darnell, David Y.	A/295	White
August 16th 1867 - Page 20		
Kitchens, Kincher	A/296	White
James, Robert	A/296	White
Miller, Joseph	A/297	White
McKelvey, Alex	A/297	White
Enterkin, John	A/298	White
B--tley, Tiny D.	A/298	White
Enterkin, Samuel R.	A/299	White

Parker, John J.	A/299	White
Enterkin, Thomas A.	A/300	White
Kenedy, John J.	A/300	White
Goodson, Michael J.	A/301	White
Mobbs, (sic) Joseph	A/301	White
Mobbs, (sic) Killis B.	A/302	White
Alexander, Jno B.	A/302	White
Linsday, James A.	A/303	White
House, George	A/303	Colored
Holliman, Robt.	A/304	Colored
Carnes, Jabez	A/304	Colored
Farmer, Peter	A/305	Colored
Farmer, Robt.	A/305	Colored
Williams, William	A/306	Colored
Middlebrooks, Green	A/306	Colored
Williams, Isaac	A/307	Colored
Miller, David	A/307	Colored
Clinton, Jas. S.	A/308	White
Enterkin, Fletcher	A/308	White
Mattox, Early J.	A/309	White
Michael, John	A/309	White
Goodson, Andrew J.	A/310	White
Holoman, Saml.	A/310	White
Morrow, Hillian (sic)	A/311	White
Morrow, Jas. R.	A/311	White
Garman, James	A/312	White
Robbins, Daniel	A/312	White
McKelvey, Isaac	A/313	White
Allen, George	A/315	White
Stewart, Perry. G.	A/315	White
Trapp, Asa C.	A/316	White
Baggett, John	A/316	White
Feely, John	A/317	White

August 16th 1867 - Page 21

McLarty, Oliver	A/317	Colored
Polk, Peter	A/318	Colored
McLarty, Bailey	A/318	Colored
Polk, Mann	A/319	Colored
McLarty, Henry	A/319	Colored
Jones, Jesse	A/320	Colored
McLarty, Clark	A/320	Colored
McKinney, Squire	A/321	Colored
Darnell, David	A/321	White
Brown, Wm. H.	A/322	White
Hurt, Jas. W.	A/322	White
McWhorter, Marion	A/323	White
Butler, Martin G.	A/323	White
Freeman, Linsday	A/324	White
Bntley, (sic) Wm. T.	A/324	White
McClung, Samuel	A/325	White
Hicks, Thomas	A/326	White
Meadows, David S.	A/326	White
Endsly, Clarke	A/327	Colored
Henderson, Jackson	A/327	White
Newton, Henry	A/328	White
Mattox, Elijah N.	A/328	White
Polk, James E.	A/329	White
McLarty, Thos. A.	A/329	White
Dorris, Wm C.	A/330	White
Lindlay, James	A/330	White
Wynn, Geo. A.	A/331	White
Blachard, Thos. J.	A/331	White
Dorris, John M.	A/332	White
Vansant, Noah	A/332	White
Vansant, John	A/333	White
Vansant, Michael	A/333	Colored
Maxwell, John G.	A/334	White
Biggers, Saml. W.	A/335	White

McElreath, Jas. M	A/335	White
White, Saml. J.	A/335	White
House, Micajah G.	A/336	White
McKenney, Alex G.	A/336	White
Weddington, Charley W.	A/394	White
August 24th 1867 - Page 22		
Vansant, Young	B/188	White
Hartsfield, Richard M.	B/189	White
McElwreath, Carson	B/189	White
Ergle, John	B/190	White
Pool, Wm. A.	B/203	White
Lindley, Aquilla	B/211	White
April 6th 1868		
Clinton, Wiley A.	D/99	White

12

The Southern Claims Commission

"I was present and saw two men dressed as United States soldiers take and carry away three horses and a mule about daylight on Sunday morning in June 1864. . .

General Stoneman's troops, under the command of Major Terry Williams — William T. Sherman's Army was forging in the area of Sandhill in Carroll and Campbell Counties while other calvary units were at Villa Rica and Dark Corner. He visited the home of Green and they took what they needed and went back to where they were camped on Dog River.

They also visited the home of John J. Kennedy, taking his horse, corn, and fodder, bacon and other stores.

In Villa Rica, four miles west of Dark Corner, the foraging Union Army visited the home of Allison Cheves taking a fine mare worth $200.00. Kilpatrick's troops, took the horse back to where they were stationed—at Wadkin's. Kilpatrick went on to raid in Powder Springs and Dallas.

Claimant: Nancy Stewart for $600.00

The United States, ***To Nancy Stewart***				**1864**
Item 1	*2 fine Mules*	*valued at*	*$150.00*	*$300.00*
Item 2	*2 fine horses*	*valued at*	*$150.00*	*$300.00*
			Balance	*$600.00*

To the Commissioner of Claims, (under Act of 3d of March , 1871.) Washington, D.C.

The PETITION of . . . ***Nancy Stewart. . .*** respectfully represents:

That your petitioner is a resident of the county of . . . ***Campbell. . .*** in the State of . . . ***Georgia:. . .*** that her post-office address in . . ***Dark Corner. . .***in said County and State: and that at the time his claim and each item thereof as above set forth accrued he was a

resident of the county of . . . ***Campbell. . .*** and State of ***. . . Georgia. . .***
that he is the original owner of said claim: that he has never sold, assigned or transferred the same or any part thereof to any person; that no mortgage, bill of sale or other lien of like nature has at any time rested upon it, or any part thereof, nor has it been attached, or taken in execution; that the same has not been paid by the United States or any of their officers or agents, nor have the United States any legal offset against the same or any part thereof; that he is the sole owner of the said claim, no other person being interested therein: that said claim does not contain any charge for property which was destroyed or stolen by the troops or other persons: that the rates or prices charged are reasonable and just, and do not exceed the market rate or price of like stores or property at the time and place stated; all of which your petitioner states of his own knowledge.

Your petitioner further states that she is now and was at the time the several items of her said claim accrued, as stated therein, a citizen of the United States; that he remained a loyal adherent to the cause and Government of the United States, during the war of 1861, etc: and was so loyal before and at the time of the taking or furnishing of the property for which this claim is made.

And your petitioner father represents, and of his own knowledge state, that on the ***8th*** day of ***June*** A. D. 186***4***, at ***her residence*** in the State of ***Georgia*** the following property or stores were taken from your petitioner for the use of the Army of the United States, and for which payment is claim, via: ***which is above described***
which said property or stores being of the kind, quantity, quality and value above stated was taken by—***General Kilpatrick*** **belonging to the** ***Cavalry*** Department of the United States Army, in the service of the United States, whose rank was ***General of Cavalry*** **of the Regiment of . .** ***not known.*** **acting as** ***General of Cavalry*** **...** who, as your petitioner has been informed and was stationed at . ***Sweet Water factory*** **. .** under the command of ***. . . General Wm. T. Sherman . . .*** who at that time had command of the United States forces in the District in which said property was taken —.

And your petitioner further represents that he had been informed and believes that the said stores or property was taken from your petitioner as above stated and removed to **. . . .** ***.Sweet Water factory. .*** for the use of Company of the Regiment of ***. not known;*** that at the taking of said property, or stores, no vouchers, receipt or other writing was given therefor by the person taking the same as aforesaid or received at any time by your petitioner.

Your petitioner further states that the claim, within and above mentioned has (*) ***never heretofore been presented to any officer agent or department of the Government or to Congress or to any Committee thereof and there never has been any decision or action concerning it in any way whatsoever.***

Claimant's Statement:

"I resided from April 1, 1861, to June 1, 1865 in Campbell now Douglass County Ga in my own land; I owned there two hundred acres; I cultivated about twenty acres of this farm; half of the farm was in woodland; This farm is situated at Sweetwater Creek a mile and a quarter from Dark Corner Post Office. I was carrying

on a small farm during the war; I did not move or change my business during the war.

"I had four or five head of cattle pressed by the rebel army and not paid for.

"I had three sons - Francis M., George W. and James L. Stewart - in the rebel army; G. W. resides now in Douglass County and the other two are dead; gave them a little money & something to eat and some clothing; Gave them no military equipment; sent them also some provisions.

"I sympathized at the beginning of the rebellion with the Union cause. I felt and talked in favor of the Union, I had no influence or vote.

"Adhered to the Union cause after secession.

"I do solemnly swear that from the beginning of hostilities against the United States & (illegible) thereof my sympathies were constantly with the cause of the United States; that I never of my own free will & accord did anything or offended or sought or attempted to do anything by word or deed to injure said cause or retard its success. I was not willing to have aided and assisted the cause of the union on its supporters against 'our people.' I am now single, my husband having died in 1860. I have nine living children, their names and ages are as follows:

Elizabeth Winn	*age*	*42 years*
Caroline Humphreys		*40*
George W. Stewart		*32*
Nancy Winn		*30*
Rhoda Winn		*28*
Lovina Fur		*26*
Malinda Hughey		*34*
Jesse D. Stewart		*22*
Savannah McClarty		*20*

"One of the above, George W. was in the Confederate army and two who are now dead as aforesaid; I bought the property specified at the sale of my deceased husband's property; no one but myself has any interest in this claim;"

In answer to questions as to the property:

"I did not see the property taken or after it was taken; the property was gone about the 12th day of June 1864; I had two mules and two horses.

"The horses were a Claybaun' (sic) and a grey; the Claybaun' was going on 4 years old, large size, in good order, sound and worth two hundred dollars. The gray horse was going on 5 years, large size, in good order, sound and worth two hundred

dollars. Got the gray horse back again.

"There was a mare taken at the same time; this mare was a sorrel, 7 years old, large size, in good order, sound & worth two hundred dollars;

"The mules were, one, 4 years old, large common size, in good order, sound & worth two hundred dollars, the other 7 or 8 years old, common size, in good order, sound and worth two hundred dollars.

"My husband owned these at the time he died; Received no showing for the stock.

"There were no United States soldiers camped near our place at the time these mules and horses were taken."

Nancy (her mark X) Stewart

Sworn to and subscribed before me in Douglass County Georgia this June 18th, 1872.

Jno L. Conley
(illegible)
(illegible initials)

Witness for the Claimant Nancy Stewart:

Erasmus F. Potts being duly sworn deposes and says:

In answer to questions by the (illegible) Committee

"My name is Erasmus F. Potts, my age 50 years, my residence Paulding County Ga, my occupation a farmer; I am not related to the claimant & have no interest in this claim.

"I was present and saw two men dressed as United States soldiers take and carry away three horses and a mule about daylight on Sunday morning in June 1864; these men came to the house late at night, and asked for the stock and told claimant that they would go out and get the stock and give her a showing to hold to and give her the money for the balance; the stock was hid out about two miles from the house; the soldiers took a negro with them to show the stock & when they got there they took the horses and the mule and went off just as I got within sight; I do not believe these men were horse thieves but only that they took the stock without authority; there were no soldiers camped then nearer to claimant than six miles; Claimant afterwards recovered one of the horses; the other mule was tied out in the bottom & somebody took it and went off; I know nothing about the taking of this mule; the soldiers who got the

stock were not armed.

"The mare was worth two hundred dollars; the horse was worth a hundred & fifty dollars as was the first mule the other mule was worth seventy-five dollars.

I was overseeing for claimant."

Erasmus (his X mark) F. Potts

Sworn to and subscribed before me in Douglass County, Georgia this June 18th 1872.

Jno. L Conley
N. S. (illegible
(illegible initials)

Witness for Claimant Nancy Stewart:

Harrison Furr being duly sworn deposes & says:;

In answer to questions by the (illegible)

"*My name is Harrison Furr, my age 29 years, my residence Douglass County Ga, my occupation a farmer, am son-in-law of claimant & have no interest in this claim.*

"I was present & saw five head of stock belonging to the claimant in the possession of the United States soldiers; the soldiers were riding four head of the stock & the other mule was tied to a sapling in their camp; this was seven miles from where the claimant lived, there was quite a crowd of soldiers along when I saw the stock; I do not know what command it was; I said nothing to the soldiers who had the stock; I was a prisoner at the time & stopped in the road to rest & the stock passed by; I do not remember what day or month it was; I think it was in July 1864; I am positive it was claimant's stock; I was within ten or twenty feet of the stock as they passed slowly by;

"I know nothing as to the age or value of the stock; The soldiers were going toward Atlanta. There were three horses and two mules."

Harrison Furr

Sworn to & subscribed before me in Douglass Co Ga this June 18th 1872

Jno L. Conley
N. S. Com (?)
N. D. S.

Claimant Levi Holoway (Dark Corner, Georgia) for $200.00

The United States, . . . ***To Levi Holoway . . .*** **1864**

Item 1	*1 fine horse*	*valued at*	*$200.00*

To the Commissioner of Claims, (under Act of 3d of March , 1871.) Washington, D.C.

The PETITION of . . . ***Levi Holoway. . .*** respectfully represents:

That your petitioner is a resident of the county of . . . ***Douglas . . .*** in the State of . . . ***Georgia:. . .*** that her post-office address in . . ***Dark Corner. . .***in said County and State: and that at the time his claim and each item thereof as above set forth accrued he was a resident of the county of . . . ***Campbell. . .*** and State of ***. . . Georgia. . .*** that he is the original owner of said claim: that he has never sold, assigned or transferred the same or any part thereof to any person; that no mortgage, bill of sale or other lien of like nature has at any time rested upon it, or any part thereof, nor has it been attached, or taken in execution; that the same has not been paid by the United States or any of their officers or agents, nor have the United States any legal offset against the same or any part thereof; that he is the sole owner of the said claim, no other person being interested therein: that said claim does not contain any charge for property which was destroyed or stolen by the troops or other persons: that the rates or prices charged are reasonable and just, and do not exceed the market rate or price of like stores or property at the time and place stated; all of which your petitioner states of his own knowledge.

Your petitioner further states that she is now and was at the time the several items of her said claim accrued, as stated therein, a citizen of the United States; that he remained a loyal adherent to the cause and Government of the United States, during the war of 1861, etc: and was so loyal before and at the time of the taking or furnishing of the property for which this claim is made.

And your petitioner father represents, and of his own knowledge state, that on the ***9th*** day of ***July*** A. D. 186***4***, at ***his residence*** in the State of ***Georgia*** the following property or stores were taken from your petitioner for the use of the Army of the United States, and for which payment is claim, via: ***which is above described*** which said property or stores being of the kind, quantity, quality and value above stated was taken by—***General Stoneman raid*** **belonging to the** ***Cavalry*** Department of the United States Army, in the service of the United States, whose rank was ***General of Cavalry*** **of the Regiment of . .** ***not known.*** **acting as** ***General of Cavalry*** **...** who, as your petitioner has been informed and was stationed at ***. . Israel Causey's (***at Austell***) . .*** under the command of ***. . . General Wm. T. Sherman . . .*** who at that time had command of the United States forces in the District in which said property was taken —.

And your petitioner further represents that he had been informed and believes that the said stores or property was taken from your petitioner as above stated and removed to ***. . . . Israel Causey (***at Austell***). .*** for the use of Company of the Regiment of ***. . not known***; that at the taking of said property, or stores, no vouchers, receipt or other writing was given therefor by the person taking the same as aforesaid or received at any time by your petitioner.

Your petitioner further states that the claim, within and above mentioned has (*) ***never heretofore been presented to any officer agent or department of the Government or to Congress or to any Committee thereof and there never has been any decision or action concerning it in any way.***

I expect to prove my loyalty by the following witnesses and others:
. . . . . .***Perry Stewart.*** . . . . residing in ***Dark Corner, Ga.*** . . . .
. . . . . .***Frank M. Mitchell.*** . residing in ***Powder Springs, Ga.*** . . .
. . . . . .***Henry Mitchell*** . . . . residing in ***Powder Springs, Ga.*** . . .
and also expect to prove the other facts alleged in the foregoing petition by
. . . . . ***Josiah Burge (?)*** residing in ***Powder Springs, Ga.*** . . .
. . . . . ***Thomas C. Holoway*** residing in ***Brownsville, Ga.*** . . .

My Post Office address is ***Dark Corner, Ga.*** . . . .

My Counsel is ***C. W. Bennett.*** . . . Esq., whose Post Office address is ***Washington, D. C.***

Claimant John W. Humphries (Salt Springs) for $1,263.00

The United States, . . . ***To John W. Humphries*** **. . . 1864**

Item 1	*1 mule*	*valued at*	*$150.00*
Item 2	*280 bushel corn*	*$100*	*$280.00*
Item 3	*3500 ms Fodder*	*$150*	*52.50*
Item 4	*80 bushel Oats*	*75.*	*60.00*
Item 5	*2,850 ms Pork Hogs*	*14 ct*	*399.00*
Item 6	*300 ms Bacon*	*20 ct*	*60.00*
Item 7	*150 bushels of wheat*		*225.00*
Item 8	*100 ms Tobacco*	*25 ct*	*32.00*
	Balance		*1,263.00*

To the Commissioner of Claims, (under Act of 3d of March , 1871.) Washington, D.C.

The PETITION of . . . ***John W. Humphries.*** . . respectfully represents:

That your petitioner is a resident of the county of . . . ***Douglas*** . . . in the State of . . . ***Georgia:*** . . . that her post-office address in . . ***Salt Springs.*** . . in said County and State: and that at the time his claim and each item thereof as above set forth accrued he was a resident of the county of . . . ***Campbell.*** . . and State of . . . ***Georgia.*** . .
that he is the original owner of said claim: that he has never sold, assigned or transferred the same or any part thereof to any person; that no mortgage, bill of sale or other lien of like nature has at any time rested upon it, or any part thereof, nor has it been attached, or taken

in execution; that the same has not been paid by the United States or any of their officers or agents, nor have the United States any legal offset against the same or any part thereof; that he is the sole owner of the said claim, no other person being interested therein: that said claim does not contain any charge for property which was destroyed or stolen by the troops or other persons: that the rates or prices charged are reasonable and just, and do not exceed the market rate or price of like stores or property at the time and place stated; all of which your petitioner states of his own knowledge.

Your petitioner further states that she is now and was at the time the several items of her said claim accrued, as stated therein, a citizen of the United States; that he remained a loyal adherent to the cause and Government of the United States, during the war of 1861, etc: and was so loyal before and at the time of the taking or furnishing of the property for which this claim is made.

And your petitioner father represents, and of his own knowledge state, that in the month of ***July*** A. D. 18***64***, at ***his residence*** in the State of ***Georgia*** the following property or stores were taken from your petitioner for the use of the Army of the United States, and for which payment is claim, via: ***which is above described***
which said property or stores being of the kind, quantity, quality and value above stated was taken by—***General Kilpatrick & Col Adams*** **belonging to the** Department of the United States Army, in the service of the United States, whose rank was ***General of Cavalry*** **of the Regiment of . .** ***not known.*** **acting as** ***General of Cavalry*** ... who, as your petitioner has been informed and was stationed at **. .** ***Cox's Cross Roads*** under the command of . . . ***General Wm. T. Sherman*** . . . who at that time had command of the United States forces in the District in which said property was taken —.

And your petitioner further represents that he had been informed and believes that the said stores or property was taken from your petitioner as above stated and removed to . . . . . ***Cox's Cross Roads . . .*** for the use of Company of the Regiment of **. . . . . . .** that at the taking of said property, or stores, no vouchers, receipt or other writing was given therefor by the person taking the same as aforesaid or received at any time by your petitioner.

Your petitioner further states that the claim, within and above mentioned has (*) ***never heretofore been presented to any officer agent or department of the Government or to Congress or to any Committee thereof and there never has been any decision or action concerning it in any way whatsoever.***

Claimant Roswell Strickland for $150.00

The United States, ***To Roswell Strickland*** **1864**

Item 1	***1 fine Mare***	***valued at***	***$150.00***
		Balance	***$150.00***

To the Commissioner of Claims, (under Act of 3d of March, 1871.) Washington, D.C.

The PETITION of . . . ***Roswell Strickland. . .*** respectfully represents:

That your petitioner is a resident of the county of . . . ***Douglas. . .*** in the State of . . . ***Georgia:. . .*** that his post-office address in . . ***Villa Rica. . .***in said County and State: and that at the time his claim and each item thereof as above set forth accrued he was a resident of the county of . . . ***Carroll. . .*** and State of . . . . . . ***Georgia. . . . .*** that he is the original owner of said claim: that he has never sold, assigned or transferred the same or any part thereof to any person; that no mortgage, bill of sale or other lien of like nature has at any time rested upon it, or any part thereof, nor has it been attached, or taken in execution; that the same has not been paid by the United States or any of their officers or agents, nor have the United States any legal offset against the same or any part thereof; that he is the sole owner of the said claim, no other person being interested therein: that said claim does not contain any charge for property which was destroyed or stolen by the troops or other persons: that the rates or prices charged are reasonable and just, and do not exceed the market rate or price of like stores or property at the time and place stated; all of which your petitioner states of his own knowledge.

Your petitioner further states that he is now and was at the time the several items of his said claim accrued, as stated therein, a citizen of the United States; that he remained a loyal adherent to the cause and Government of the United States, during the war of 1861, etc: and was so loyal before and at the time of the taking or furnishing of the property for which this claim is made.

And your petitioner father represents, and of his own knowledge state, that on the . . . ***(illegible). .*** day of ***July*** A. D. 186***4***, at ***his residence*** in the State of ***Georgia*** the following property or stores were taken from your petitioner for the use of the Army of the United States, and for which payment is claim, via: ***which is above described*** which said property or stores being of the kind, quantity, quality and value above stated was taken by—***General Stoneman . .*** **belonging to the** ***3rd Division . . Cavalry . .*** Department of the United States Army, in the service of the United States, whose rank was ***General of Cavalry*** **of the Regiment of . .** ***not known.*** **acting as** ***General of Cavalry ...*** who, as your petitioner has been informed and was stationed at ***. .Wadkins . .*** under the command of ***. . . General Wm. T. Sherman . . .*** who at that time had command of the United States forces in the District in which said property was taken —.

And your petitioner further represents that he had been informed and believes that the said stores or property was taken from your petitioner as above stated and removed to ***. . . . . Wadkins. . .*** for the use of Company of the Regiment of ***. . . not known. . .***; that at the taking of said property, or stores, no vouchers, receipt or other writing **was** given therefor by the person taking the same as aforesaid or received at any time by your petitioner.

Your petitioner further states that the claim, within and above mentioned has (*) ***never heretofore been presented to any officer, agent or department of the government or to Congress or to any Committee thereof and that there never has been any decision or action concerning it in any way whatsoever.***

13

Pioneer Families Mentioned in Chapter 16

"Thomas M. Holloway and Mary Jane Lowry was married in the big road by Wylie Roberts a couple of weeks ago since. Milton Winn and Nancy Stewart was married in the big road near Roberts some two months ago. Washington Clinton (George's son) Sarah Smith (big Polls gal) was married in the big road near Roberts some three weeks ago."

Baggett

Stephen Baggett, born December 29, 1784 in Anson, North Carolina, died February 19, 1877 in Winston, Georgia, was the son of Allen Baggett (a Revolutionary veteran). Stephen Baggett moved from North Carolina to Walton County, Georgia about 1825, then settled in Campbell County, about 1828. Stephen served on the grand jury in Campbell County in 1828. He is shown on the 1830, 1840, 1850 and 1870 Campbell County Federal Census. He married Sarah Sikes (February 10, 1791 - October 9, 1881) in North Carolina in 1811. He moved to Paulding Co., shown on the 1860 Paulding County Census, and then back to Dark Corner after the Civil War.

Stephen and Sarah Baggett's children:

1) William, born 1810 North Carolina, died 1895 Tennessee;

2). **Jackson Baggett,** born October 1, 1812 in Anson, North Carolina, died May 3, 1863 while serving as Corporal in the Georgia 35th, Regiment of Infantry. His wife was Nancy N., August 2, 1817 - November 20, 1869. She is buried at the Sweetwater Church Cemetery in Paulding County.

3). Martha, born January 1, 1814, died November 18, 1905. She married William M. Thomason;

4). Prudence Amelia, born January 8, 1816 in Campbell County, died March 25, 1894 in Cobb County; she married John Willingham Moon in 1843.

5. **John Baggett,** was born on December 27, 1817 in North Carolina, and died on January 9, 1893 in Winston, Douglas County, Georgia; he married on January 9, 1842 to Ruth S. **Camp**, who was born December 1, 1825 and died on February 24, 1881. She was the daughter of Thomas and Letitia Lindley Camp. Both John and Ruth Baggett are buried at the Baggett Cemetery.

6). Mary Flora, born April 6, 1820 in North Carolina, died December 17, 1902 in Douglas County, Georgia; unmarried.

7) Elizabeth, born May 5, 1822 in Campbell County, died September 16, 1903. She married W. N. **McGouirk**;

8). Susan, born February 21, 1825 in Campbell County, died January 31, 1905 in Douglas County; unmarried.

9). Allen Jacob born December 12, 1828 in Campbell County, married on October 14, 1848 in Fulton County, Georgia to Elizabeth A. James, January 29, 1830 - June 6, 1922. He enlisted March 20, 1863 as Private, Co. F, 30th Regiment of Georgia Volunteers. He died June 29, 1863 at Newton Station, Mississippi, relapsing from having the measles. **Note**: Jackson and Allen, both sons of Stephen and Sarah Baggett, died in the Civil War within two days of each other.

10) Wiley C. Baggett, born March 22, 1830 in Campbell County, died December 3, 1908 in Douglas County, married on October 7, 1855 to Louisa C. Scoggins, May 27, 1828 - Mary 21, 1914. Wiley Baggett's occupation was a carpenter. Wylie enlisted as Private on May 12, 1862, Co. F (then Co. C) 30th Regiment Georgia Volunteer Infantry. Absent-has-not-come-to-camp on roll call for May-June 1862. Enlisted as Private in Co. D 2d Regiment Georgia State Guards Cavalry August 1, 1863. Present January 31, 1864.

11) Charles B. Baggett, April 13, 1832 in Campbell County, died October 30, 1920 in Douglas County. He married in 1858 to Mary E. **Arnold**, 1840-1888, daughter of Alston Arnold. Charles served in the Civil War as 2nd Lieutenant, 1st Georgia Cavalry, CSA. After Mary's death, he married a second time; in 1889 in Campbell County, he married Mary A. Hood, 1847-1921. She is buried in Palmetto, Georgia at Ramah Cemetery.

12). Sarah J., born July 12, 1835 in Campbell County, died July 11, 1883 in Douglas County.

An icon of Dark Corner is a corncrib built by the Benson family who lived on LL 199 and 198. It was moved about 1960 to this present location - close to the intersection of Mann and Cedar Mt. Roads. Photo: John Bailey, 2014.

Benson

Reuben Benson (1786 - June 16, 1864) who was born in South Carolina, moved to Gwinnett about 1818, then to Cobb County about 1830. He was married to Elizabeth Kemp who was born, July 16, 1793 and died 1833 in Campbell County. Reuben drew an original land grant for Campbell County, Dark Corner, LL #198 on September 14, 1831. After Elizabeth died, Reuben married again between 1833 and 1836 to Mary Stepp who was born in 1770 in Virginia; Mary died between 1850 & 1860. Reuben is buried in Paulding County. Elizabeth is buried in the Benson Cemetery, Douglas County.

James LaFayette Benson, (son of Reuben & Elizabeth Benson) was born April 15, 1822 in Gwinnett County, Georgia. On March 26, 1844, he married Harriet Caroline **McLarty**, (daughter of John McLarty). Harriet was born January 31, 1826 in Mecklenburg, N. C. and died April 07, 1896 in Douglas County, Georgia.

James and Harriet Benson moved to Paulding Co. about 1849. On the 1860 and 1870 Federal Census Record, they lived in Paulding County at the Brownsville

Community. On the 1880 and 1900 census the family lived in the Conners District of Douglas County where he died on May 9, 1902. James LaFayette and Harriet Benson's children:

1) **John Reuben Benson** was born March 14, 1845, in Georgia and lived in the Dark Corner later Conners' District of Douglas County on Land Lot # 198 where he died on May 8, 1905. He married Lucy Caroline Umphrey (July 1844-1905) on August 13, 1869 in Paulding County, Georgia.

2) Samuel Wilson Benson August 9, 1846 - August 3, 1848;

3) Martha Elizabeth Benson, born January 7, 1849, died February 2, 1926 who married James W. Anderson - her second husband was James M. Dorris;

4) Mary Virginia Ann "Mollie," born October 23, 1852 and died August 7, 1940 in Winston, married James A. Sayer (1849-1922).

James Endsley

James Preston Endsley, Jr. born November 22, 1802 in Laurens County S. C. and died March 13, 1889 in Cass County, Texas. He married Mary Ann Couch (June, 1806 - September 5, 1876) in 1828 in South Carolina. They are shown on the 1830 and 1840 Federal Census in Coweta County, Georgia. In 1846-1848, he was a soldier in the Mexican-American War, serving through the entire war.

The family is on the 1850 and 1860 Federal Census for Campbell County, Georgia and on the Georgia Property Tax Digest, paying taxes on LL # 165. He enlisted September 25, 1861 as Private, Company F, 30th Georgia Infantry Regiment, Campbell County. James was present in August of 1867 to sign an Oath of Allegiance and to register to vote in Campbell County. They lost two sons in the Civil War - Matthew and Manning. James and Mary Ann Endsley's children are:

1) Leander (1826-1890);

2) Matthew, born 1829 in South Carolina, married Mary Ann Miller in Campbell County on November 29, 1853. He enlisted as Private on April 25, 1862 in Co A, 56th Regiment Georgia Volunteer Infantry; died from having the measles at Lookout Mt. Georgia hospital on August 30, 1862.

3) Caroline, 1830-1881, married John W. Thomas on October 5, 1856 in Campbell County;

4) Lucinda Ann, born 1834-1918 married Benjamin G. Miller on October 3, 1854 in Campbell County, Georgia;

5) Eliza Jane Endsley, 1834-1923 married Eli Vansant on August 13, 1858 in Fulton County, Georgia;

6) Manning Endsley, born Coweta County, in 1835; enlisted on September 25, 1861 in Co F. (later Co. C.) 30th Georgia Volunteer Infantry - "Campbell Sharpshooters;" died from disease on May 14, 1862 at Camp Hardee, near Savannah, Chatham County, Georgia.

7) James Preston Endsley, III born 1837 in Coweta County, married Arminda Morris on July 23, 1865 in Campbell County. He enlisted in Co. E, 30 Georgia Regiment. He died in 1882 at Savannah, Chatham County, Georgia.

8) Joseph Preston Endsley born November 17, 1841 in Campbell County, married Nancy Jane Thomas, February 19, 1871 in Miller County, Arkansas; he died August 31, 1898 in Texas;

9) Berry "Bud" Endsley, born July 1843 in Campbell County, died in 1928 in Texas;

10) Elenor (Ellender) Endsley, born January 1850 in Campbell County died 1910 in Texas;

11) Malissa Endsley born 1851 in Campbell County married Alexander Couch January 3, 1868 in Campbell County, died 1919 in Texas.

David Enterkin

David Enterkin was born in Laurens County, South Carolina about 1788, died about 1860 in Campbell County, Georgia. His wife Mary **Winn**, born about 1793, died about 1870. They moved from Laurens County to Dark Corner in the 1840s. Their children are John, Martha, Samuel Kanady Enterkin, David Fletcher Enterkin, and Thomas Asbury Enterkin.

1) John Enterkin 1815-1873, was born in Laurens, South Carolina, married Mary **McElreath**, 1820-1882, in 1843 in South Carolina, and came to Campbell County about 1846. The family settled on Land Lot #157 and were there in 1855 and 1861 and are listed in the 1870 Dark Corner Federal Census Records.

John Enterkin enlisted in the 41st Regiment, Georgia Infantry, Company A, as Private on March 4, 1862. He mustered out December 8, 1862.

Their children:

a. Samantha, born 1847;
b. Matilda, born 1850;

c. John Quincy Enterkin, born February 17, 1857, died December 6, 1918; married Laura Middlebrooks;

d. Thomas M. Enterkin, born 1851, married in 1870 to Frances, daughter of Robert H. **Weddington**.

Enterkin Family about 1907. L-R F Row: 5th - Flossie Ethel Miles Enterkin; husband John Pierce Enterkin; her mother Martha Gable Miles. Photo: Courtesy Billie Lee.

e. Lourentha E. married in 1869 to Edwin L., son of Artemus Ergle.

f. Mary Angeline, 1844-1926 married Noah Vansant;

g. Luda Stephen Enterkin born October 9, 1854; died February 7, 1927 in Winston, Georgia, married Mary Ann **Winn** on May 8, 1875 in Douglas County, Georgia. Mary Ann Winn, born April 11, 1854, died 1945, was the daughter of James Henry **Winn** and Sarah Ellen **Polk**. Children of Luda and Mary Enterkin: Willis born 1877 - 1976, married Mattie Causey; Carrie Odessa., born 1876 who married Allen Waldrop; John Pierce, born 1880 who married Flossie Ethel **Miles**; Sarah, born 1882 who married George Smith; Annie Pearl born 1884 married Samuel Lee; Lilly Mae, born 1890, married Robert McBrayer; Jennie Maude born 1892; Clyde, born 1898 married Ruby Daniels; and James Marvin, born 1887 who married Grace Barrow.

2) Martha Enterkin, born 1823, married late in life in 1880 to Eli Edmondson,

born 1825 who was living near Winston in 1880.

3) Samuel Kanady Enterkin was born August 13, 1825 in Laurens, South Carolina, died April 13, 1888, in Douglas County; married on November 22, 1847 to Esther Virginia **McLarty**, May 1, 1830 - July 28, 1906, daughter of John McLarty, Jr., and Martha White.

4) David Fletcher Enterkin, born September 1838, married in 1858 to Mary Leathers; married 2nd to Polly Virginia **McLarty Hartsfield**, 1838 - 1912, daughter of Stephen Harvey McLarty and widow of George W. Hartsfield.

5) Thomas Asbury Enterkin, 1828-1880, married in 1871 to Mary Elizabeth Lindley Morse, born June 1843, died December 29, 1931. She was the daughter of Aquilla Lindley and had married 1st in 1865 to Samuel F. Morse, a Confederate veteran and native of Newton County. Thomas A. Enterkin enlisted on April 25, 1862 as Private in the Civil War, Co. A, 56th Georgia Infantry. Discharged, furnished Clark C. Talbert as substitute, in 1862.

Hartsfield

Moses Hartsfield was born in South Carolina in 1763; he married before 1816 to Clement who was born in Virginia in 1788 and died after 1870 in Douglas County. Moses Hartsfield was in Lenoir County, North Carolina in 1800; in Oglethorpe County, Georgia in 1802; in Clarke County, Georgia in 1804; in Jasper County, Georgia in 1821; on the 1830, 1840, 1850 and 1860 Federal Census of Campbell County, Militia District #730. He drew LL # 197 on February 14, 1853 and is listed on the Campbell County Census for 1860. He died in Campbell County, District 2, January 19, 1865 at age 102. Moses and Clement Hartsfield's children:

1. Samuel R. Hartsfield, born August 9, 1806 in Clark County; he purchased LL # 219 on February 4, 1851 in GMD #730; he died December 21, 1886 in Texas.

2. Leroy Hartsfield, born 1815 in Georgia; married Melinda Hicks on July 25, 1839 in Carroll County. His family is listed on the 1840, 1860 & 1870 Federal Census Record for GMD #730. On February 17, 1851, Leroy Hartsfield purchased LL #231 in GMD #730, Campbell County.

3. Mary Ann was born June 5, 1818 in Jasper, Georgia; died April 22, 1902 in Lamar County, Alabama.

4. Clementine born 1820-1825 in Georgia; died 1852-1860 in Campbell Co.

5. Chafin S. Hartsfield born 1823 in Georgia married Jane Ann Matthews. He

is listed in Militia District #730 for the 1855 Georgia Tax Digest.

6. George W. Hartsfield, born 1828 in Georgia married Mary **McLarty**; he is listed on the 1850 Carroll County Census and the 1860 Campbell County Census. George W. Hartsfield enlisted as Private on April 25, 1862 with Co. A 56th Georgia Infantry; **Memorial marker in McLarty Cemetery;**

7. Richard M. Hartsfield born July 1831 in Georgia, married Charlotte Beggs (born 1838) on December 21, 1856 in Campbell County; he is listed on the 1860 Federal Census for Campbell County, #730 Militia District. He enlisted as Private on April 25, 1862 with Co A, 56th Georgia Infantry.

Maxwell

Dr. Edwin Wilson Maxwell was born May 16, 1805 in Charlotte, North Carolina and died on August 16, 1873 in Bastrop Co., Texas. He married Caroline Margaret **McLarty**, on June 19, 1832 in Mecklenberg Co. N. C. Margaret McLarty (born April 24, 1814, N. C., died April 15, 1866, Dark Corner, Campbell Co., Georgia) was the daughter of John McLarty and Mary Wilson McLarty. The Maxwells followed the McLarty to Georgia in the 1830s, settling in Dark Corner, Campbell County and lived on LL # 159 in 1855. Children of Dr. Maxwell and Margaret:

1) Mary Cornelia Maxwell, born December 24, 1833 North Carolina; died 1881 in Bastrop County, Texas; married Thomas L. Bowen;

2) Magnum Calhoun Maxwell, born March 18, 1836 in N. C.; married Eveline C. Mattox, 1840-1912, daughter of Early J. Mattox of Carroll County; they married October 11, 1856; he enlisted March 4, 1862 in Campbell County as Private., Co. K 41st Georgia Infantry. He died in the hospital at Oxford, Mississippi, June 30, 1862. **Memorial marker in McLarty Cemetery**.

3) Elizabeth Ann Maxwell, born May 18, 1838 in Campbell County; died August 27, 1839.

4) Letitia Caroline Maxwell, born August 9, 1840, married Emmanuel Vansant who was enlisted as Private on April 25, 1862, in Company A 56th Regiment Georgia Volunteer Infantry. He was killed in action. After the war she married a Confederate veteran named Martin G. Butler. Letitia died October 27, 1935. Both Martin and Letitia Butler are buried at Bright Star Methodist Cemetery in Douglasville.

5) John Guy Maxwell, born March 4, 1843 in Campbell Co; died May 29, 1909 in Douglas County. He enlisted September 25, 1861 as Private, Co. C, 30th

Georgia Infantry. He was captured on July 19, 1864; took the Oath of Allegiance to the U. S. Government at Camp Douglas, Ill.; mustered into the 6th Regiment U. S. Infantry on March 26, 1865. In 1868, he married Louisa R. Malone, 1845-1885. In 1887 he married Mary Catherine "Kate" **Polk**, 1857-1939.

6) Margaret Elizabeth Ann Maxwell, born September 29, 1845; married Colonel Joseph S. James, first mayor of Douglasville.

7) William Archibald Maxwell, September 17, 1848-1881.

8) David Alexander Maxwell, born April 11, 1851; died January 12, 1881; he was a store clerk, boarding with his brother-in-law Joe James in 1880.

9) Edwin Wilson Maxwell. Jr., born September 12, 1855; died 1939, married in 1878 to Julia Skinner, 1859-1931.

Dr. Edwin Wilson Maxwell enlisted Sept. 25, 1861 as Private in Co. F Georgia 30th Infantry, CSA and during his service was promoted to full surgeon. After his wife's death in 1866, he married again and moved to Arkansas.

Dr. Maxwell, in an 1859 letter to George W. Lowery, tells of the many things that were taking place in Dark Corner. "Your brother James" referred to in Dr. Maxwell's letter is James Madison Lowery who married Avarilla Matthews in Campbell County in 1856. She died after giving birth to twins in 1858. The twins also died.

"Dark Corner Campbell County Ga
April 25th, 1859

George W. Lowry, Esqr.
Dear Sir:

I received a letter from you some three weeks since and was glad to hear of the welfare of yourself and family. I also got one from you last year and lost it after reading it and showing it to your friends. Lucinda carried it and showed it to your mother and the rest of the family. My family are all in good health. Your father-in-law's family are well. James and family the same and all your acquaintances as far as I know.

I am not aware that you have ever heard of your brother James wife and two children. She was brought to bed with twins. Had Middlebrooks with her until she was delivered of one dead on Sunday morning on Sunday night I was sent for and I had to deliver her with instruments. Both of the children ought to have been delivered on Saturday before and they would have been alive. She died on the next Saturday night following. James married again and remains at his old stead attending Ruben

Merchant Mill. His wife was by the name of Coggin, a very nice Woman.

Thomas M. Holloway and Mary Jane Lowry was married in the big road by Wylie Roberts a couple of weeks ago since. Milton Winn and Nancy Stewart was married in the big road near Roberts some two months ago. Washington Clinton (George's son) Sarah Smith (big Polls gal) was married in the big road near Roberts some three weeks ago. Dr. John Middlebrooks and Rody Jane Stewart was married on last (Sunday/Thursday?) at home. M. H. Woodall and Miss Adleline Adderholdt was married some four weeks ago. He has a store at widow Watsons. Old Joseph Summerlin and Susan Bomar was married about five weeks since.

Alek McLarty and Joseph Farmer and Robert McLarty have all got home from Arkansas. Robert and his family live in Grandmas home and I sold Farmer my lower place for $1500.00 and Alek has moved again with old David and Frazier Trentham to Alabama. Frazier married Nancy Griffin in the big road too. Joel Rice is dead. Also Mark McElreath also old Billy Neal. And old George Moore will die in forty eight hours from drinking whiskey.

Fletch Enterkin is married to a Miss Leathers and gone to farming and (reverend) Bull (sic) (Asbury) and old Martha hang on to the blessed state of celibacy. Eli Vansant is married to one of old Jim Endsleys girls and old man Dorman is married to Ann McKelvey. Your mother come out close concerning that nary a fact of your Fathers estate at the March term of our Superior Court. Her and Tom Holloway and Jasper are living on the lot of land she bought after your fathers death.

Your other single brothers I know nothing concerning them. Your father-in-law is determined to move this fall to Arkansas, whether he sells or not. He is selling off his stuff and offering it for sale privately. Lee Stone will go with him.

We have a cold dry spring, though wheat looks well. I will now come to a close complying with your request concerning a recipe for my preparation of Flux medicine, viz:

Take of . . ? . . . 2 oz; Spirits of Camphor 1 oz; Sweet tincture of rhubarb 8 oz; Aqua Amonia (?) 1/2 oz; Oil of peppermint 120 drops. Of this mixture give to a grown person one teaspoonful every fifteen minutes until all nausea subsides and all pain ceases and then proceed with salts, if pain returns after the salts have operated, you must resort to the above medicine. It should be taken in warm sweetened water. May it prove a blessing to you and family if needed.

Give my respects to your wife and children and may God bless you and yours.

I remain yours respectfully.

E. W. Maxwell

P. S. Joe Payne married one of the Coggins girls who had a couple of children as a start so him and Jim are brother-in-laws.

E. W. M."

McGouirk

William N. McGouirk, born April 21, 1821 in Jasper County, Georgia, died June 3, 1897 in Douglas County, Georgia. William N. was the second of six children of Seth and Lydia Mills McGouirk. Seth McGouirk was born in North Carolina in 1794; died in 1827 in Jasper County. His widow Lydia (born in 1794 - died 1860 in Campbell County, Georgia) moved to Campbell County with her children. Their son, William N. married Elizabeth Baggett, daughter of Stephen **Baggett**, on July 21, 1844, in Campbell County; Elizabeth was born June 5, 1822 and died September 16, 1903 in Douglas County.

William McGouirk served as sheriff of Campbell County for eight years before the Civil War and for two years afterward. During the war, he was Captain of Company C (F), 30th Georgia Infantry in the "Campbell County Sharpshooters." He resigned, because of illness, at Morton, Mississippi in August 1863. He was a Baptist deacon, served as State Representative of Douglas County 1878-1879, and was an original county commissioner of the county. William and Elizabeth's children are:

1) Sarah F., born 1846, died 1893; married James Blair;

2) Stephen Harry, born 1848, died 1893; married Theresa;

3) John W., born 1849, died 1902; married Helena Bowen in Campbell County, Georgia in 1874;

4) Seth Alexander, born December 29, 1852, died April 22, 1932; married Etta Redema Vansant on February 2, 1879;

5) Charles W., born January 19,1853, died June 29, 1930; married Jesse Winn on October 26, 1899;

6) Martha born 1856 in Campbell County, married William K. Glover in 1874;

7) William, born 1857;

8) Caleb Perry Bowen McGouirk, born 1859, died 1904;

9) Thurza, born 1876, died 1910.

McKelvey

John McKelvey, "a planter" from Laurens County, South Carolina left a will dated September 29, 1824 which names his wife, Mary, and children. Mary is age 74 on the 1850 Laurens County Census and was John's 2nd wife. Their children:

1) Thomas McKelvey was born 1806 in South Carolina and lived in Campbell County in 1850; died after 1860.

2) Alexander McKelvey was born about 1810 in South Carolina and moved to Campbell County about 1840 with wife Eleanor or Ellender who died June 28, 1884, age about 67 years. In 1850 Alexander was a trustee of Flat Rock Methodist Church. Alexander and Eleanor had no children and he died about 1870.

3) Ann McKelvey was born about 1815 and married Alfred Dorman in Campbell County on January 3, 1853.

4) Isaac W. McKelvey, born February 2, 1820, died July 22, 1902, married Elizabeth Polk who was born January 28, 1832 and died June 12, 1912. She was the daughter of Ezekiel **Polk**. Both Isaac and Elizabeth are buried at the Douglasville City Cemetery. "Ike" McKelvey came to Campbell County about 1840 and was a merchant at Dark Corner in 1850. In 1855, he paid taxes on 202 1/2 acres of LL # 131 and 101 1/4 acres of LL # 158. As a merchant, this puts him in the community of Dark Corner, near the post office, school, and first Brush Arbor Church. "Uncle Ike" was also a trustee at the Flat Rock Methodist Church in 1870.

McLarty

John McLarty was born either December 21, 1776 or December 25, 1775; his tombstone reads, "died January 21, 1853, aged 77 years." He married Mary Wilson on November 23, 1795 in Mecklenburg, North Carolina. She was born March 15 (or 21), 1776 in Scotland and died February 3, 1866. Mary and John McLarty's children:

1) Alexander McLarty 1797-1888; married Rebecca Eliza Parks in 1821 (Alexander is the only sibling who didn't stay in Georgia.) Alexander's children:

1A. John Parks McLarty 1822-1883; Pvt., Co. A, 8th Mississippi Cavalry, enlisted August 7, 1863 at age forty.

1B. Mary Amanda McLarty 1824-1830.

1C. Mary Ann McLarty 1826; married Albert B. Martin - Pvt. C. B, 4th Miss Infantry.

1D. William LaFayette McLarty 1829-1862; Pvt., Co. B, 4th Mississippi Infantry,

died March 12, 1862; **Memorial marker in McLarty Cemetery**.

1E. Wilson L. McLarty 1831-1862, died March 12, 1862; **Memorial marker in McLarty Cemetery.**

1F. George Washington McLarty 1833-1894.

1G. Margaret Indiana McLarty 1836-1898. She married Henry Isaac "Jack" Latham, who enlisted as Private, Co. B, 31st Mississippi Infantry on September 18, 1863 in Columbia, TN. He was sent to Camp Chase, Columbus, Ohio on January 23, 1865 and died of pneumonia March 19, 1865.

Unknown McLarty daughter/grand-daughter.
Photo: Courtesy Sandy Whittington.

1H. Harvey T. McLarty 1839; 1st Lieutenant, Co. A, 4th Mississippi Cavalry.

1I. Alexander W. McLarty 1842-1864; Pvt. 2nd Lieutenant, Co. B, 31 Mississippi Infantry, Enlisted March 4, 1862 in Choctaw County; wounded in the left hand July 20, 1864 at the Battle of Peachtree Creek and hospitalized in Atlanta; Killed in action Franklin, Tn. November 30, 1864; **Memorial marker in McLarty Cemetery.**

1J. James K. Polk McLarty 1844-1862; Corporal, Co. A, 29 Mississippi Infantry, enlisted March 15, 1862 in Lexington, Mississippi, Killed in action at Murfreesboro, TN (in the corn field) either December 29, 1862 or December 31, 1862; **Memorial marker in McLarty Cemetery.**

2) Samuel Wilson McLarty 1799-1863; married Mary **Polk**, Charity **Rice**, and Sarah Biggers **White**. Purchased LL #s 160, 199, 182 and 200 in Dark Corner. Samuel's children:

2A. Charles Bingley McLarty 1827-1882; Pvt. Co. E, 10th Texas Infantry, enlisted in Houston, October 23, 1861.

2B. Mary Amanda McLarty, 1829-1906; married Williamson Parks Strickland, 1822-1897.

2C. John Columbus McLarty 1831-1862; died of measles August 26, 1862 in Dallas County, Texas.

2D. George Wilson "California George" McLarty 1834-1893; enlisted in Co. D 7th Georgia Infantry on May 4, 1861; elected 3rd Lieutenant on February 12, 1862; resigned and not on rolls after May 1862.

2E. Hannah C. McLarty 1836-1852.

2F. Samuel Marion McLarty 1839-1864; Pvt. Sgt., Co. C 30th Georgia Infantry; enlisted September 25, 1861 in Campbell County; wounded in Jackson, Mississippi, July 16, 1863; Killed September 20, 1864; **Memorial marker in McLarty Cemetery.**

2G. Sophia Caroline McLarty 1841-1922; married Thomas Jefferson Perkerson 1834-1926; Pvt., Co. F 41st Georgia Infantry, enlisted September 1, 1863 in Greenville, GA, hospitalized near Macon in December 1863.

2H. Harvey Ezekial McLarty, born 1843, Pvt., Co. A, 12th Georgia Cavalry, enlisted December 9, 1862 at Camp Randolph (Dalton); served as a blacksmith; captured May 1864; took the Oath of Allegiance at Chattanooga May 17, 1864.

2I. Martha Jane McLarty 1846-1925; married John Dempsey Perkerson; Pvt., Co. F, 41st Georgia Infantry. He enlisted March 1, 1862 in Greenville, Georgia. Detailed as wagoner. Captured/hospitalized, Vicksburg July 14, 1863; paroled July 16, 1863.

2J. William Wallace McLarty, born about 1860; son of Samuel and Sarah Biggers **White**.

3) John McLarty Junior was born March 7, 1802 in Mecklenburg, County, North Carolina, died March 14, 1856 in Campbell County, and married Martha **White** on November 18, 1824, in North Carolina. She was born November 11, 1801, in North Carolina, and died November 11, 1842, in Campbell County. She was the daughter of Samuel and Esther White. John McLarty, Jr. moved from North Carolina to Georgia between 1832-1836. His second wife was Sarah McLarty **Anderson**. John McLarty, Jr. and Martha had eight children:

3A. Harriet Caroline McLarty; January 31, 1826 - April 07, 1896; on March 26, 1844, she married James Lafayette **Benson,** April 15, 1822 - May 8, 1902.

3B. Samuel Alexander McLarty, February 24, 1828 - February 4, 1901, married Mary

Elizabeth **Hildebrand**. He enlisted August 6, 1862 at Calhoun, Georgia as Private in Company C, 30th Georgia Infantry, CSA. He is buried at Ephesus Church in Winston.

Samuel and Elizabeth (Hildebrand) McLarty had a daughter Mary Ellen McLarty who was born October 15, 1851 and died July 12, 1917. On March 3, 1870, she married Wilson Vansant who was born March 11, 1849 and died June 3, 1919. Both Samuel and Elizabeth are buried at Chapel Hill Road Baptist Church.

At Left: Mary Ellen McLarty (1851-1917) and husband Wilson Vansant (1849 - 1919). They married in Douglas County in 1870.
Photo Courtesy Sandy Whittington.

3C. Esther Virginia McLarty was born May 1, 1830 in North Carolina, died July 28, 1906 in Douglas County; married Samuel Kanada **Enterkin** 1825-1888.

3D. Mary Wilson McLarty; January 20, 1832 - November 12, 1842.

3E. Margaret Ann McLarty; January 15, 1834-1880; married Rev. Miles Edwards 1825-1885; Lieutenant - Captain, Co. H 19th Georgia Infantry. Margaret is buried at Pleasant Hill Cemetery in Cobb County; Miles in Buchanan City Cemetery, Haralson County, Georgia.

3F. John Jackson McLarty; August 10, 1838-1895; Pvt., Co. C 30th Georgia Infantry; buried at Bethel Methodist in Paulding County.

3G. Martha Jane McLarty, born August 10, 1838, married James Fletcher McLarty 1836-1906; Pvt., Co. K 41st Georgia Infantry.

3H. Dr. George Washington McLarty; September 30, 1840-1919; Private, Co. C 30th Georgia Infantry; died in Okaloosa County, Florida.

3I. Mary Catherine McLarty; 1846-1885; married Posey Newton **Brown** 1849-1896.

3J. Thomas Shelby McLarty; 1848-1920; died in Ochiltree County, Texas.

L-R Front row: Joseph, James Alexander McLarty, (son of John Jackson 3F above) Lizzie Mae, Baby - Fred, Ida Maroney McLarty, John A. L-R Back row: James Walter, Florence, Leota (center of photo), Carl; Cavella (Carl's wife). Photo: Courtesy Dianne McLarty.

4) George Washington McLarty 1804-1885; married Charity **Bates,** January 12, 1813 - October 25, 1882; both are buried in the Old Villa Rica Cemetery. See Chapter 6 on Dark Corner Settlement for more family history.

5) Stephen Harvey McLarty 1806-1864; married Mary Annie **Weddington**. They were buried on their property (Land Lot #186) on Mann Road, directly under the current power lines. Georgia Power Company destroyed their graves in the process of erecting the power lines, about 1940s. Stephen and Mary's children:

5A. William Alexander McLarty 1828-1862; Pvt., Co. A 56 Georgia Infantry; enlisted April 28, 1862; died in Tennessee November 6, 1862; **Memorial marker in McLarty Cemetery.**

5B. Margaret C. McLarty born 1830, married William N. Norton, born 1825.

5C. Mary Polly Virginia McLarty 1832-1833.

5D. Jane Melvina McLarty, born 1834, married James A. Rogers Senior, born 1810.

G. W. McLarty Home (#4 on opposite page) location unknown.
Photo: *McLarty & Family of Kintyre.*

5E. John Harvey McLarty, born in 1836; enlisted as Private in Co. A 56 Georgia Infantry on April 28, 1862; captured/paroled in Vicksburg; took the Oath of Allegiance in August 1864. He died in Arkansas in 1917.

5F. Mary Polly Virginia McLarty, 1838-1912 married George W. Hartsfield and David Fletcher Enterkin. George W. Hartsfield; Pvt., Co. A 56th Georgia Infantry; enlisted April 25, 1862; **Memorial marker in McLarty Cemetery;** David Fletcher Enterkin born 1836; Pvt., Co. D 2nd Georgia Cavalry (State Guards); enlisted August 1863 in Campbell County; mustered out at Camp Lane, January 31, 1864.

5G. Hannah Louise McLarty born 1840; married Alexander Rodgers, born 1832.

5H. Sarah Ann McLarty 1843-1920, married William H. Mattox 1842-1883; Sergeant - Lieutenant, Co. H, 3rd Georgia Cavalry (State Guards); enlisted August 23, 1863 in Elberton, Georgia. Promoted September 15, 1863.

5I. George Wilson McLarty, December 11, 1844 - January 25, 1916; enlisted as Private on August 31, 1864, at age 19, promoted to Sergeant, Co. A, 181st Ohio Infantry

Regiment; buried at Ephesus Church in Winston; grave is marked with GAR (Union) marker.

5J. Archibald Green McLarty 1846-1923; Pvt., Co. B 4th Georgia Reserves; enlisted May 10, 1864 in Atlanta; buried in Ozan Cemetery - Bengin, Arkansas.

5K. Emily Rushbrook McLarty 1849-1908; married Alexander Z. Chambliss.

5L. Martha Elizabeth McLarty born 1852; died before 1910; married Simmeon Edwards.

5M. Charles Stephen McLarty born 1854.

6) Polly Caroline McLarty 1809-1885; married John F. **Morris**, Senior 1801-1888. (See Morris below.)

7) Archibald Newton McLarty 1812-1867; see Chapter 16 for family of A. N. McLarty.

8) Margaret McLarty 1814-1866; married Dr. Edwin Wilson **Maxwell** 1805-1873. Buried in Douglasville City Cemetery. (See Maxwell above.)

Morris:

John F. Morris born August 30, 1801 in Mecklenburg County, North Carolina, was the ancestor of the Morris families of "Morristown" on Chapel Hill Road in the Interstate 20 area in Douglas County, Georgia. He was the son of Philemon Morris who married Mary Shaver in 1794 in North Carolina. John F. Morris married Mary Caroline "Polly" McLarty on July 22, 1830 in Mecklenburg and came to Campbell County, Georgia with the McLarty family in the mid-1830's. Their children:

1) Mary Morris, May 15, 1831 - March 11, 1887, married December 10, 1856, Campbell County, to Reuben Perry Bullington who was born February 23, 1829 in Spartanburg, South Carolina and died October 31, 1911. Reuben Bullington was a veteran of Co. C 30th Georgia Infantry, CSA. He married a second time to Franciney Smith Stewart. He died at the Confederate Soldiers Home in Atlanta. Children of Reuben and Mary Bullington:

1A. David A. Bullington married 1881 to Jo Harris.

1B. J. William Bullington married 1885 to M. E. Thompson.

1C. Newton J. Bullington.

1D. Joseph B. "Joe" Bullington, November 10, 1874 - September 11, 1960, buried at New Hope with wife Viola, January 17, 1869 - April 5, 1963.

1E. Benjamin J. "Ben" Bullington, November 10, 1874 - August 7, 1919, buried New

Hope Church.

2) James Columbus Morris, September 8, 1834 - June 19, 1903 married Sarah E. **Polk**, April 16, 1843 - October 22, 1909. James Columbus Morris served in the Civil War as a Private - Sergeant, Co C. 30th Georgia Infantry; enlisted September 25, 1861; promoted May 1, 1862; wounded in Jackson, Mississippi on July 16, 1863 and again in Calhoun, Georgia in May of 1864. Their children:

2A. Harriet C. Morris, February 9, 1875 - October 16, 1945, married in 1892 to Emanuel T. Vansant, 1870-1962; both buried at Ephesus Baptist Church Cemetery.

2B. Katherine "Kitty" Morris, January 10, 1878 - May 29, 1969, married September 13, 1894 to John Thomas Feely, December 11, 1872 - March 20, 1953.

2C. Nora Mary Morris, born 1880, unmarried.

2D. Nellie Morris, 1887-1964, married June 16, 1907 to William W. Winn, born 1883.

2E. Minnie C. Morris born 1883 married John Thomas Camp, 1882-1951, buried at Ephesus Church Cemetery, son of John T. and Jane Duke Camp of Paulding County.

3) Edwin Alexander "Sandy" Morris, April 20, 1837 - August 10, 1914, married January 27, 1859 in Campbell County to Permelia Camp, February 20, 1839 - December 24, 1913. Edwin A. Morris served in the Civil War as Private, Co. K, 1st Georgia Cavalry; enlisted May 3, 1862 at Camp Morris (Cartersville); captured October 14, 1864 at Snake Creek Gap (Resaca); sent to Elmira Federal Prison in New York; discharged May 17, 1865. He and his wife are buried at the Douglasville City Cemetery. Children:

3A. William L. Morris, December 16, 1859 - March 19, 1939, buried in the Douglasville City Cemetery with wife Alice Tapp, August 31, 1859 - March 14, 1925.

3B. Thomas Edwin "Ed" Morris, March 5, 1862 - June 16, 1937, married November 15, 1883 in Campbell County to Georgia Mae Camp, May 1, 1866 - October 6, 1964, daughter of Sheriff John L. Camp. Ed. Morris served as Douglasville City Clerk. He and his wife are buried in the Douglasville City Cemetery.

3C. Joseph Benjamin Morris, born 1867, died 3 July 1928, married Ada Tapp, born 1868.

3D. John C. Morris, 1871-1928, married October 20, 1897 to Jenny Camp, 1876-1942, daughter of Sheriff John L. Camp of Campbell County.

4) William J. Morris born June 26, 1839.

5) Margaret Ann Morris born May 21, 1844 married a Jones.

6) John McLarty Morris July 27, 1846 - February 25, 1926 married Sarah C.

McElreath, January 24, 1846 - April 24, 1925. They married on July 5, 1868. Both are buried in the Douglasville City Cemetery, Douglasville, Georgia.

7) Philemon Newton Morris born November 4, 1848.

8) Simon Morris born May 5, 1853.

Polk

Ezekiel Polk, was the son of Charles Polk, 1784 - 1829, and Eleanor Shelby 1783- 1855, daughter of Thomas Shelby, all from North Carolina. Ezekiel was born September 5, 1808 in Mecklenburg, North Carolina and died January 6, 1886, in Winston, Douglas County, Georgia. He is buried in the Douglasville City Cemetery with his wife Melissa Jane who was born June 3, 1809, in Cabarrus, North Carolina and died February 19, 1893 in Winston, Douglas County.

Ezekiel Polk, one of the largest Plantation owners in Dark Corner. Photo: Courtesy Elaine Steere.

Melissa Jane was the daughter of William and Mary Weddington; Ezekiel and Melissa Weddington Polk married October 11, 1828 in Cabarrus, North Carolina. They came to Campbell County about 1834. In 1860, Ezekiel's real estate value was $10,700 and value of personal estate was $12,000. Ezekiel and Melissa's children were:

1) Mary Ellen, born 1829 in North Carolina; died June 1, 1856 in Paulding County; she married in 1848 to Jeremiah Wesley Clonts, 1821 - 1864.

2) Anna Elizabeth "Hannah," born January 28, 1832 in North Carolina, died June 13, 1914 in Douglas County; she married in 1849 to Isaac W. **McKelvey**.

3) Sarah Evelyn, born May 8,1834 in Campbell County; died September 8, 1925 in Winston; she married James Henry **Winn** on December 30, 1852 in Campbell County.

4) Charles Marion Polk was born 1836 in Campbell County. He married Ritha Caroline "Mittie" Carnes, born in 1841 in Carroll County, daughter of John Thomas

and Mary M. Ann Carnes. Charles M. Polk enlisted April 25, 1862 as 2nd Lieutenant in Co A, 56 Regiment Georgia Volunteer Infantry; he was elected 1st Lieutenant on August 20, 1862. He was captured at Vicksburg, Mississippi on July 4, 1863 and paroled there July 8, 1863. He died at the Battle of New Hope Church, Paulding County, Georgia in May 25, 1864. His widow later married John Bradley Sheffield.

5) Nancy J., born 1841, died August 1910, unmarried.

6) William Hale Polk, born June 1, 1843, married Georgia Ann Darnell; he enlisted in Co. A., 56th Regiment Georgia Infantry on April 25, 1862. He died August 6, 1862 at Camp Tazewell, Cairborne County, Tennessee, of Typhoid Fever.

7) Martha Ann Polk was born June 13, 1846 and married John Thomas Feely on February 17, 1867. She died March 3, 1925 in Winston, Douglas County;

8) Amanda Pauline Polk born June 6, 1850 in Campbell County; died June 14, 1937 in Fulton County, Georgia; she married 1st William David McGuire, 2nd William A. Taylor.

9) Margaret Viana Polk, born September 30, 1853, married on April 9, 1866 to James Malmoth Darnell who died at Dark Corner in the 1870's. Then Margaret married a 2nd time to Nicholas J. Neely. She died about 1939 in Fulton County, Georgia.

Charles Shelby Polk, brother of Ezekiel, was born May 29, 1814, died July 10, 1879, married Catherine, 1821-1907, daughter of James and Sarah Ellen (Shelby) McLarty. Sarah Ellen was a daughter of Thomas and Sarah (Helms) Shelby of Mecklenburg County, North Carolina. In 1860, Charles S. Polk's real estate value was $3,600 and value of personal estate was $6,600. Charles Polk died of cholera, as shown on the 1879-80 mortality schedules of Douglas County and had been a county resident for 45 years. Children of Charles S. and Catherine Polk:

1. Sarah E. Polk married 1st George W. **McLarty**, Jr. on October 11, 1860 in Fulton County, Georgia, 2nd James Columbus Morris.

2. James E. Polk, 1845-1888, unmarried.

3. Charles Thomas Polk, 1860-1916, married in 1872 to Margaret A., 1855-1907, daughter of Madison Freeman.

4. Mary Catherine Polk, March 6, 1857 - June 25, 1939, married John Guy **Maxwell**, March 4, 1843 - May 20, 1909; both are buried in Douglasville Cemetery.

5. Henrietta Elizabeth, born 1859 married James Beasley, born 1861.

Siblings: Mary Polk, 1810-1848, sister of Ezekiel and Charles S., was the wife of Samuel Wilson **McLarty.**

Hannah Polk, 1812-1874, another sister, was the wife of A. G. **Weddington**.

The head of the household for the Polk, McLarty, and Weddington families were on the 1830 Mecklenburg, North Carolina U. S. Federal Census and all were early settlers of Dark Corner coming, about 1834.

Asa Sewell

Asa Sewell was born in Franklin County, Georgia, on November 11, 1802, and died in LaFayette County, Arkansas on June 27, 1862. He married Nancy Maria Mitchell on October 8, 1829 in Franklin County. She was born November 13, 1809 and died February 13, 1871 in Arkansas. Asa and Nancy Sewell and family are shown on the Campbell County, Georgia Census in 1850, and on the LaFayette County, Arkansas Census in 1860. In 1855, they lived on 202 1/2 acres on LL # 161 in Campbell County, and their children attended Dark Corner school in 1855. Their children:

1) Martha Theresa born December 20, 1831 in Franklin, Georgia and died May 23, 1883 in Texas; Martha married George Wilkie Lowery born September 12, 1831 in Gwinnett County; died December 28, 1911 in Erath, Texas.

2) Elizabeth Jane born 1831 in Franklin, died in Texas.

3) Harriet H. born 1837 in Campbell County, died in Lewisville, Arkansas in 1865;

4) Orra S. born 1839 in Campbell County;

5) James H. Sewell born about 1840 in Campbell County;

6) John James Sewell born November 29, 1841, died about March 1, 1928 in Texas;

7) Mason Perry Sewell born March 23, 1844 in Campbell County, died 1906 in LaFayette, Arkansas;

8) Nancy C. born March 25, 1846 in Campbell County;

9) William Asa C. Sewell, born September 13, 1848, died January 25, 1924 in Arkansas;

10) Henry G. Sewell born 1853 in Campbell County;

11) Willie Sewell born 1854 in Campbell County.

A Southern Claims commission suit was filed on September 21, 1871 against the United States Government for $498.50 by an Asa Sewell of Fairburn, Georgia, Campbell County for goods taken by the Union Troops from his premises on August

29, 1864. This suit may have been filed and signed by his son William Asa C. Sewell because Asa Sewell died in 1862 in Arkansas. Witnesses for the claimant lived in Fairburn. It is unclear if the Union Army foragers took goods from his residence on LL # 161 in Dark Corner or from his son's premises in Fairburn, Georgia.

James Stewart

James Stewart was born in South Carolina on June 6, 1804 and is shown on the Campbell County 1830 Federal Census. His wife, Nancy Miller, was born in September 19, 1810. He died on September 8, 1860. Their children:

1) George W. Stewart, February 13, 1838 - June 11, 1914, married September 1, 1859 to Amanda Weddington (daughter of A. G. **Weddington**), August 11, 1837 - August 10, 1927. George W. Stewart enlisted on September 25, 1861 in Co. C., 30th Regiment Georgia Volunteer Infantry. Both are buried in the Douglasville Cemetery.

2) Elizabeth Jane Stewart, born September 27, 1828, married on February 3, 1850 to William P. **Winn**.

3) Mary Caroline Stewart, born April 26, 1830, married in 1853 to John L. Umphrey, 1832-1864.

4) Martha Malinda Stewart, was born on June 13, 1834, died August 6, 1911, married May 9, 1858 to John Mason **Huey** (1828-1891); both are buried at County Line Church, Lithia Spring, Georgia.

5) Sarah Ann Stewart, August 9, 1836 - December 3, 1858, married March 12, 1856 to John Harvey **McLarty**, (1836-1917), son of Stephen H. McLarty. Sarah Ann Stewart McLarty is buried in the Stewart Cemetery on Maroney Mill Road near Walton Store Road, north of Douglasville.

6) Nancy Jane Stewart, born May 23, 1842, married Francis M. **Winn**, 1836-1924, on January 2, 1859.

7) Rhoda Jane Stewart, 1842 - 1910, was married first to Dr. John Middlebrooks, 1833-1863, of Powder Springs. She married the second time to Amos Hamilton Winn, 1841 - 1929.

8) Margaret Lovina Stewart, who was born on May 7, 1846 and died May 17, 1910, married Harrison "Dick" Furr (August 5,1843 - April 1, 1910) on October 29, 1865; both are buried in the Douglasville City Cemetery.

9) James LaFayette Stewart born April 12, 1844; enlisted as Private, March 4, 1862 in Company F, 40th Regiment Georgia Volunteer Infantry, Paulding County,

Georgia; died at Baker's Creek, Mississippi on May 16, 1863.

10) Francis Marion Stewart, born May 23, 1832, died December 26, 1871, married March 10, 1853 to Martha Elizabeth Weddington, September 30, 1834 - September 11, 1886, daughter of A. G. Weddington. F. M. Stewart enlisted as Private on May 13, 1862 in Co. F, 40th Regiment Georgia Volunteer Infantry, Paulding County. He was captured at Baker's Creek, Mississippi on May 16, 1863; paroled at Fort Delaware, Delaware on July 3, 1963; and exchanged at City Point, Virginia on July 6, 1863. December 31, 1863, shows absent without leave.

11) Jesse DeKalb, born October 13, 1850.

12) Emily Savannah, born September 3, 1852, died in 1883; married Dr. George W. McLarty, (1840-1919) son of John McLarty, Jr.

Roswell Strickland

Roswell Strickland born about 1810 in Georgia, lived in Campbell County in 1840 and 1860 and at Villa Rica in 1850 and 1870. He married in February 11, 1832 in Campbell County to Lena Flanagan, 1814 - 1870. His second wife was Emiline.

Roswell and Lena Strickland had eight children, all born in Campbell County: 1) Thomas William, born 1832; 2) Jasper, born 1835; 3) Elizabeth, born 1836; 4) Nancy, born 1837; 5) Bethena, born 1842, died in Carroll County, May 17, 1912; 6) Louvena, born June 27, 1842 - November 10, 1912; 7) George Newton, born 1843, who married Julia Ann Henderson; and 8) Martha Ellen, born 1847.

Roswell Strickland is listed on the 1855 Tax Digest for district #730 but no land lot number is shown. In 1871, he filed with the Southern Claims Commission for compensation from the United States Government for good taken from his premises in July 1864 by the Union Army, during the Civil War. See Chapter 12.

Simeon & Parkes Strickland

Reverend Simeon E. Strickland was born in Gwinnett County, Georgia on April 24, 1801 and died in Cobb County on June 6, 1853. On August 11, 1819, he married Matilda **Bates**, who was born January 7, 1803 and died January 13, 1855 in Cobb County. She was the daughter of Mathias **Bates** and Matilda Fountain Bates. Simeon Strickland is listed on the 1830 Census for Campbell County, District 10. In 1831, he drew LL #222 in District #730; one of the witnesses was his father in-law Mathias Bates.

Williamson "Parkes" Strickland, one of Rev. Simeon Strickland's seven children, was born July 22, 1824 in Lawrenceville, Gwinnett County, Georgia and died April 3, 1897 in Douglasville, Douglas County, Georgia. "Parkes" married Mary Amanda **McLarty**, who was born July 1, 1829 in Mecklenburg, North Carolina and died June 18, 1906 in Douglas County. They married on April 23, 1845 in Fulton County. In 1850 and 1860, they lived in District 10, Campbell County.

"Parkes" enlisted March 4, 1862 as first Lieutenant, 41st Regiment, Georgia Infantry, CSA. In 1870 the family lived in the Chestnut Log District and on the 1880 Federal Census, the family is listed in the Salt Springs District of Douglas County. In the 1880s, he served as a city councilman in Douglasville and made his home on Strickland Street.

Watson

Samuel H. Watson, Sr. and Martha Motley Watson were the parents of prominent early settlers of Campbell County. After Samuel, Sr. died in 1827 in Morgan County, Georgia, Martha, Feb 7, 1791 - February 24, 1881, and her children moved to Walton County, then, about 1840 to Campbell County to the Brownsville-Powder Springs Road area where Martha is buried at Pleasant Hill Church. Samuel and Martha Watson's children:

1) John Pendleton Watson, September 29, 1809 - December 20, 1889 is buried at New Hope Church at Chapel Hill. He was an ensign in the Campbell County Militia in 1836 and operated a general store at Dark Corner in 1854. He owned a cotton factory on Sweetwater Creek. John P. married three times. His first wife, Louisa Camp, born about 1815; died October 6, 1840; she was the daughter of Judge Joseph Camp. Louisa Watson is buried in the Holly Springs Cemetery in Douglas County.

John Pendleton Watson married again on November 20, 1842, in Campbell County, to Elizabeth Goolsby, January 20, 1827 - March 2, 1869. She is buried at Neal Cemetery. J. P. Watson's third wife was Eustacia Caroline, March 8, 1834 - April 13, 1910 whom he married before the 1870 Federal Census was taken.

2) Permelia Watson, 1811 - 1849, married Nathan Camp, son of Judge Joseph Camp. She is buried at Holly Springs.

3) Elizabeth, 1821 - 1889 is buried at Midway Church, Marietta - Dallas Road, Kennesaw, Georgia.

4) Martha Watson, born about 1814, who married January 24, 1842 at Dark

Corner to William Peter Goolsby.

5) James Motley Watson, February 9, 1825 - February 14, 1899, married Elizabeth, May 30, 1831 - October 29, 1915, daughter of Jacob Clonts. He was a merchant at Brownsville; he is buried at Bethel Methodist Church in Brownsville.

6) Samuel H. Watson, Jr - see Chapter 6.

Francis & Mahalia Winn/Wynn

John Wynn an early Georgia pioneer who came from South Carolina and

Front L-R: Natilda James, Manroe Gore, Martha Shipley James, Vassie James Smith, Mattie James Winn, Etta James Causey; Back L-R: J. F. "Jim" Winn, Howard Causey, Robert E. "Bob" James, William A. "Bill" James. Photo: Douglas County Public Library.

settled in Gwinnett County, drew Campbell County Land Lot numbers 223 in 1830, 224 in 1832, and 193 in 1834. In his will dated January 20, 1849, he left the land in Campbell County to sons **(A)** Francis and **(B)** Allen B. and to his son **(C)** John J. A. Winn's widow, Mahalia Winn and her orphans. Witnesses of the will were Samuel H. Watson, Archibald N. McLarty and Asa Sewell. His son Francis and his daughter-in-law, Mahalia lived in Campbell County, Dark Corner District, with their many descendants.

(A) His son, Reverend Francis Winn, born about 1798-1801, died March 1862, and is buried at the Winn-Watson Cemetery on North Flat Rock Road, in Douglas County. Rev. Francis Winn established what is now the First Methodist Church of Douglsville. He and his wife, Drucilla, (1802 - 1870) arrived as pioneer settlers at Dark Corner about 1828 and lived there as late as 1870 as they are shown there on the 1870 Federal Census. Reverend Winn was pastor on March 16, 1850 when Thomas Enterkin deeded 10 acres for the church on present-day Bright Star Road to the trustees of the Methodist Episcopal Church - South at Flat Rock: David **Enterkin**, Samuel W. **McLarty**, Alexander **McKelvey**, Mark **McElreath**, and William C. Wright. In 1855**,** Francis Winn paid taxes on LL # 223. John and Drucilla's children:

1) Margaret C. Winn, married in 1870 to Burrel M. Malone.

2) Allen B. Winn, born 1841, was a Private in Company F, 30th Georgia Infantry and taught school at Brownsville in 1870.

3) Thomas O, Winn, born about 1845.

4) William P. Winn, born 1830, married in 1850 to Elizabeth Stewart, daughter of James **Stewart**.

5) George A. Winn, February 28, 1836 - August 12, 1876. On November 3, 1870, he married Nancy Ann Mozley, daughter of Isaiah Mozley. George Winn is a veteran of Company K, 41st Georgia Infantry, CSA. He is buried in the Old Salt Springs Campground Cemetery at Lithia Springs, Georgia.

6) James Henry Winn, January 29, 1828 - April 29, 1896, married on December 3, 1852 to Sarah E. **Polk** (May 8, 1834 - September 8, 1925), daughter of Ezekiel Polk. Both J. H. and Sarah Winn are buried in the Enterkin - Winn Cemetery at Winston, Georgia. He was the first postmaster and merchant at Weddington, later named Winn, then the name was changed to Winston. J. H. Winn was the Captain of the #730 Militia in 1860. He was an original county commissioner of Douglas County and later operated a cotton gin and grist mill at Winston along with his store.

7) Mary Isabelle Winn, 1831 - 1910 married in 1848 to Madison Freeman; she is buried in Douglasville City Cemetery, Douglas County, Georgia.

8) Newton Francis Winn, born about 1836,

9) Ann Winn - wife of Perry G. **Stewart**,

10) Nancy E. Winn - born about 1839, married Michael Madden

11) Ellen D. Winn, 1844 - 1923 married David Smith, 1836 - 1907.

12) John W. Winn, born about 1832.

(B) Allen Winn

(C) John J. A. Winn, born August 10, 1811 and died in November 21, 1848 married Mahalia (Barnett) Winn born November 14, 1805 - 1874. She was the daughter of Amos and Hannah Barnett of Pendleton District, South Carolina. After she became the widow of John J. A. Winn, she raised her children and farmed on the land her father-in-law, John Wynn, left to her husband. In 1855 and in 1861, Mahalia Wynn paid taxes on LL #s 193 and 224. Their children:

1) Drucilla Caroline, born June 22, 1834; married in 1855 to Isaac Bentley, son of Elijah Bentley of Carroll and Haralson Counties.

2) John C. Winn, born September 29, 1835; enlisted September 25, 1861 in Company F, 30th Georgia Infantry which became Company C, 39th Regiment Georgia Infantry; after March - April 1862 he was transferred to 1st Battalion. After May 1862, he was back to Company C 30th Georgia Infantry. He died in the Civil War in 1863.

3) Henry A. Winn born December 5, 1838; he married in 1860 to Mary A. Mattox; their daughter was Ida M. Winn. He enlisted in the Civil War in Company K, 41st Georgia Infantry, from Salt Springs on March 4, 1862. He is listed as wagoner, then teamster; captured at Vicksburg, Mississippi, July 4, 1863; paroled and signed Oath of Allegiance to the Union Army on July 17, 1863; died August 17, 1863. On July 16 1864, his wife, Mary, filed a claim for a deceased soldier, her husband, Henry A. Winn.

4) Mary Ann Winn born May 5, 1839; married in 1862 in Campbell County to Samuel A. Wood, born 1840, a shoe and bootmaker.

5) Amos Hamilton "Hamp" Winn, born May 4, 1841; married in 1865 to Rhoda J. Stewart Middlebrooks, widow of Dr. John Middlebrooks and daughter of James Stewart. He enlisted in Campbellton, Campbell County, Georgia, on September 25, 1861, the same time as his brother, John C. Winn, in Company F, 30th Georgia that became Co. F 39th Regiment Georgia Infantry. On May 1, 1863 he was received in transfer to 1st Battalion, then back to the 30th Georgia. "Hamp" Winn died in the Confederate Soldiers' Home in Atlanta in 1929.

6) Andrew Jackson Winn, born September 16, 1847; died April 1883; married Nancy Lucinda Harbin, December 22, 1850 - Feb 17, 1920.

7) Francis Milton "Uncle Milt" Winn was born on October 29, 1836; he

married Nancy Jane **Stewart**, daughter of James Stewart. An 1873 Douglas County deed shows that Francis M. Winn was deeded land in land lots #193 and #224 by his mother, Mahalia, and names his brothers and sisters. He was named as guardian of Ida M., minor, orphan of Henry A. Winn. He is buried in the Stewart Cemetery with an updated Confederate marker. F. M. & Nancy's children:

A. James F. Winn was born on December 17, 1860 and died July 18, 1915. In 1886, he married Mattie James, 1861 - 1946, daughter of Stephen James. Their children were Alva who married T. P. Huckaby, Jamie who married Lee Morris, and others including Frank Winn who was born in 1894 who married Mary Peace. Frank Winn was Douglas County Clerk of Superior Court.

B. Lura A. Winn married in 1882 to N. S. Lipscomb.

C. Sarah E."Sallie" Winn, 1867 - 1951, who married Henry Reuben Barrow, 1862 - 1958.

D. Atticus P. Winn, 1871 - October 2, 1942, married Ethel McKelvey who was born June 6, 1877.

E. Jessie A. Winn, 1872 - 1964, married Charles W. McGouirk

F. Savilla Winn married John Wesley McKelvey.

G. Marvin Winn was born in 1875.

H. Arthur Winn was born in 1879; a sawyer and logman in Douglas County in 1900.

I. Willie May, born 1881, was a teacher in Douglas County in 1900.

14

More Pioneer Families

Federal troops took a horse, a few hundred bundles of fodder and bushels of corn, chickens, whatever they could find.

Brittain

Alfred Tyre Brittain, born October 15, 1865 at Newnan, Georgia, died November 20, 1942, Douglas County, Georgia married Mary Frances **Kennedy**, born January 26, 1873 and died January 27, 1953, in Douglas County. They had thirteen children, all born in Douglas County in the Dark Corner Community.

1) Fannie Lou Brittain, born February 9, 1889, married Horace **Darnell**.

2) Tyre Aubrey Brittain, born February 9, 1891 (same birthday as sister), married Alma Carnes, then 2nd marriage Elizabeth Dodson, born March 11, 1904.

3) Aulton Kennedy Brittain, born February 27, 1893, was killed in World War I, November 6, 1918, in Achen, France.

4) Bernard Harrison Brittain, born December 19, 1894, married Grace Poe, died May 20, 1953.

5) Hester Annie Brittain, born May 10, 1897, married William Riley Thomas.

6) Gladys Mae Brittain, born May 1, 1899, married Reece Hamby, died September 1923.

7) Gertie Maude Brittain, born April 29, 1901, married James Ernest Gibbs.

8) Cecil Brittain, born June 11, 1903, died July 30, 1990; married February 26, 1922 to George Harlin Culpepper.

9) Mary Elizabeth Brittain, born October 16, 1905, married October 3, 1929 to Eugene Camp Dodson, died March 10, 1971.

10) Virginia Brittain, born March 2, 1908, married Glen Hay.

11) John Ralph Brittain, born December 16, 1910, married September 3, 1942 to Ella Gilland.

12. Lorena Brittain, born May 29, 1914, married Paul Tidwell.

13. Mabel Blanch Brittain, born March 27, 1916, married Howard Kennerly.

Brown

William Hardy Brown was born February 27, 1811 in South Carolina; he was married in Gwinnett County, Georgia on December 6, 1836 to Irena Matthews who was born January 5, 1813 in South Carolina also. In 1855, five of their children are listed on the Dark Corner School class roll: J. M., Narcissa, W. H., P(osey) N(ewton) and Irene Brown. This family is listed on the 1870 and 1880 U. S. Federal Census for District #730, Campbell County. William, died March 12, 1895; Irena, died February 23, 1884. Children: A) John Morton Brown, born in Gwinnett County, Georgia on December 2, 1837; died June 4, 1914 in Paulding County, Georgia;

Posey Newton Brown and wife Mary Catherine McLarty Brown
Photo: Courtesy Linda Willoughby Leatherman.

B) James F. Brown, born January 5, 1839 in Gwinnett County; died October 8, 1908 in Carroll County, Georgia;;

C) Narcissa A. Brown, born November 13, 1840 in Campbell County; died August 3, 1908 in Villa Rica, Georgia; married Jasper S. Smith.

D) William Hardy Brown, Jr., born May 28, 1842 in Campbell County; died in Bartow County, Georgia; married Sarah A.

E) Parker Northcutt Brown, born June 13, 1844 in Campbell County; died November 20, 1920 in Douglas County, Georgia; Parker enlisted on December 13, 1862 with the "Campbell County Sharpshooters" - Co F 30th Georgia Volunteer Infantry. He was captured in Campbell County, Ga on July 16, 1864; took the Oath of Allegiance to U. S. Government at Louisville, Kentucky and released August 3, 1864 to remain north of Ohio River during the war. He married Artemesia Hendricks.

F) Irena R. Brown, born February 1, 1847 in Campbell County; died March 16, 1919 in Douglas County;

G) Posey Newton Brown born June 13, 1849 in Campbell County, District #730, married Mary Catherine **McLarty** born in Georgia 1846, the daughter of John McLarty, Jr and his second wife, Sarah Eleanor. They married October 28, 1872. Posey died July 17, 1896 and Mary Catherine died April 30, 1885. Both died in Douglas County and are buried at the McLarty Cemetery at Dark Corner. Their Children: 1) Charles Newton, 1874 - 1912; 2) Posey Columbus, 1876 - 1945; 3) James Anderson, 1879 - 1962; 4) Marion Napoleon, 1880 - 1950; 5) Arthur Brown, 1882 - 1964; 6) Poly Cleveland, 1885 - 1885.

H) Lousesa Brown, January 1, 1851 in Campbell County; died November 28, 1878 in Douglas County;

I) Hattie Amanda Brown, born January 16, 1854 in Campbell County, died August 14, 1877 in Douglas County.

Camp

James Seaborn Camp, who was the father of twenty-three children, was born 1813 in Georgia and died July 6, 1900 in Clayton County and is buried in east Jonesboro, at the old homeplace. Seaborn's first wife was Mahaley Beavers whom he married in Henry County on January 10, 1833. His second wife was Sissillia Elizabeth Parish. Seaborn and Sissillia Parish Camp's son, John Thomas Camp, Sr. (who was born in June 10, 1855 in Henry County Georgia, and died January 3, 1939 in Douglas County) came to Campbell County before 1880.

John Thomas Camp, Sr. married in 1879 to Martha Jane Duke. Martha's parents were John Monroe Duke and Sarah Ann Beck Duke. Martha was born October 21, 1861 and died May 16, 1934. John Camp was born June 10, 1855 and died February 27, 1941. Both are buried at Friendship Church Cemetery in Paulding Co. John and Martha Camp had 10 children all of whom were born in Clayton County.

1) William "Will" Robert Camp, born May 30, 1880, died January 3, 1939 and is buried in Paulding Co. at Friendship Church Cemetery; he married Mary Savana Garner. **2)** John Thomas, Jr. Camp born, October 15, 1882, died April 23, 1951, married Minnie Carmen Morris on December 24, 1902 in Douglas County. Minnie and John had eleven children, all born in Douglas County and for four generations have lived in Dark Corner: a) John Thomas "Jim" born October 4, 1903; b) Charles "Shelby" born June 6, 1905; c) Oscar "Frank" born July 8, 1907; d) William "Fred" born Nov. 18, 1909; e) Hulan Jackson "Streak" born June 29, 1912; f) "Ruby" Pearl, born June 29, 1914; g) John "Lewis" born August 21, 1916; h) Ruth Lee, born Oct 2, 1918, i) Sarah "Allene" born, March 18, 1922; j) Audrey Virgie "Mutt" born October 19, 1924; k) Raymond, b. Oct. 24, 1927.

John Thomas Sr, and wife Martha Jane Duke Camp
Photo: Courtesy the Camp Family

3) Sebran I. Camp, born January 1, 1885, died as an infant in February 1885.

4) Sarah Elizabeth "Lizzie" was born June 8, 1886 and died May 10, 1964 in Douglasville, Douglas County. She married Jessie Leon Pilgrim on October 16, 1904.

5) Elijah Malone "Lone" Camp was born September 16, 1888 and died October 27, 1967 in Douglas County. He married Della Rice in 1909.

6) Cornelia "Gennie" born, September 8, 1891, died in 1982. She married Henry Grady Thompson on November 9, 1915.

7) Melinda "Lindy" Camp was born on September 8, 1894; she married Clestor Taylor on October 12, 1927.

8) James Walter "Walt" was born April 25, 1897 and died April 21, 1988 in Douglasville. He married Elbertice Gibson on December 10, 1916 in Douglas Co.

9) Henry Lovett was born on September 10, 1899; died September 9, 1936; he married Lola Mae McMichens on Sept 20, 1925.

10) Mittie Ioma "Omie", born June 17, 1902, married Ray Henter 1/12/1919.

Peter Carnes

Peter Carnes was a mulatto slave who was born March 1833. He was bought by John Thomas Carnes and brought home to the Carnes farm, then in Carroll County, (after 1870, Douglas County). Peter grew up working on the Carnes farm; then he learned the trade of blacksmith. When his master, Thomas Carnes, allowed him to do spare jobs, Peter saved enough to buy himself freedom and after the Civil War, took the surname Carnes.

Peter, along with other members of his family, all of whom were slaves before the Civil War, Nathaniel Hawkins, Neal Hart, George Weddington, Clark McLarty, and Perry Thrasher, all worked several years, after slavery, for Ezekiel Polk. About 1875, Peter Carnes became his own employer with his own employees. In time, Peter married Sophia Polk. They had one son, Peter James Carnes, born on November 17, 1882, but died the same day. Peter buried his son in the McLarty Cemetery. Peter had two daughters, Sarah Carnes born in 1852 who was also listed with her father Peter in the "Will of John Thomas Carnes of Villa Rica, Georgia." Sarah Carnes married Nathaniel **Hawkins**.

Peter's second daughter, Ida Carnes, was born in 1873; she married Albert Scales on July 27, 1889. Their children: 1) Walter Scales, born April 3, 1890; 2) W. H. Scales, born September 16, 1891; 3) Mattie Lillian, born September 16, 1893; 4) William England Scales, born October 15, 1896, married Lillian Sinkfield, on March 31, 1918; 5) Lester Scales, born Sept 1898; 6) Lizzie, born 1901, married James McCoy; 7) Paul M. "Freeman" Scales, born March 22, 1903, married Fannie Mae Wysinger; 8) Lena, born 1905, married Charley Bell; 9) Pete Scales, born January 28, 1907; married Oleen Johnson; 10) Addie B., born July 24, 1910, married Jodie Jones; and 11) Velma, born Oct 18, 1912, married Otho Merritt.

When Ezekiel Polk died in 1886, Peter and his family members: Neal Hart, Clark McLarty, Peter Polk, Nathaniel Hawkins, Sarah Hawkins, and Bob Baker all attended his estate sale and bought a part of the Polk plantation. Years later Peter

Carnes would buy more of the old Polk plantation. Peter Carnes was family to both the black and white families of Dark Corner.

When Peter died in August 30, 1920, he was the owner of a Ford automobile, a two story house, acres of land and had many grandchildren and great grandchildren. One of Peter's last wishes recorded in his will was to be buried at what was once known as the McLarty Grave Yard and during his final years the black families in the Dark Corner area had referred to it as the Old Mountain Top Grave Yard. His wishes were carried out and his grave was marked with a double headstone for him and his wife, Sophie Carnes who would die in 1927. Peter had purchased additional acreage at the top of the McLarty Cemetery for the black families in Dark Corner to continue to be buried there. And so it was—well into the 1940s though the white families had stopped using this site for burial.

When Peter Carnes left this earth, he left behind many friends who included the families of the Carnes, Polks, Weddingtons, McLartys, Darnells, Harts, Bakers, Enterkins, Clintons, Pounds, Kirbys, Morris, Waldrops, Harpers, Pooles, and many more—both black and white. Peter's descendants through Sarah Carnes Hawkins still own the old part of the Polk plantation that Peter Carnes bought, ages ago.

Darnell

David Z. Darnell (Darnold) was born in 1783 in Mecklenburg, North Carolina and died in 1851 in Dark Corner, Campbell County Georgia. He married Lucinda Lusky (Luskie) Acorn in 1808, in Mecklenburg N. C. In 1820, they resided in Morgan County Georgia then in 1840, District #736 Campbell County, Georgia and then in 1850 District 10, Campbell County. They had three children:

1) Lucinda Polk Darnell (1809-1879), married James Burson;

2) James Melton Darnell (1818-1888); and

3) David Young Darnell, born in 1816 in Georgia, and died in 1866 in Campbell County, Georgia. On March 22, 1838 in Campbell County, David Y. Darnell married Lucinda **Hightower** who was born in 1816 in North Carolina. He drew LL# 136 in Dark Corner in the Richardson - Conners' Road area that was later, Winston. He is listed paying tax on LL #136 on the 1861 Georgia Property Tax Digest. David Young and Lucinda Hightower Darnell had ten children:

1) Nancy J. Darnell born 1834;

2) James Melmeth Darnell, born 1839, and he died in 1879;

3) John G. Darnell, born 1840, died 1899;
4) Georgia Ann Darnell, born 1843;
5) David Darnell, born 1844 - died 1898;
6) Joseph G. Darnell, born 1845;
7) Robert Joshua Darnell, born January 7, 1849 Campbell County, died September 2, 1928 in Douglas County, married in 1875 to Malissa (1855-1944). Children: Wilson, Eudilla, Burnice, Ocilee and Horace Darnell, Jr. - born May 31, 1877; died August 20, 1962. Horace lived in the Dark Corner area all his life. He married Fannie Lou **Brittain**, born 1889 - died 1990;
8) Millard Darnell, born 1853 - died 1899;
9) Mary Darnell, was born in 1855;
10) Charles Darnell, was born in 1856.

David Z. Darnell 1783 - 1851
Photo: Courtesy Darnell family.

A Tall Tale told by Roy Black about Buddy - a real character from Dark Corner.

"Every community has its characters who tell tall tales. Downtown Dark Corner had Buddy. His family lived on a farm way out in the country where they raised cotton and corn. Buddy had one older brother and two older sisters. He was left there on the farm to do what young, country boys do, growing up. When he got about 13, he was a big old boy - a long tall long-legged boy. Buddy had never had any shoes. The other boy around there had shoes. Buddy got to noticing the girls. Buddy told his daddy one fall when they were ready to sell the crops, that he wanted a pair of shoes along with his new overalls that he got once a year. Mr. Darnell told Buddy, 'you can have one of the two but you cannot have both. Take your choice - shoes or overalls, there is no money for both.' Buddy had grown about a foot that year and his overalls came down just below his knees. But he wanted those shoes because the other boys (his age) had shoes. 'Just buy a new pair of shoes,' Buddy told his Dad - cause he had never had any. So they went to Douglasville to Mr. Huffine's warehouse. In the hardware (part) they saw the shoes. They were pretty too. There were great-ole-big

ones, medium ones, and small shoes. So Buddy picked out the biggest size and put them on. Never had socks. Buddy's feet were tough. He had walked through briars, down the country roads and railroad tracks. Nothing bothered his feet. They were hard and even cracked. Socks? They could not afford any. Just the new shoes.

"So they went back home. It was Saturday. Buddy put on those brogans and walked to Winston. He wanted those people in Winston to see his new shoes. Buddy walked down the county road, proud of his new shoes. They even had checks on the bottom. These boots were made out of rawhide with a big brass brad on each of them. He walked in the sand on the dirt road - backward so he could see those pretty marks - those pretty tracks his boots made in the sand. He went to the post office and all the people there were looking at his new shoes - they never had seen Buddy with shoes on. He was so proud of those new shoes - he walked everywhere.

"So about four or five weeks later something happened to his shoes. He went in to show his daddy. They were still making those pretty tracks like they had done. But a hole had come into the bottom of each of his shoes. 'Look Daddy, something has happened to my shoes!' Come to find out that Buddy's feet were so tough that he had worn his shoes out from the inside! So that's the story of Buddy and his shoes."

Dorris

Rev. John McKensie Dorris, born May 13, 1806 in South Carolina, died May 13, 1883 (birth month and day same as death month and day) in Paulding County, Georgia. He married on August 5, 1830 in Carroll County, Georgia to Elizabeth L. Clements who was born November 25, 1806 in Georgia and died January 24, 1899. Both are buried at Sweetwater Baptist Church Cemetery in Paulding County, Georgia.

In 1830 and 1850, the Dorris family lived in Carroll County, in 1840 in Cherokee County, and in 1860 and 1870, in Campbell County living along Dorris Road that runs North to South along LL #s 221 and 228 then extends northward, over the line into Paulding County.

On 1880 Federal Census Record, John M. is shown as a widower living in Paulding County with his son, J. B. Dorris. John and Elizabeth Dorris' nine children:

1. Martha Emaline Dorris, born May 14, 1832, died November 22, 1914. She is buried at Poplar Springs Church in Paulding County.

2. James McKensie Dorris, born September 2, 1833, died January 24, 1889. James married Martha Jane

Norton on March 17, 1867; Martha, was born on September 14, 1848, and died January 5, 1931. She was the daughter of Daniel W. Norton, of Paulding County.

3. Mary Frances "Molly" Dorris, born March 4, 1835, and died November 21, 1911 was never married.

4. William Clements Dorris was born May 22, 1837, and died July 8, 1917. He married Matilda Lowe on February 20, 1868; Matilda, born March 6, 1847, died August 25, 1931, was the daughter of John C. and Elizabeth Bates Lowe.

James and Martha Jane Dorris

Photo: Courtesy Marcyln Martin

5. Elizabeth S. Dorris, born March 14, 1841, died May 28, 1863, married Milton M. Davis. She is buried at Sweetwater Church in Paulding County.

6. Winifred Dorris, born 1843, married John Baker.

7. Hester A. Dorris, born on November 25, 1845, died July 2, 1895, married John Johnson Kennedy (1835 - 1905) on February 27, 1862.

8. Vernialli J. "Mollie" Dorris, born March 3, 1847, died October 20, 1907, married in 1869 to G. T. McClung, October 18, 1846 - January 24, 1901.

9. John Benjamin Dorris, born March 22, 1851, died December 4, 1919, married on November 11, 1873 to Mary Tallula "Lou" Laird, September 12, 1854 - October 22, 1932.

Littleberry Hawkins

Littleberry Hawkins, was born October 12, 1805 in Buncombe, North Carolina and died in November 1866 in Stilesboro, Bartow County, Georgia. He bought LL # 217 in District #730 on October 31, 1834 and LL # 216 on October 3, 1845; he is shown on the 1840 U. S. Federal Census for Campbell County, Militia District #730, listed next door to Alexander Green Weddington. About 1828, Littleberry married Campassy Seaborn, born 1810 in Greenville, Spartanburg County, South Carolina and died after 1866 in Bartow County, Georgia. On the 1850 Paulding County Census for Militia District #985, Campassy's mother, Mary Seaborn (born in N. C, in 1760) is listed next door. The value of their real estate is shown as $4,000. The 1860 Census for Cass County, Georgia shows the value of their real estate was $8,000 and value of personal property was $3,200. Their children and some of the grandchildren:

1) George Washington Hawkins was born in 1829 in South Carolina. On December 1, 1848, he married Mary Ann Weddington, (daughter of Alexander Green Weddington and Hannah Polk) who was born September 26, 1830 and died in 1918. He enlisted as a Private, May 1862, in Co. I, 43rd Regiment Georgia Infantry; later he was promoted to Lieutenant. George Washington Hawkins fought in the Battle of the Wilderness and died from a gunshot wound in the head on May 6, 1864.

Mary A. Hawkins settled the estate of her late husband, George Washington Hawkins. An inventory and appraisal was done on the estate of G. W. Hawkins on June 4, 1866 in Paulding County, Georgia

2) Hannah Louise, was born in 1830 in Greenville, Spartanburg County, South Carolina; she married Seaborn Edwards, on January 11, 1857.

3) Benjamin Franklin Hawkins was born on April 22, 1831 in Greenville, South Carolina and died on February 9, 1912 in Rockmart, Polk County, Georgia. He married Drucilla Jane McGregor, 1839-1918. He served in Company B of Phillips Legion of Volunteers. Benjamin Hawkins was named in Littleberry Hawkins' will as executor of the estate.

4) John Ranson Hawkins was born in 1833 in South Carolina; he married Sarah Dodson. He enlisted on May 6, 1862, at Camp Prichard, as Private in Company O (originally Company E) of 1st Confederate Regiment Infantry, Phillips Legion. John was killed on September 14, 1862 in the Battle of South Mountain, also called the battle of Boonesboro Gap, near Boonesboro, Maryland.

5) Augustus M., Hawkins was born in 1835 in South Carolina and died in 1861 in Knoxville, Tennessee.

6) Sarah M. Hawkins was born in 1838 in Georgia. She died before 1866.

7) Emily Josephine, born July 10, 1842 in Villa Rica, Carroll County, Georgia, died December 6, 1905 in Stilesboro, Georgia. On March 12, 1863, she married Captain Henry John McCormick, 1838-1929.

8) Louisa Nancy, born July 17, 1846 in Georgia, died December 18, 1920, in Carroll County. She married a Muse.

9) Thaddeus S. Hawkins, born 1850 in Paulding County, died April 30, 1938 in Bartow County. He married Susan T. McCormick on March 13, 1873.

From a Littleberry Hawkins' will dated January 31, 1866, Bartow County, Georgia, the following grandchildren were named: Emily Elizabeth, Hannah Campasia, Sarah Caroline, Louisa Jane, George Alexander, Louisa Kennedy, Jesse Kennedy, Alfred and Benjamin Kennedy.

This family lost three sons to the Civil War: George Washington Hawkins, Augustus M. Hawkins and John Ranson Hawkins.

Harriet Hawkins

Harriet Weddington Hawkins, born in Georgia in 1824, grew up a slave working in Dark Corner. She married John Hawkins, who was a slave of Littleberry Hawkins and later his son George Washington Hawkins. After 1870, Harriet lived with her daughters and granddaughters, and at her death, she was living with her daughter, Patsey Blanchard, in Marietta. According to family stories, she lived to be 103, but her death certificates indicates she lived to be 98; she died July 23, 1922. Harriet and John had five children: Nathaniel, Nicey, Louisa, Minerva, and Patsey—all shown on the Campbell County 1860 Slave Schedule belonging to George Washington Hawkins.

I - Nathaniel "Hal" Hawkins was a slave of George Washington Hawkins. In 1871 after the Civil War and after the Freedman's Act was passed, he worked for Ezekiel Polk. Nathaniel was born October 7, 1849 in Campbell County and died November 15, 1902 in Winston, Douglas County. He married Sarah Carnes who was a former slave of Thomas Carnes. Sarah Carnes was born March 1852 and died February 9, 1942 in Villa Rica, Douglas County. Nathaniel and Sarah had six sons and seven daughters, all born in the Dark Corner area:

1) Emma was born in 1873 and died July 31, 1942, in Douglas County. She married Robert Baker;

Marion H. Hawkins & wife Willie Mae
Photo: Courtesy Greg Dansby

2) Josephine was born in 1874 and died in 1916. She married Henry Poole;

3) Emily was born in 1875 and died in 1898. She married Edmund Johnson;

4) Frances was born in 1877 & died in 1945. She married Jackson Holliman;

5) Peter James Hawkins was born in 1879 and died in 1912;

6) George Washington Hawkins, was born on May 27, 1871 and died on August 20, 1944. He married Amanda Reeves.

7) Twin - Marion H. Hawkins, born on August 5, 1883, and died November 17, 1963, in Winston. Marion H. Hawkins married Willie Mae Hart. She was the granddaughter of Neal Hart and daughter of Samuel Hart, Sr., who, most likely, was a slave of Samuel Hart, owner of a large plantation in Villa Rica. Willie Mae's brother was Samuel "Son" Hart Jr., a tenant farmer on the corner of Mann and Cedar Mt. Road on the Kennedy, later the Winn property, for many years.

8) Twin - Mary who was born on August 5, 1883 and died on August 10, 1927, in Winston. She married Columbus Jones;

9) Mattie was born in 1885 and died in 1949. She married Thomas Mathis;

10) Minnie was born in 1887 and died in 1904;

11) William Harris Hawkins was born on November 26, 1889 and died March 7, 1923. William Harris Hawkins was a World War I veteran.

12) Benjamin Curtis Hawkins was born on December 30, 1891 and died 1952.

13) Leonard Boyd Hawkins.

II - Nicey Hawkins born about 1858 and died in 1912. Nicey married William H. McLarin on March 11, 1877. Nicey and William had one daughter, Odessa McLarin who married Charley Johnson on October 22, 1905.

III - Louisa "Lula" Hawkins born about 1854 married Joseph McLarty around 1871. Lula and Joe had 12 children. Ella McLarty was born about 1872, married Tom Holliman; Mollie McLarty, born about 1874 married Comer Parker; Reverend Tobe B. McLarty, born December 20, 1877, died June 16, 1938. He married Bertha Mitchum. Tobe attended Morehouse College in Atlanta. He was also the contractor for the 1st *New* Mt. Top Baptist Church in Winston. Joe F. McLarty, born about 1878; Lizzie McLarty born about 1880; Carrie McLarty born about 1881, married George Dorsey; John McLarty born about 1883; William A. McLarty, born about 1887 - October 25, 1931; Matthew McLarty, born about 1888; Samuel McLarty, born about 1890; Hattie C. McLarty, born about 1894; and Fred McLarty born about 1897.

Reverend Tobe B. McLarty
Photo: Courtesy Fred Sparks.

IV - Minerva Hawkins born about 1856 married Robert Holliman on February 11, 1879. Their children were Della Holliman who married Henry McLarty on December 16, 1882; Savannah Holliman who married Charlie McKoy; Tom Holliman who married Ella McLarty about 1891; Daisey Holliman who married William Mapp; Glenn Holliman; Jewel L. Holliman; Bert Howell Holliman. Minerva died in Knoxville, Tennessee on March 24, 1938.

V - Patsey Hawkins born about 1858, died January 23, 1940. She married 1st to William Jones on April 15, 1875 by Randle Gamble, Minister of the Gospel. By 1910, Patsey was a widow. She married a 2nd time to Dolph Blanchard on December 31, 1913. She died on January 23, 1940. She had no children.

Hightower

Henry R. Hightower was born in Pennsylvania and about 1800; migrated to Oglethorpe County, Georgia, then moved to Campbell County, about 1850 where he died in 1857. He married Temperance “Tempie” Ray who was born about 1800 in Georgia. They married in Clarke County on January 13, 1820. Their children:

1) Isaac born about 1830 in Georgia;

2) Amanda born about 1834 in Georgia;

3) Hilliard born about 1835, in Georgia;

4) Nancy D. born about 1837 in Georgia;

5) Herby born about 1842.

6) John Dickson Hightower who married Roanisa Teal;

7) Elberry W. (Littleberry) "Berry" Hightower born 1842 in Ga.; married Martha Ann "Mattie" **Weddington**, daughter of Robert Hale Weddington and Clemmie (**Hartsfield**) Weddington on March 24, 1865 in Paulding County, Georgia. Elberry (L.B.) Hightower enlisted as Private on March 4, 1862 in Co. F. 40th Regiment Georgia Volunteer Infantry, Paulding County. He was captured at Vicksburg, Miss. on July 4, 1863 and paroled July 6, 1863; captured in Campbell County, Ga. on July 16, 1864. He took the Oath of Allegiance to the U. S. Government at Chattanooga, Tenn. on July 26, 1864, and was sent to Louisville, Kentucky where he took the Oath again on August 3, 1864 and was released to remain north of Ohio River during the war.

Hildebrand

John (Johannes) Hildebrand, who was of German descent, was born October 31, 1798 in Burke, North Carolina and died August 8, 1866 in Villa Rica, Georgia. He married in North Carolina on January 27, 1830 to Anna Van Horn who was born May 17, 1812. She was the daughter of John Van Horn of North Carolina. She died on August 24, 1877 in Villa Rica, Georgia.

On February 19, 1830, John purchased Land Lot #203 in Carroll County (later Douglas County) located on Brewer Road. John, a surveyor, came to this area about the time the land was being surveyed into land lots. He was a road commissioner for District #642—Villa Rica and the Carroll County portion of Dark Corner—from 1836-1842. He was paid for resurveying the "Town of Carrollton" around 1836-37. John and Anna Hildebrand's children:

1) Mary Elizabeth, born March 24, 1831 and died May 11, 1925, married Samuel Alexander **McLarty** on February 24, 1850. He was born February 28, 1828 and died February 9, 1901.

2) Sarah "Sallie" Minerva, born February 18, 1833 in Carroll County, died January 10, 1933. She married James William White on February 27, 1857. James was born July 24, 1833. He enlisted as Private in Co. I, 56th Regiment Georgia

Hildebrand siblings, 1924: L-R FR: Elizabeth McLarty, 93; Minerva White, 91; Mandy Hallman, 82; Margaret Willoughby, 79; BR Jane White, 87; Martha Leathers, 74, William; Josie Leathers, 72; John Hildebrand, Jr. Two sons killed in Civil War - not shown. Photo, courtesy: Sandy Whittington

Volunteer Infantry on May 10, 1862. He died May 3, 1863 at Enterprise, Mississippi during the Mississippi campaign.

3) John H. Hildebrand Jr, born July 4, 1835 in Carroll County, died May 10, 1912. He married Eliza Caroline White on January 6, 1859 in Paulding County. Caroline was born December 27, 1840 in Campbell County and died May 15, 1923 in Tallapoosa, Haralson County, Georgia.

4) Nancy Jane, born November 24, 1838 in Carroll County, died December 7, 1924 in Douglas County. She married Samuel Jefferson White on August 2, 1855. Samuel was born November 5, 1836 in Powder Springs and died June 27, 1884.

5) Isaac Newton Hildebrand was born March 19, 1840 in Carroll County. Enlisted as Private on September 25, 1861 in Co F, later Co. C, Campbell County Sharpshooters, 30th Georgia Volunteer Infantry; died July 20, 1864 in Pulaski, Tennessee

from wounds incurred during battle.

6) Alfred Green Hildebrand, born October 1, 1842 in Carroll County, enlisted May 10, 1862 as Private in Company I, 56th Regiment Georgia Volunteer Infantry, CSA, from Carroll County, Georgia; killed July 3, 1863 in the Vicksburg, Mississippi.

7) Amanda C. was born December 8, 1844 in Carroll County, died August 9, 1930. She married Henry Hallman on February 7, 1861. Henry was born January 8, 1828 and died November 5, 1908.

8) Margaret Catherine, born May 9, 1847, died August 18, 1936 in Villa Rica, Georgia. She married William James **Willoughby** on December 15, 1864. He was born May 29, 1841 in England and died November 1, 1923 in Villa Rica, Georgia.

9) Martha Ann, born January 19, 1850, died August 17, 1929. She married Peter Kennedy Leathers on December 9, 1869. Peter Leathers was born April 1, 1850 and died May 27, 1918.

10) Josephine, born June 1, 1852, died January 24, 1939. She married William Franklin Leathers on December 9, 1869. He was born October 8, 1848 and died December 22, 1918.

11) William H. Hildebrand, born May 19, 1854, married Barbara Conners on January 8, 1874. She was born in 1852 and died in 1936. William died on October 22, 1928 at the age of 74. William was a blacksmith at Winston, before moving to Villa Rica in 1900.

This family lost two sons and one son-in-law to the Civil War: Isaac Newton Hildebrand, Alfred Green Hildebrand and James William White.

Keaton

For the story on the Keatons as early settlers, see Chapter 3. Kader Keaton, 1769-1820 married Sarah Rebecca Peacock Keaton who was born September 3, 1776 in South Carolina and died August 24, 1867. Their son William K. "Jesse" Keaton, was born August 2, 1813 in Washington County, Georgia and died May 19, 1890 in Douglas County, Georgia. He is buried in the family cemetery near Keaten Creek. William married Susan D. Butler (June 1, 1816 - March 26, 1851) on January 5, 1838 in Paulding County, Georgia. William and Susan's children:

1) John (Daniel) de Lafayette Keaton, born February 8, 1839 in Carroll County, died February 2, 1888 in Douglas County, married 1863 in Carroll County, to Sarah M. Williams, born January 10, 1840, died July 10, 1910;

2) William M. Keaton, born May 20, 1840, died June 2, 1848.
3) Keader Isham "Kaiser" Keaten, born January 9, 1842 in Carroll County, died October 11, 1920 in Douglas County, married Sarah J. 1850-1920. He was a Private in Company I, 56 Georgia Infantry. K. I. Keaten was a Justice of the Peace in Douglas County. Keader I. is buried at New Hope Church Cemetery in Villa Rica, Georgia.
4) Martha, born January 11, 1844, died December, 1908, married John P. Carnes, Jr and is buried in the Keaten Family Cemetery.
5) Henry Hudson Keaten, born February 14, 1846 in Carroll County, died May 6, 1914 in Douglas County, married Margaret Cansler, 1841-1932.
6) Mary Ann, born 1848, died October 31, 1862 in Douglas County.
7) Susan Hester, born January 27, 1850 in Carroll County, died May 21, 1920 in Douglas County, married Beaten S. Daniell.

William's second wife was Elizabeth Styles Keaton, born August 25, 1831 in Campbell County, died February 15, 1880 in Douglas County. Their children:
1) Nancy Jane, born January 8, 1853 in Carroll County, died November 13, 1862 in Carroll County;
2) Mary, born 1855;
3) Joseph D. Keaton, born June 1859 in Carroll County, died April 8, 1920, married on September 30, 1880 to Nancy Mabry Long, daughter of Esther Daniell Long;
4) Julia Emmaline, born 1861, died 1906, married in 1880 to W. L. Brown;
5) Mary Elizabeth, born 1864;
6) Amanda Kay, born November 22, 1869, died May 1, 1906, married in 1886 to J. T. Saylor.

In 1864, at age 49, William K. "Jesse" Keaton, is listed in the Carroll County Re-organizing the Georgia Militia.

John Kennedy (Canady)

John Harrison Kennedy came with his wife, Elizabeth, and children to Dark Corner in the spring of 1828, settling on LL #201. Of the 202 1/2 acres acquired at the time, the family, now six generations later, still own all of the original land grant except for 30 acres sold during the depression years of the 1930s.

John was born in South Carolina in April 1791 and died in Campbell County October 28, 1848. His wife, Elizabeth Carroll Kennedy, (daughter of Ginny Carroll) was born January 3, 1796 in South Carolina and died January 2, 1874 in Douglas County. Their children:

1. James Kennedy was born April 4, 1817.

2. William Kennedy was born October 15, 1818.

3. Harrison Kennedy was born August 15, 1823 in Campbell County and died September 7, 1856 in Red River, Arkansas.

4. Penelope Kennedy was born June 27, 1825.

5. Nancy Sims Kennedy, born January 15, 1826 in Campbell County, died May 10, 1901 in Villa Rica, Georgia married John Nalley on November 13, 1842.

6. Georgia Ann E. Kennedy was born October 9, 1837 and died April 26, 1929 in Winston, Douglas County, Georgia. She married 1st G. A. Hassell who died in the Civil War. Then she married James M. Alexander, 1840 - 1915.

7. Polly Ann Kennedy married Peter K. Leathers on December 29, 1839 in Campbell County.

8. John Johnson Kennedy was born September 27, 1835 in Campbell County, and died April 25, 1905 in Winston, Douglas County, Georgia. In 1862, he married Hester Ann Dorris, born November 25, 1845, died July 2, 1895. Their children:

A) Nancy Penelope, born July 24, 1870, died 1943, married in 1890 to J. J. Kirby, then divorced. J. J. Kirby became the first mayor of Winston when it was incorporated in 1906.

B) William Harralson Kennedy, born April 15, 1865, died about 1870 of spinal meningitis at about age five.

C) Mary Francis Kennedy, born January 26, 1873 in Douglas County, died January 27, 1953 in Winston, Georgia. She married Alfred Tyre Brittain who was born October 15, 1865 and died November 20, 1942.

D) Elizabeth Ella, born December 3, 1862, died July 7, 1951 and married in 1882 to Charles Wesley **Winn**. They divorced before 1900.

E) Barbara Kennedy married in 1890 to James Pilgrim.

"The John Kennedy family had lived on LL # 201 working the land, growing cotton and corn with the help of a few slaves. Their land prospered and the children multiplied. When John Kennedy died in 1848, the land was divided into 9 equal portions, but then the children signed the land back to their mother on August 11, 1849 and she continued to run the farm with her slave labor.

Her youngest son, John J. Kennedy married during the first of the Civil War.

John & Hester then took over the farm and added several improvements, including a gin house where two branches came together on the west side of the property.

During the first part of the Civil War, John J. Kennedy was able to send his nephew, A. H. Kennedy, as a substitute so that he could stay on and run the farm.

The slaves stayed on through the war and farming was continued as usual as much as possible. Not being on any main battle grounds the Kennedys were harassed mainly by foraging troops of both armies. On several occasions, Confederate troops came by to catch chickens. Federal troops who came through took (his horse, some bacon) *a few hundred bundles of fodder, and bushels of corn. In return for this they gave the farmers script that could have been redeemed for money had the Kennedys presented it after the war.*

Cotton production was not great during the war years due to the need for food stuffs, but there were two bales stored in the gin house when a party of Federal troops came by. Not taking time to destroy the cotton, they simply cut the bands on the bales and left it. After the war Kennedy repacked it and sold it in Atlanta.

As the end drew near, the Confederates pressed every available man into service. John J. Kennedy had to leave his farm to his wife and ageing mother and joined the Third Regiment of the The Georgia Infantry.

After Lee's surrender at Appomattox Court House, Virginia, on April 9, 1865, John J. Kennedy was allowed to come home on parole on May 16th contingent upon taking the loyalty oath, which he did on September 9, 1865 at Marietta.

As it was for most farmers of the state, reconstruction was a difficult period for the Kennedys. Most of the emancipated slaves stayed on and worked for wages. One old Negro woman stayed until 1870.

Mrs. Elizabeth Kennedy died on January 2, 1874. Most of John J. Kennedy brothers and brothers-in-law had farms elsewhere, and some had moved as far away as Hopkins County, Texas enabling him to buy up the shares of the other heirs a ninth of the lot at a time. He had been doing this since 1857 at approximately thirteen dollars an acre. He acquired the entire lot at the time of his mother's death in 1874, accomplishing a task at which he had been working ever since he had been grown."

Mann

Hiram T. Mann was born in South Carolina about 1795. He married Tabitha Everett on March 20, 1831 in Carroll County. She was born in Georgia about 1814.

He and his family are shown on the 1850 Carroll County Federal Census. His occupation was a carpenter. On the 1860 Federal Census Hiram's occupation is shown as miner. All their children were born in Georgia: John, born about 1832; Thomas, born about 1834; Henry, born about 1836; Elizabeth, born about 1839; Mary, born about 1841; James, born about 1844; William, born about 1846; Sarah, born about 1850; Ben born about 1852; Lucy, born about 1852; Louisa born about 1854; Florence born about 1856, and Martha M., born about 1860.

The oldest of these thirteen children, John Everett Mann was born May 29, 1833 in Carroll County and died August 10, 1912. He married Anna Eliza Bivins who was born November 1835 and died 1910. Both John and Anna Mann are buried at the Old Town Cemetery in Villa Rica, Georgia.

John Everett Mann enlisted in Co. I, 56 Georgia Regiment as a Private on May 10, 1862. He was captured at Baker's Creek, Mississippi on May 16, 1863, imprisoned at Camp Morton, Indiana and Fort Delaware, Delaware where he was paroled for exchange July 3, 1863. He was received at City Point, Virginia on July 6, 1863; captured at Dalton, Georgia on May 18, 1864; imprisoned at Louisville, Kentucky and at Rock Island, Illinois, where he was released on June 22, 1865.

John Everett and Tabitha Mann's children were all born in a section of Villa Rica, which before 1870 was in Carroll County and after 1870, is in Douglas County, Georgia:

1) JoAnn, born about 1852, died in 1857 at Villa Rica in Carroll County.

2) John E. Mann was born about 1852 and died in 1852, an infant.

3) Washington N. Mann, born about 1855, died in 1895; married Ida Moon.

4) Margaret Indiana Mann, born about 1859; died 1894; buried at Old Town Cemetery, in Villa Rica.

5) John Henry Mann, born December 30, 1861; died December 26, 1946; he married Elizabeth Drucilla **Willoughby** on October 29, 1901. She was born March 18, 1871 and died November 27, 1963, both are buried at Friendship Baptist Church. On the 1910 Census, this family lives on Stone Road listed in margin next to **Dark Corner Road** in Conners' District #1259.

6) Alice Lenora Mann, born June 8, 1864, died January 3, 1952 in Salt Lake City, Utah; married Thomas Andrew Pannell who was born on January 18, 1871 and died August 31, 1918.

7) Nancy Mann was born about 1866.

8) Louellen Mann born about 1868; married Rufus M. Hicks, born 1839.

9) Mary Elizabeth Mann born about 1870; died 1892; married a Rogers.

10) Minnie, born about 1872. 11) Mattie, born about 1874. 12) Lottie, born about 1876.

McElreath/McElwreath

Michael McElreath (McElwreath) was born about 1759 in Ayrshire County, Scotland, and in 1785, he married Jenice Carson who was born 1764 in Dublin, Ireland. They moved from County Antrim, Ireland, then arrived in the United States at Charles Town, South Carolina and lived in Spartanburg County, South Carolina in 1800. On the 1840 Campbell County Census for District # 730, Michael McElwreath is listed as 70 to 80 years old and his oldest son, James McElwreath, also a head of the household, is listed as 30-40 years old.

Goat in Wagon. Courtesy McElreath Family.

Michael McElreath is shown on the 1850 census for the Oregon District of Cobb County, as born in Ireland, age 84. In 1857, he died at age 91 and is buried at Lost Mt. in Cobb County, Georgia. BUT on his tombstone, no birth or death date is given but the statement, ". . . died at the home of his son, John McElwreath, at the age of one hundred years." His wife, Jenice, died June 1840 and is buried at Lost Mt. also. They had ten children:

1. Jane Jenice, born in Spartanburg, South Carolina in 1790; died on July 10, 1871 in Pickens, South Carolina; married Joel Jones.

2. Anna, born 1795 in Spartanburg, South Carolina; died in 1874, in Carroll County, Georgia

3. Mary Rachael "Polly," born 1797 in South Carolina; died August 12, 1865; married Joel Daniel Leathers of Carroll County.

4. James Michael McElreath was born December 19, 1802 in Spartanburg, South Carolina. He is listed on the 1840 Federal Census for District #730, Campbell County; died July 17, 1886 in Winder, Barrow County.

5. Elizabeth "Betsy" McElreath, born 1803 in South Carolina; died 1894 at Lost Mt., Cobb County, Georgia; married Thomas Whitehead of Cobb County.

6. Nancy, born in 1809 in Spartanburg, South Carolina; died 1889 in Powder Springs, Georgia; married Peter P. Hewitt, 1815 - 1894.

7. Martin, 1810 - 1891, married Sarah Blair, 1826 - 1917, in Carroll County in 1844. She was the daughter of Joseph Blair, 1801 - 1871, of Douglas County.

8. John, born 1812 in Spartanburg, South Carolina; died 1894 at Lost Mt., Cobb County, Georgia; married in 1839 in Campbell County to Ann Eliza McClung, 1818 - 1896. He is buried at Midway Church in Cobb County.

9. Infant born 1814.

10. Marcus "Mark" McElreath, born June 1, 1811 in Spartanburg, South Carolina, married Jane **McLarty**, born June 1, 1823, daughter of James and Sarah (Shelby) McLarty. They married about 1842 in South Carolina and the family is shown in 1850, District 10, Campbell County, in the Dark Corner Community. He died February 21, 1858; Jane died May 22, 1878; both are buried in the McLarty-Benson Cemetery, Douglas County, Georgia. Their children:

a) Carson S. McElreath, born March 27, 1842 in Mecklenburg, South Carolina; died November 13, 1881 in Douglas County, Georgia; married on January 13, 1867 to Martha A. Vansant, who was born May 14, 1845 and died on October 22, 1882. She was the daughter of Young Vansant. Carson S. McElreath enlisted as Private in Company A, 56th Georgia Volunteer Infantry, CSA on April 25, 1862. Both Carson and Martha McElreath are buried at the McLarty-Benson Cemetery.

b) James M. McElreath, January 26, 1844 in Douglas County; died July 24, 1917; married on October 20, 1870 to Mary O. Blanchard, December 10, 1852 - January 26, 1912, daughter of Thomas Blanchard. Both are buried at the Douglasville, City Cemetery.

c) Sarah C. McElreath, born January 24, 1846; died April 24, 1925 in Douglas Co; married in 1860 to William W. **McLarty**. Sarah's second husband was John McLarty **Morris**.

d) John Thomas McElreath, born December 4, 1851 in Campbell County, Georgia; died January 24, 1924; married in 1879 to Frances, May 16, 1854 - July 9, 1923, daughter of Josiah Hatchett. Both John and Frances McElreath are buried in the Douglasville City Cemetery.

e) Samuel A. McElreath, born March 12, 1854; died July 9, 1886; he married Sarah Emma. Samuel McElreath was a city councilman in the 1870s and 1880s and a partner in Price & McElreath General Store in 1879 and partner with Price on the *Weekly Star* newspaper - all in Douglasville. Samuel and Sarah McElreath's son, Paul, was born 1883 and died 1884. Both he and Samuel A. McElreath are buried at the Douglasville City Cemetery. A second son, Glen, was born in 1885. After Samuel's death in 1886, Sarah married Robert A. Massey who died in 1890. Sarah became emotionally distraught and disappeared in 1891 (noted in Ordinary's Minutes). Her son, Glen, was raised by his uncle, John McLarty Morris, who was appointed guardian in 1891.

f) William M. McElreath was born in July 1854 and died in 1905. He married Lois B. May, in 1884.

Miles

James Elijah Miles married Nancy Elizabeth Gibson. Her father was Andrew Jackson Norton who was born January 20, 1832 in Paulding County and died January 1862 in Paulding County. Her mother was Mary Jane Rhodes who was born March 5, 1840 in Chambers County, Alabama and died December 12, 1930 in Douglas County. James and Nancy's children:

A) John H. "Uncle Buddy" Miles, December 13, 1859 - September 13, 1950, is buried at Ephesus Church.

B) Joseph Abner Miles was born on April 21, 1861 and died February 26, 1908. On December 23, 1883, he married Martha Melinda **Gable**, born January 29, 1861, died May 21, 1953, daughter of Harmon and Delia Jane (Cook) Gable. Joseph and Martha Miles had a daughter: Flossie Ethel Miles, born January 28, 1886, died July 8, 1965, who married on October 22, 1901 to John Pierce **Enterkin**. He was born April 10, 1880 in Douglas County; died January 4, 1957 in Villa Rica, Georgia; he was the son of Luda S. Enterkin.

L-R James, Mattie, Bertie May, Florence, Docia holding John Marion and Jeff. Photo: Courtesy Alyce Dodson King.

C) James Taylor Miles, born October 9, 1865 in Carroll County; died June 28, 1940, in Douglas County. On January 25, 1887, he married Theodocia Norton who was born May 11, 1867 in Paulding County and died August 22, 1945 in Douglas County. They are both also buried at Ephesus Church Cemetery. All their children were born in Douglas County:

1) Jefferson Davis Miles, born February 19, 1888, married Lillie Mae Kinney on October 15, 1911;

2) Mittie Florence, born August 11, 1890, married Charlie W. **Waldrop**;

3) Emer Lieu, born January 1, 1892, died June 2, 1892;

4) Bertie May, born May 3, 1894, died November 1, 1918. She was the wife of Horace J. **Baggett**, born 1892, son of B. J. "Bud" Baggett;

5) Mattie Aldora, born March 9, 1897, married a Baggett;

6) John Marion Miles, born December 27, 1899; died December 5, 1918.

7) Gibbie Elizabeth, born January 5, 1902, married Noah Adolphus New;

8) Mary Ruby, born April 10, 1904, married George Fred King;

9) James William, born July 18, 1907; died December 27, 1923.

Nalley

John Baylis Nalley, born April 18, 1814 in Anderson County, South Carolina, died December 5, 1884 in Villa Rica, Douglas County, Georgia, married wife, Nancy Canady (Kennedy), born January 15, 1826 in Georgia, died May 10, 1901, in Villa Rica. They married November 13, 1842 in Carroll County. John B. Nalley is listed on the 1844 Georgia Property Tax Digest living on LL# 204 in Carroll County that became Douglas County when Douglas County was created in 1870. Both are buried at New Hope Church, Villa Rica. Children:

1) William H. Nalley, born August 17, 1843, died May 14, 1909, married Louisa, daughter of Thomas **Willoughby**, born April 8, 1846, died March 31, 1916. William was a Private in Co. I, 56th Georgia Infantry, CSA.

2) Ambrose Jefferson Nalley, born May 14, 1845 in Carroll County, Georgia, died June 30, 1905 in Villa Rica, married Emmie **Willoughby**, born July 14, 1854.

3) John Kennedy Nalley, 1851-1927, married Sarah Stone, 1850-1910.

4) Hannah L. Nalley, born December 2, 1847, died November 21, 1917, married in 1868 to Thomas Carnes, born 1846.

5) James D. Nalley, was born in 1862. In 1886, he married Mollie L. Kilgore, 1870-1909.

6) Elizabeth M. Nalley, born October 23, 1849, died March 19, 1947, married Alexander P. Sewell, 1847-1901. They lived near Winston in 1900.

7) Julia Nalley, born June 12, 1854, died September 3, 1936; she married Thomas Edwards.

8) Mary Lura Nalley, born 1859, died October 31, 1948.

9) Georgia S. Nalley, born April 21, 1864, died January 9, 1912, married Homer T. Shockley.

Peter Polk

According to the 1870, 1900, and 1910 U. S. Federal Census Records, Peter Polk was born about 1825-1827 in Georgia. But family stories tell that he and his mother, Harriet, were bought at a Virginia Slave Market by Ezekiel Polk who brought them to Georgia when Peter was about four years old. Peter married in 1865 to Harriet Endsley, daughter of John Endsley (1810-1870) and Jane Endsley (born 1813 in Virginia, died July 12, 1886). Harriet Endsley, born in 1848 in Georgia and died about 1920 in Georgia was a former slave of Jane Weddington Polk.

According to family history, "after the Civil War, when slaves were freed, 'Marse Zeke' told them that they were free to go or to stay, and if they chose to stay, they would be paid for their work. Peter chose to remain on the Polk farm for a few years. He is shown on the Freedman's list of 1867 and 1868 as working for Ezekiel Polk; he also worked for Charles Polk. In his later years, Peter said his master—Ezekiel Polk—was a kind and good man, who taught his slaves right from wrong.

In 1870, Peter and his family lived in Carroll County; in 1900, they lived in the Crombie District of Douglas County. In 1882, Peter Polk bought 202 1/2 acres, LL #149, in Carroll County, and in 1910, they lived on Winston Road in Douglas County. Peter and his mother and other family members are buried at Ephesus Cemetery.

Peter and Harriet had five sons and six daughters: 1) James "Jimmy," born in 1867 married Maggie Crow on October 20, 1894; 2) Samuel Abraham, born 1872, married Nina Endsley; 3) Hayes, born 1877, married Lucille. Hayes served as a minister of Shady Grove Baptist Church for thirty years beginning in 1925; 4) Lewis; 5) Heron "Jack" Polk who was born December 25, 1892 and died August 15, 1986; 6) Millie A., born Sept 1883; 7) Frances, born May 1885; 8) Julia A., born December 1887; 9) Sarah; 10) Ann; and 11) Julie.

Rice

Joel E. Rice was born 1811 in South Carolina and died before 1870 in Campbell County, Georgia. He married Caroline or Karline Vansant, sister of Young Vansant. Caroline was born in 1813 in Lexington, South Carolina and died about 1909 in Douglas County at age 96.

The 1850 Federal Census for Lexington South Carolina shows: Joel, age 39 and Caroline, 37; their children Louisa S. 19; Barbara A., 11; J. Godfrey, 8; Christina, 6; James P., 5; Emanuel H., 2; and Siducia M., age 1.

Joel and Caroline Rice came to Campbell County before 1855. He is shown on the Tax Digest for LL #132 in 1855; he also paid taxes on 101 1/4 acres of LL# 101 in 1855. In 1861, 1867 and 1871, the tax digest lists Caroline Rice for the same LLs.

On the 1870 census for Dark Corner Militia District, # 730, of Douglas County shows: Caroline, age 59; Louisa, 28; Barbara, 27; Nancy, 24; Jas, 23; Manual, 22; Sadetha, 21; and Martha, 17.

Their son, Jay Godfrey Rice who was born on July 16, 1842 in Lexington, South Carolina, married in Campbell County on May 20, 1865 to Sarah Jane "Sallie"

Roberts who was born December 18, 1847 in South Carolina and died May 1, 1935 in Douglas County. J. G. Rice is listed on the tax digest for LL #125 in 1869 and 1871 and LL # 126 in 1869.

Jay G. Rice died in Atlanta in 1906 after surgery for injuries sustained during the Civil War. Both Jay G. and Sallie Rice are buried at Bright Star Church Cemetery. Their children:

1) James T., 1868-1932, buried at Bright Star with wife Margaret L. Bullington, 1865-1908.

2) Jay W. Rice, 1877-1948 buried at Bright Star with his wife Mary E., 1882-1965, daughter of J. Luther Ergle and Bertha S. Thompson, 1876-1899.

3) Margaret Marcella, born April 10, 1866, married William J. Lowery, born 1859.

Sarah Elizabeth "Lizzie" Rice
Photo: Courtesy Mildred Thompson

4) Sarah Elizabeth "Lizzie" Rice who was born July 15, 1870 in Douglas County, died November 17, 1938 in Winston, Georgia. Lizzie married Charlie Olin Enterkin, Sr. (April 24, 1864, Campbell County - April 2, 1906 Winston, Douglas County) son of Samuel Kanady **Enterkin**.

5) John Emanuel Rice was born September 18, 1872.

6) Carrie Caroline, born November 18, 1874, married Ector F. Pope.

7) Joel Wilson Rice, born July 20, 1879, died 1900.

Roach

George Washington Roach was born in 1811 in Queens County, Ireland, the son of Edward Roach, born 1774 and Ann, born 1776. George W. Roach immigrated to New York then moved to Campbell County about 1840. On February 16, 1840, he married Temperance Dollison in Campbell County. She was born in 1822 and died on December 6, 1843 in Campbell County. George and Temperance had two children:

1) Nancy Jane Roach was born on December 5, 1842 in Campbell County. She died November 24, 1913 in Merkel, Taylor Co, Texas.

George Washington & Jemima Bailey Roach
Photo: Courtesy Debra Munn

2) Clarinda Lerrett, born about 1843. After Temperance Dollison Roach's death, George W. married a second time to Jemima E. Bailey on December 7, 1843. She was born May 18, 1825 and died January 31, 1912. She and George had seven children.

1) Carolina Elizabeth, born April 28, 1845 in Campbell County and died May 12, 1928 in Glenwood, Wheeler County, Georgia.

2) Sarah Margaret, born December 23, 1846 in Georgia and died April 26, 1923 in Eastland County, Texas.

3) Martha Ann, born 1848 in Campbell County, Georgia and died in Comanche County Texas.

4) William Henry Roach, born September 2, 1850 in Campbell County. He died March 11, 1918 in Kansas City, Jackson County, Missouri. He married Catherine Louise Weddington (1851-1947) who was the daughter of Alexander Green Weddington and Hannah Polk.

5) Annie M., born 1853, is shown on the Douglas County Census for 1880.

6) George Roach, Jr., born February 1853 in Georgia, died October 26, 1916 in Merkel, Taylor County, Texas.

7) John Roach, born 1856 in Campbell County, is shown on the 1880 Douglas County Census; he died in Texas.

George Roach died February 16, 1900 in Eastland County, Texas.

Stanley/Murdoc

George Washington Stanley was born on January 31, 1811 in Georgia and died July 11, 1893, in Douglas County, Georgia. He is buried at Ephesus Church with his wife Matilda Pugh Haynes who was born November 12, 1815 and died April 22, 1909, in Douglas County. They married about 1837 in Campbell County, lived in Gwinnett County, Georgia in 1838, in Macon County, Alabama in 1840 and Coosa County, Alabama in 1860. George Stanley is shown on the 1866 Property Tax Digest for Dark Corner, Campbell County, but no LL is listed. In 1870 they owned land that borders Paulding County. In 1880 they live in Conners, District 1259 in Douglas County. George and Matilda and daughter Lilla, age 25, lived next door to daughter Josephine with her husband George Wilson McLarty and their daughter May M. age 13. George and Matilda Stanley's children:

Josephine Murdoc Huckeba
Photo: Courtesy Nancy Huckeba

1) Mary E. Stanley, born May 1838 in Gwinnett County, Georgia, died May 30, 1923 in Douglas County, married Milus "Miles" W. Murdock on August 6, 1857 in Macon County, Alabama, where they lived in 1860. He was born in Gordon County, Georgia on February 26, 1832. On May 19, 1862, he enlisted as Private in Company G, 45th Alabama Regiment CSA. He died July-August 1862 in Lauderdale Springs, Mississippi while serving with the Confederate Army. After his death, Mary moved to Douglas County and is shown on the 1870 Dark Corner Census as a widow with four children:

1A) Josephine "Josie" Murdock was born February 16, 1857 in Alabama and died about 1890, in Winston. Josephine Murdock married John Luke Huckeba on December 26, 1878 in Douglas County;

1B) Georgia Murdock, born 1860, Campbell County, died 1891 Douglas County, married William Merrell Watkins, 1857-1944, about 1878 in Douglas County.

1C) Mary W. "Willie Mae" Murdock, born January 1861 in Campbell County, died August 20, 1943 in New Orleans, Louisiana, married on December 27, 1884 in Carroll County to William A. Huckeba, born July 5, 1860 in Randolph County Alabama, died October 30, 1924, in Fulton County, Georgia;

1D) Benjamin Alonzo Murdock, born March 17, 1864 in Georgia, died 1951 in Villa Rica, Carroll County. In 1894, he married Ella M. Chambers, 1870-1950.

2) Josephine Bonaparte "Josie" Stanley, born July 24, 1842 in Campbell County, Georgia, died April 23, 1929 in Villa Rica, Carroll County and is buried at Ephesus Church Cemetery, in Winston. On March 22, 1866 in Campbell County, Josie married George Wilson **McLarty**, December 11, 1844 - January 25, 1916.

3) Early Jasper Stanley, born December 24, 1847 in Alabama, died May 22, 1939 in Marshall County, Alabama married in 1877 to Fannie E. Stovall.

4) George Washington Stanley, Jr was born February 1848 in Alabama and died July 21, 1933 in Morgan County, Alabama. He married E. E. Umphrey in 1856. He paid taxes on LL # 138 located in Conners' District, #1259 in 1884.

5) Lilla Matilda Stanley, born September 1857 in Alabama and died 1905 in Douglas County, Georgia, married on June 13, 1880 in Douglas County to Allen Campbell Watkins 1859 - 1930.

Thompson

Thomas N. Thompson was born in 1833 in Newton County Georgia, and on December 16, 1852, he married Emily Kinney who was born June 1827 in Newton County. Before 1860, they moved to the Pumpkinvine district of Paulding County, near Dark Corner and there they had three children: Martha A., born 1855, Lemuel R., born 1856, and Robert Alexander, born 1858. Thomas N. Thompson enlisted in the Confederate Army on March 4, 1862,

Lenora Young Thompson, Courtesy Ed Thompson

serving with Co F, 40th Regiment Georgia Volunteers, Paulding Washington Guards. He was present on a muster roll for March 10, 1865. He is not on the 1870 census, so he apparently died at the end of the Civil War or sometime before 1870.

Emily raised the children alone and did not remarry. She died before 1900 in the Conners District #1259, of Douglas County at age 73.

Their son Robert Alexander "Alex" Thompson was born April 8, 1858 in Dark Corner, Georgia and died there on March 26, 1915 at age 56. On September 19, 1880, he married Lenora Octavia "Nora" Young born July 14, 1857 in Georgia. She was the daughter of Allen J. **Young** and Hulda P. Edwards who married in Carroll County in 1857. Lenora died April 1, 1924 in Dark Corner at age 66. Robert and Lenora Thompson's children were:

Robert W. Thompson railroad foreman
Photo: Courtesy Ed Thompson

1) Thomas Alexander Thompson was born on July 14, 1881; **2)** Lemuel L. Thompson was born on October 16, 1883 **3)** Robert Wesley Thompson, born February 13, 1886, married Leona Enterkin, daughter of Charlie Olin Enterkin, Sr. and Sarah Elizabeth **Rice**. Leona Enterkin Thompson, born July 6, 1890 in Winston, died August 9, 1991 in Douglas County at age 101.

4) Martha Eugenia Thompson was born on December 5, 1888;

5) An infant who was born on May 1, 1889;

6) William Alexander who was born on November 4, 1891;

7) Fanny Lew who was born on March 2, 1894;

8) Lizzie May who was born on April 17, 1897.

Waldrop

Abraham Waldrop wore this hat, 1862-1864 while fighting in the Confederate Army. Photo: Courtesy Allen Waldrop

Allen Christian Waldrop, and wife, Grace “Gracie” Richardson Waldrop, were both born in South Carolina. He was born in 1810; she was born in 1819 and died after 1900. They settled in 1835 on LL # 154 in Campbell County in what was later known as the Winston area of Douglas County.

A) Abraham James “Abe” Waldrop (Waldrup), Allen and Gracie Waldrop’s first son, was born January 12, 1836 in Campbell County, Georgia and died in 1923. On July 22, 1857, Abraham married Eliza Jane Hallman, 1832-1930, who was the daughter of Christian Hallman. Abraham enlisted in Co. K 42nd Georgia Infantry. He was with The Army of Tennessee, serving at the Battle of New Hope Church in Paulding County. After the battle, Abraham took leave and returned to his home in Winston. It was on the Waldrop Farm that Abraham was captured by Union troops as they were making a series of wide flanking movements south, in preparation for the siege on Atlanta. The family story:

“Abraham was plowing the cotton field after taking leave for a few days to help his wife, Eliza, with the farm, when he was surrounded and taken prisoner by Yankee troops who where moving through the area. Eliza, who was making lye soap in the yard fought the Yankees to the best her ability, even throwing hot lye soap on the approaching troops. But to no avail. The Waldrop Farm was ransacked, with all their possessions either stolen or destroyed by the Yankee troops who even took the mule Abraham was plowing.”

After the war, Abraham returned home, and began to pick up the pieces of the life he had known. The family, five generations later, still live on the same Waldrop Farm in Winston today. Abraham and Eliza’s children:

1) John W., born before 1860, is shown on the 1880 census.

2) Mary Ellen, 1861-1891, buried at Ephesus Church in Douglas County.

3) Joseph A. Waldrop, was born April 1, 1863 and died October 2, 1912. In 1882, he married Emma Polk who was born January 2, 1862 and died August 13, 1942. Their children: Charlie, born 1883; John C., born 1885, who married Beulah M., born 1888 - died 1933; Jane, born 1888; Mary, born 1889; Elder Rader, born 1894, who married Eva, daughter of Owen Tyson; Bessie, born 1895; Charlie who married Jimie Strawn and Marvie, born 1899.

4) William H. Waldrop, 1858-1932, married Martha E. 1862-1932; both are buried in Hillcrest Cemetery at Villa Rica. Martha was the daughter of Talton and Elizabeth Woods Grubbs. Children: Joe, Prude, and daughter, Eliza Jane, born 1885 who married Jesse Tolbert.

5) Margaret A., 1867-1896, is buried at Ephesus Church Cemetery.

6) Allen Christian Waldrop, born June 15, 1872; died 1934; married Carrie Odessa, March 7, 1876 - 1959, daughter of Luda S. **Enterkin**. Both Allen and Odessa are buried at Ephesus Church Cemetery. Among their children are Nettie L., Guy, Ray, Steve, Minnie Faye, Eva Mae, and Thomas Hayne Waldrop.

7) Rebecca, 1872-1947, married Charles Edwards.

8) Milton T. Waldrop, 1877-1912, who married Dula Christiana, 1880-1968, daughter of James W. **Willoughby**. Their son, James E., born 1905, was State Representative of Douglas County in 1949. Other children of Milton and Dula: Irene T. born 1903; Robert R. born 1907 and Margaret D. born 1910.

9) Thomas M., born about 1878.

10) Louisa Waldrop, December 24, 1882-1960, married Oliver O. Morris. He was born August 17, 1877, died 1947. Both are buried at Ephesus Church Cemetery.

B) William A. Waldrop, born May 12, 1847, in Newton County, died October 15, 1918 in Douglas County and is buried at New Hope Church in Villa Rica. (These dates are shown on his tombstones.) His first wife was Lucetta S. Carnes, September 19, 1843 - January 1, 1903, who is buried at New Hope. In 1908, he married his second wife, Emma V. Mize, 1864-1946. William's children: Julia, born 1870, who married J.D. Bivins; John P., born 1875, who married in 1897 to Mina Henslee; Emma A., born 1873; and Thomas W., born 1880, who married in 1897 to Ila Maroney, born 1882, daughter of James L. Maroney.

C) Harmon Waldrop, who was born May 7, 1840 and died April 6, 1924, is buried at New Hope Church at Villa Rica. In Carroll County in 1867, he married Emily Hallman who was born December 21, 1839 and died February 8, 1937. She was the daughter of Christian Hallman. Harmon Waldrop (Waldrup) enlisted as Private on June 22, 1861 in Co. I, 19th Regiment Georgia Volunteer Infantry, "The Villa Rica Gold Diggers." On September 26, 1862, he was in the Confederate Hospital at Culpepper, Virginia with pneumonia. He was captured at Fredericksburg, Virginia on December 13, 1862 and paroled there for exchange December 17, 1862. Pension records show he was at home on furlough for 30 days at the close of the war. Harmon and Emily's children: Henry N., born 1877 who married Lola **Winn**; Sarah E., born 1871; Annie, born 1878; and Rebecca born 1872 who married Charles Edward.

D) Nancy E. Waldrop, born 1842 who married Miles D. **Carnes** in Carroll County in 1868.

Weddington

William Weddington, born about 1782 in North Carolina, married Mary "Polly" McLarty, born about 1782, daughter of Alexander McLarty and Jennie Morrison McLarty; they married in Cabarrus County, North Carolina, January 7, 1806. His father was William who had settled in Mecklenburg County in the 1740s. William and Mary Weddington moved to Cobb County about 1840 and settled in what became the Weddington district of Paulding County. William died in 1850; his will states he owned three slaves. In 1860, Mary lived in Dark Corner with her son-in-law Ezekiel Polk; she died after 1860. Both Mary and her husband, William Weddington, are buried in the Winn-Watson Cemetery in Douglas County. Their children:

1) Alexander Green Weddington was born October 30, 1806 in Concord, Cabarrus County, North Carolina and died September 2, 1893 in Douglas County, Georgia. He married Hannah Elizabeth **Polk,** daughter of Charles Polk, who was born September 1,1812 in Cabarrus, North Carolina and died August 27, 1874 in Dark Corner, Georgia. They married in Cabarrus, North Carolina, December 15, 1828. In 1840, Alexander Green Weddington is shown in the Campbell County Census and is shown on the 1861 Georgia Property Tax Digest, living on land lot #198 in Militia District #730—Dark Corner. A. G. Weddington was a large landowner in the Dark Corner section and is said to have amassed a fortune in gold mining. Both Alexander and Hannah Weddington are buried at the Winn-Watson Cemetery. Alexander

Green and Hannah Weddington's children:

a) Mary Ellen "Polly" Weddington was born August 11, 1827 and died 1927 in Paulding County, Georgia; she married George Washington **Hawkins**.

Moses Barnett White b. 1822
Husband of Jane Weddington White.

Jane Weddington White b. 1832
Photos: Courtesy Debra Munn

b) Jane Ellen Weddington was born August 15,1832 in Cabarrus County, North Carolina and died May 18, 1910 in Paulding County, Georgia. She married Moses Barnett "Barney" White (January 13, 1822 - November 6, 1891) on September 21, 1848.

c) Martha Elizabeth Weddington was born September 9, 1834 in Campbell County, Georgia and died on September 11, 1886.

d) Hannah Amanda Weddington was born August 11, 1837 in Dekalb County, Georgia and died February 26, 1927 in Fulton County, Georgia.

e) Alexander Green "Sandy" Weddington, Jr. was born December 22, 1839, Dekalb County, Georgia and died May 10, 1903 in Douglas County, Georgia. He married Luvenia A. "Lou" Blanchard, March 24, 1846 - December 6, 1924, on August 11, 1863 in Campbell County, Georgia. Luvenia was the daughter of Thomas Blanchard. A. G. Weddington, Jr. served in the Civil War, enlisting September 25, 1861 as Junior 2nd Lieutenant, Company F, 30th Infantry Regiment, Georgia. On August 5, 1863, he was promoted to full 1st Lieutenant. He was, for three years, a partner with Arch W. McLarty in a Douglasville store.

f) Charles William Weddington was born in 1843 in Campbell County, Georgia and died July 4, 1925 in Fulton County, Georgia; he married Virginia Louanna Watson, daughter of Samuel H. **Watson**.

g. Camparapy Viannah "Campie" Weddington was born October 18, 1848 in

Campbell County, Georgia; died July 20, 1917; she married Samuel M. McBrayer in 1866 in Paulding County.

Catherine Weddington Roach
Photo: Courtesy Debra Munn

h. Catherine Louise Weddington was born on December 10, 1851 in Campbell County, Georgia and died May 28, 1917 in Amarillo, Texas. She married William Henry **Roach** on February 1, 1871.

Other children of William and Polly Weddington:

2) Melissa Jane was born 1809; died in 1893; married Ezekiel Polk in 1828.

3) Betsy remained in North Carolina.

4) Annie C. was born, 1811; died 1898; married Stephen Harvey McLarty.

5) Rachel married George Washington Blair; they moved to Texas.

6) Sarah was born in 1819 and died in 1873; she married William G. Black of Dark Corner in 1835.

7) Robert Hale Weddington, 1817-1896, married on July 27, 1837 to Mary Clementine "Clemmie" Hartsfield; they lived in Cobb County in 1850 and in Campbell County in 1860. His second wife was Rachel Lee whom he married on May 23, 1858. In 1880, this family lived near Winston. His third wife was Evelyn C. Mattox Maxwell. Children of Robert H. Weddington include:

a. Sarah was born in 1842 in Cobb County.

b. Martha Ann was born in 1845 in Cobb County. She married in 1865 to Littleberry **Hightower** who was living in Campbell County in 1860 with widow Temperance Hightower. He is shown as "Elsberry W." Hightower on the 1850 Campbell County Census with parents Henry and Temperance Hightower.

c. William Moses Weddington, born 1847 in Cobb County, married Elizabeth Conner.

d. Mary Ann was born in 1848 in Cobb County.

e. Frances was born in 1852 in Cobb County and married Thomas M. Enterkin, son of John Enterkin.

f. Emily was born 1853 in Cobb County, married William Jackson Bullington.

g. Georgia was born in 1860 in Campbell County.

h. Alexander Weddington was born in 1861 in Campbell County.

i. Etta Weddington, 1866-1945, married W. H. Williamson who was born June 22, 1846 and died January 13, 1912.

j. Cecil Cleveland Weddington was born May 5, 1868 in Campbell County.

k. William Jefferson Weddington was born about 1862 in Campbell County.

l. Jossie was born in 1873 in Douglas County.

m. Santia, born 1874, Douglas County, married James W. Brooks.

Thomas H. Willoughby

Thomas H. Willoughby, born November 27, 1818 in Redruth, Illogan Parish, Cornwall County, England, came to Villa Rica, Georgia in 1852 to mine for gold. He worked and earned enough money to have his family join him around 1855. His wife Christianna Pascoe Willoughby, born 1816, traveled to the USA with their seven children. He reunited with his family in Villa Rica, where their last child was born. As was true in England, the older boys also worked at the mines.

Thomas, Christianna & children: Joseph, Liggas & Emmie
Photo: The Willoughby Family

1) Thomas H. Jr, born September 9, 1840, married Amanda Kennedy on December 17, 1861. After returning to Georgia after the War, he sold his land to his brother William James and took his family to Davis/Cass County, Texas around 1869. He died March 9, 1919 and is buried at Sugden Cemetery in Jefferson County, Oklahoma.

2) William James, May 29, 1841, died November 1, 1923 and is buried in

Friendship Primitive Church Cemetery in Paulding County. He married Margaret **Hildebrand** on December 15, 1864. Margaret was born in Dark Corner, May 9, 1847 and died August 18, 1936 and is buried at Friendship Church Cemetery also.

3) John, born 1842, died August 27, 1862 in Virginia as a result of wounds and illness incurred during the War. He is buried in an unmarked grave around Richmond, Virginia.

4) Oliver Alonzo, born 1844, was a Private in the Georgia Militia, contracted illness, returned home and died in 1862. He is buried at Hillcrest Cemetery, Villa Rica, Georgia.

5) Louisa Jane, born April 4, 1846, died March 31, 1916. She married William H. **Nalley**, on February 2, 1867. He served in Co. I, 56 Regiment Georgia Volunteer Infantry. They are both buried at New Hope Cemetery in Villa Rica, Georgia.

6) Charles "Charlie," born November 11, 1849, died November 11, 1941, married Margaret Alvarenna Harper and lived near Winston in 1880. About 1884, he and his family moved to Sand Mountain, Alabama. He and "Renne" are buried at Skirum Cemetery, Dawson, Alabama.

7) Lydia Ann "Liggas," born February 1851, married John M. Kennedy, the brother to Thomas, Jr's wife, Amanda, in 1870 in Villa Rica, Georgia. They then moved to Davis/Cass County, Texas next door to Thomas, Jr. and Amanda. Liggas died October 23, 1944 and is buried in Smyrna Cemetery in Cass County, Texas, next to John.

8) Emeline "Emmie" was born on July 14, 1852 and died May 12, 1944. She married Amberous J. Nalley who born May 14, 1845 and died June 3, 1908. They are both buried at New Hope Baptist Church Cemetery, Villa Rica, Georgia.

9) Joseph Brown Willoughby was born August 1859 and died May 5, 1942. He married Mary Garmon and lived near Winston in 1880. He and his family later moved to Cullman, Alabama. He and Mary are buried at Cold Springs Baptist Church Cemetery, Cullman.

After the family farmed for a few years, the War Between the States broke out. Thomas and four of his sons served as soldiers in the Army of the Confederate States of America. One would not return; one came home, very sick, and later died in spite of the loving care his mother gave him. The mother saw such hardships during these years that she died at age 52 on August 2, 1868 and was buried at the "Chambers Burying Ground," now Hillcrest Cemetery.

In 1869, Thomas, Sr. married Amanda E. Norris in Fulton County, Georgia.

The Willoughby men soon found that their "Gold Mine" was the ability to own and farm their land. On the Georgia Property Digest for 1871, the Willoughbys are shown to own LL#s 204, 205, and 211 - on Brewer Road in the Dark Corner District of Douglas County (Carroll County before December 1870). By 1878 Thomas, Sr., had erected a two room house on Land Lot 208, which was later purchased by his grandson, William Robert Willoughby. William Robert enlarged the house, and it has housed six generations on the original "Old Willoughby farm"—to present day. Thomas Willoughby, Sr., died July 30, 1893 and is buried near Oliver and next to Christiana in the Hillcrest Cemetery in Villa Rica, Georgia.

For more on the Willoughby family during the Civil War years see Chapter 8.

William J. Willoughby

Ruby & Bertha Baggett; Lillian; Irwin; Haydan; John & Fannie Entrekin Willoughby; William J. & Margaret H. Willoughby; infant Pearl Kate; Lenord; Alonzo; Isaac; Elizabeth Drucilla; Dula Christianna; Mary & Robert.

William James Willoughby, second son of Thomas H. and Christianna Willoughby, was born on May 29, 1841 and died on November 1, 1923. He married Margaret Catherine **Hildebrand** who was born on May 9, 1847. Their children:

1) John Monroe Willoughby was in born in 1867 and died in 1947; he married

Fannie Lillian **Entrekin**, who was born on April 1,1874 and died April 7, 1959. Both are buried at Friendship Church in Paulding County.

2) Elizabeth Drucilla "Lizzie," born March 18, 1870, died November 27, 1963; she first married Joseph A. **Baggett** on September 8, 1889. After his death, in the 1890s, she married Thomas Hugh Mann.

3) William Robert, born October 5, 1872, died in March 18, 1936; on December 27, 1896 he married Mary Elizabeth McBrayer (June 20, 1887 - August 30, 1967). Both are buried at Friendship Baptist Church, Paulding County.

4) Alonzo Oliver was born on May 14, 1875, died November 26, 1954, and married Thirsie OraBell Baker, daughter of J. M. Baker.

5) Isaac Henry, born April 13, 1878 in Douglas County, died February 5, 1933 in Douglas County, married Lavarra Bagby. She was born December 16, 1878 and died August 19, 1949.

6) Dula Christina was born on November 28, 1880, died December 2, 1968 and married Milton Thomas Waldrop.

7) Leonard C., born July 18, 1884, died March 9, 1904.

For more on William Willoughby during the Civil War years see Chapter 8.

Young

Allen Jacob Young, Jr., son of Allen Jocob (sic) Young, Sr. and Mary "Mollie" Young, was born in Georgia, March 1839. On the 1850 Carroll County Federal Census, his mother, Mary, is the head of the household with several children; she was born in South Carolina in 1805; her occupation is shown as a miner; Allen is age 12.

In 1857, in Carroll County, Allen married Hulda Jane P. "Huldy" Edwards. Huldy was born in 1830 in Walton County and died in 1920 in Paulding County.

On the 1860 Federal Census, Allen Young is shown in District 2, Villa Rica, Carroll County, Georgia with wife Hulda, child, Lenora, age 3, and Wesley Young, age 32, (perhaps a brother) occupation a miner and another child, Alice, age 3.

Allen Young enlisted on March 21, 1862 as Private, Co. E., later Co. F, 1st Georgia Cavalry CSA, known as Captain Blalock's Company and then Lt. Col. Morrison's Battalion, Georgia Cavalry. He was captured in Georgia on August 14, 1864. His last muster roll was dated November—December 1864.

On the 1870 Census, this family is in Villa Rica; Allen is a farmer, age 30; Hulda, 34; Octavia, 12; Green, 10; and Thomas A., 7. In 1880 he is listed in the Conners' District, #1259, which was previously the Dark Corner District, occupation "mining."

From evidence, it seems that Allen J. Young left his family, married again and had another family. On October 4, 1891, Allen Young, who had left Douglas County, married Sarah Ellen Hampton (November 1849 - 1944) in Lawrence County, Alabama.

Allen Young is not only remembered for having left his family, but another story and a vial of mercury has been handed down for five generations. "*Allen was a gold miner in the Dark Corner area. Mercury was used by miners to collect the gold, mixed in the black sand, that was panned. The mercury was then distilled away, leaving pure gold. Of course, the mercury vapors were extremely poisonous, and mercury poisoning causes severe kidney damage. Allen Young's death certificate, dated September 17, 1911, Lawrence County, Alabama, indicates that he died of Brights Disease which is an acute and chronic disease of the kidneys. It is very conceivable that his death was caused by the mercury.*"

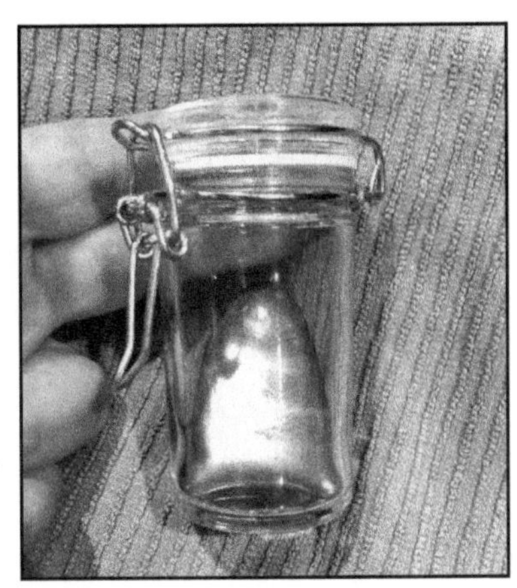

Photo of actual Vial of Mercury kept by the family for 5 generations. Courtesy: Ed Thompson

Allen and Huldy Young's daughter, (from his first family) Leonora Octavia, was born on July 14, 1857 in Dark Corner and died April 1, 1924 in Dark Corner, married Robert Alexander **Thompson**, 1858 - 1915.

15

Dark Corner Fades into History

. . . news of the Georgia Pacific Railway, (later the Southern Railway) coming to the area —within two miles of Dark Corner —really sent a bustle of activity throughout the countryside.

On October 17, 1870, Campbell County boundary lines were changed to become Douglass County. This new county was redrawn from sections of the larger Carroll, Campbell and Cobb Counties. One reason for restructure was that the larger Campbell County's county seat was about twenty-five miles from its northern boundary lines causing the settlers to travel two days journey to the courthouse and stores that were available in Campbellton. The new country seat of Douglasville was incorporated on February 25, 1875.

The small town of Weddington, was formed in the area. This town was named for the early settler and large land owner, Alexander Green Weddington, who owned LLs 218, 219, and 198, all adjacent to where the old Dark Corner Post Office was located after the Civil War.

About 1880, news of the Georgia Pacific Railway (later known as the Southern Railway) coming within two miles of Dark Corner really sent a bustle of activity throughout the countryside. There was to be a depot right on the north side of this railway giving residents access to travel anywhere the train would take them. Most were interested in day trips to Atlanta and Marietta. Things would never be the same for this small community.

On October 13, 1881, the Weddington Post Office was established. The town really began to prosper when the line of the Georgia Pacific (Southern) Railroad was completed in 1882. With a post office and a railroad station, better communication and travel became available to everyone.

Change, also, came to Dark Corner as it became more sparsely populated but remained mainly a farm community.

Weddington becomes Winn.

On October 13, 1881, James Henry Winn was appointed postmaster of Weddington. On November 15, 1882, the name of the post office—near the Railroad Station—was officially changed to Winn, named for J. H. Winn. His appointment as postmaster ended on November 15, 1883.

Dark Corner's last postmaster, Isham A. King had an appointment that began on August 31, 1881 and discontinued on January 2, 1883. Residents of the area went to Winn to post a letter or receive mail.

Some say, "I lived at Dark Corner."

A plat of Dark Corner School, dated November 6, 1928, shows the school located on Land Lot #200, and coordinates indicate the school sat back from the road facing where Cedar Mountain intercepts into Mann Road— known in years past—as the "fork in the road." Two ladies, interviewed in 2014, recall attending the 1928 Dark Corner School and remember each other:

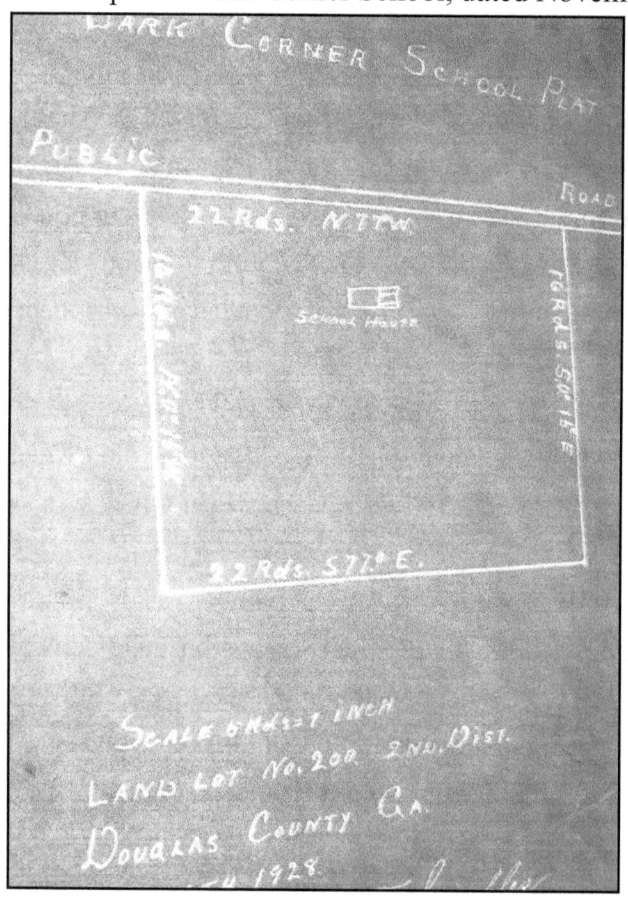

Douglas County Surveyor's Department
Courtesy: Carl Lewis

Francis Darnell Williams, age 92, attended Dark Corner School in 1928 when she was six years old. Her teacher, Mrs. Lois Cahoon, picked her up every morning in her Ford Roadster and took her to school. Francis Darnell Williams also remembers when her mother, Mrs. Darnell taught school two years earlier. "When I was four, Mother would take me to Granny Brittain's house and go across the street, near Brewer Road to teach school. There was barely the minimum amount of children to have a class, so the teacher, her mother, enrolled a five year old who attended every day. When Mrs. Darnell saw Superintendent McLarty coming toward the school to do an inspection, she sent the five-year-old out the back window of the school, to run home and not be seen by Superintendent McLarty. When he counted the children, she told him one was absent that day. Mother taught for a year until she was pregnant with my brother, Buddy."

Francis Darnell Williams

In a 2014 interview with Bertie Lee, age 93, daughter of John Pierce Entrekin and Flossie Ethel Miles, Bertie tells of her attendance at Dark Corner School in 1927. "I was too young to go to school, but I wanted to go with my older brothers. I was either 5 or 6, but I walked with them each day to and from school. The teacher there was mean to me. I got a whipping nearly every day. One day Ms. Lois Cahoon, a new teacher, replaced the mean teacher. She even picked me up in her little blue Ford Roadster and drove me to school because I was too young to walk so far with my brothers. I loved Mrs. Cahoon. But I still remember getting a whipping almost every day at Dark Corner school." In the interview, Bertie was still mad about the every-day-whippings when she was five or six. When asked what color Dark Corner School was, Bertie said emphatically, RED, like, don't you know. Bertie

Bertie Enterkin Lee

Lee is the granddaughter of Luda Stephens Enterkin and Mary Ann Winn Enterkin and great-granddaughter of John Enterkin and Mary McElreath Enterkin. On her mother's side, she is the granddaughter of Joseph Abner Miles and Martha Melinda Miles, daughter of Harmon and Delia Jane Cook. All four generations lived at Dark Corner all of their lives.

In an interview, Reverend Louis Camp, age 71, remembers that the Dark Corner children had to journey four miles to attend school at Winston in the late 1920's. But before that he remembers the Dark Corner School was a one-room red, schoolhouse offering education in the first through eighth grades. Camp estimates that the school building was standing as late as the 1930's, but does not recall what happened to the structure. There is no trace of it today.

With the building of the Georgia Pacific Railroad in June 1882, the younger

Railroad crew "kept the spikes nailed down & rails secure." Foreman, Robert Wesley Thompson, and son, Dewitt. Photo: Courtesy Mildred Thompson

generation wanted to be in the newer town of Weddington, which became Winn, then Winn Town, then Winston. Mildred Thompson remembers her grandmother Leona Enterkin (Thompson) who was born in 1890 in Winston. Mildred quotes her grandmother: Leona said, " I was raised at Winston; then I married (Robert Wesley

Thompson) and moved to Dark Corner. The Thompsons were a wonderful family. They were happy and what anyone wanted, they all worked to make it happen. But they didn't put up with any foolishness. We worked from sun-up until we closed our eyes at night. I did not want to live in Dark Corner; it was lonely there—just the sound of the morning doves cooing. It was so lonely—there were no neighbors, just the farm. I wanted to be where it was gay and lively—in Winston where you could travel on the train to Atlanta and where there was a store and post office and people coming in and out. Things were more exciting; we had get-togethers and parties." Leona and her husband moved back to town when their first child was born. Leona died in 1991 at age 101.

As the town of Dark Corner faded into history, so did our memory of the older generations. As time went by, the stories told by the elders, handed down to their sons and daughters and grandchildren, became lost or forgotten, but bits and pieces have survived. This book has put some parts of the puzzle together to give a small picture of what it was like in the early history of Campbell and Douglas County.

16

Journal of Archibald Newton McLarty

. . . we have been out of milk for some time but the old black muly had a calf to day. . .

Archibald Newton McLarty was born January 31, 1812, died October 16, 1867. He was the son of John McLarty, Sr. and Mary Polly Wilson. He married Ann Gilliam and Louisa **Vansant**. Ann was born on August 23, 1814 and died November 10, 1855 in Campbell County, Georgia. Archibald enlisted September 25, 1861 in the Civil War as a Private Co. C, 30th Georgia Infantry; appointed Assistant Commissary Sergeant on June 30, 1862; resigned November 1862. He died in Wood County, Texas; buried in Winnsboro City Cemetery. Archibald's children:

1). William Alexander McLarty 1833-1898; Cpl. - Sgt, Co. F 1st Alabama Cavalry **(US);** died in Bremond, Texas.

2). Mary C. McLarty 1835-1876; married Joseph R. Farmer; Pvt., Co. C, 30th Georgia Infantry; enlisted 9/25/61 in Campbell County; died in 1863 in Mississippi; **Memorial marker in McLarty Cemetery.**

3). Robert Wilson McLarty 1837-1907; Sgt., Co. F 1st Alabama Cavalry **(US)**; died in Stroud, Oklahoma.

4). Archibald DeKalb McLarty 1839-1862; Pvt., Co. A, 56th Georgia Infantry; enlisted 4/28/62 in Campbell County; died 8/10/62 in Lookout Mountain hospital; likely buried as unknown at Chattanooga Confederate Cemetery; **Memorial marker in McLarty Cemetery.**

5). John Stephen Harvey McLarty 1841-1903; Pvt. - Cpl., Co. A 56 Georgia Infantry; enlisted 9/25/61; mustered into Co. F, 6th **US** Volunteers 3/26/65; died at Winnesboro.

6). George Gilliam McLarty 1844-1923; Pvt., Co. C. 30th Georgia Infantry; enlisted 9/25/61; hospitalized repeatedly with malaria; died in Vernon, Texas.

Home of A. N. McLarty, built 1850 on LL# 162
Photo: ***McLarty Family of Kintyre.***

7). Samuel Washington McLarty 1846-1912 or 1926; Pvt., Co. C, 30th Georgia Infantry; enlisted 2/16/62; discharged 9/25/62 at Camp Hardee (age 16).

8. Charles Newton McLarty 1848-1930 died in Vernon, Texas.

9. Parkes Strickland McLarty 1850-1907; died in Texas.

10. Benjamin David McLarty 1852-1925; died in Texas.

11. Ann McLarty, born February 27, 1855; died as infant in 1855.

Children of Archibald and Louisa VanSant:

1. Thomas Jacob McLarty 1857-1902.
2. Rebecca Ann McLarty, born 1859.
3. Jefferson Davis McLarty 1861-1935; buried in Tallapoosa, Georgia.
4. Margaret Orpha McLarty, born 1864.
5. James Patrick McLarty 1867-1918; died on Oklahoma.

A. N. McLarty kept a journal of his daily life in the Dark Corner area from January 1, 1847 to about 1866. This journal was an 18 inch long by 6 inch wide, pasteboard backed book which had inscriptions on the inside cover: I. S. H. McLarty was born December 25, 1841; A. N. McLarty—his hand write. (sic) (The spelling, punctuation, and grammar is as he wrote it—with no corrections. Some dashes were put between phrases for clarification. Left side numbers represent entries and not necessarily dates.)

Journal of A. N. McLarty

January 1847

1. All of my family will and we grubed to day - cloudy; with rain.
2. Grubed in the morning all of the family will - Cloudy and cold with some rain, - heavy rain in the evening at home all day.
3. Sabeth morning all of the family will - Cloudy and cold with some rain, - heavy rain in the eveening at home all day.
4. Made two pair shoes - Cloudy and very stormy in the evening.
5. Made shoose - Clear day.
6. Wint to Wilsons shop - Returned home sick.
7. Made shoose-unwell all day - very stormy with snow.
8. Roled logs at Asa Sewells and then wint to George Mlarty, with Danell - very cold day.
9. Received $100 from Danell made Danell titler to no. 114-47 and I went to Squire Watsons - Returned homee - hung my meat and found Anns jar broken.
10. Sabath day - All well and at home all day - rain all day - heard a number of guns to day.
11. Made shoes - very cold and clear - we have been out of milk for some time but the old black muly had a calf to day
12. Went to Villarica - changed my money and paid all my dets and have $66.40 cents in hand yet.
13. Grubed in the morning and then went to Smiths mill.-Cloudy and cold. Returned home from mill unwell---

(entries for Jan. 15-19 are missing as the pages are torn.

20. Grubed in the morning and then went to shop in the evening - very cold wet day
21. Grubed 48 rods a peace today - very cold and clear - very tired
22. Grubed in the morning and then went to the Wilsons - Stayed all night - Bleed more at the nose that night than ever I did - clear and cold.
23. Loaded my apple trees and went to the powder Springs - Sold 250 trees and returned to John M lartys - Stayed there all rain night - William Duncan died today
24. Sabath morning returned home all of the family well - rain

Grubed all day - cloudy in the morning and clear in the evening.

25. Grubed and made one pair of shoose - grate deal of thunder and rain and very worme.

Went to Frances Winns to Machien house raised and the children grubed. Clear and cold - Mr. Clinton died today.

Took up my apple trees and rubed my trees in the orched - cloudy and very cold rain at night and stormy. (two coffins are drawn in the margin) Grubed all day - cloudy all day and cold - John Magines died today Grubed in the morning and cut and hauled wood in the evening - clear and cold

Sabath day at home all day - clear and plesent day, I am thirty five years old today.

Sixteen dry dayes and fifteen wet dayes in this month. Employed every (rest of page missing)

February 1847

1. Grubed in the morning and loaded my apple trees to go to Campbellton - clear and worme.
2. Went to Campbellton - Sold one dollars worth of trees - Macay (sp) negros sold generly very high - returned home very dark night and very wet and cold and very stormy.
3. Done no work to day - high winds today and very cold.
4. Made two pair shoes to day and the children grubed - John C. Whittley grubed today and Green Maguire - clear and cold.
5. Grubed all day - tolerable cold day - John C. Whittey and Green worked to day.
6. Grubed all day with the same hands - very plesent day - cloudy in the morning.
7. Sabath day - went to Robert Benson to see their child-found it better-stayed all night - Cloudy day and worme.
8. Returned home and grubed all day - clear and plesent day - Sold Green Wedington three dollars and half worth trees.
9. Grubed all day - very warm day - thunder and rain at night.
10. Grubed all day - clear and cold day - John C. Whittey and Green grubed to day.
11. Grubed all day - very cold to day.
12. Went to log roling at Wm. Maguires - the hands worked very lively - hevy roling finished in good time - clear and cold day.
13. Grubed in the morning and planted my irish potatoes in the evening - Clear and plesent day.
14. Sabath morning grate deal of fire in the woods moderate day to make apple trees thrive - to every gallon of soft sope, put one half pint of salt and one half pound of sulpher and paint the tree down from the fork.
15. Planted my apple seed and moved my lane fince - clear and worm day
16. Made some railes and cut logs and the boyes plowed dark wet day
17. Grubed in the morning find then plat shucks for a horse collar, but I could not make it - grubed in the evinin - rain
18. Went to smiths mill spept their after night came home at 10 a clock wet day and very worm
19. Grubed all day - cloudy with rain
20. Cut wood in the morning and wint to Entricans log roling in the evening - cloudy and very warm with rain.
21. Sabath day at home- wrote to brother Alexander to day - remarkable wet in the morning and very worm.
22. Grubed all day and mashed my nose with a stick of wood - very cold day and cloudy
23. Went to John Baggets log roling and Alexander plowed - cloudy and pleasant day

24 Wint to Jeames Endsleys log roling and father and the boys grubed - clear and cold

25. Made wagon frame and made gluts and ring mall and the boys plowed for granpap all day - clear and plesent day
26. Made shoes to day and haled wood stormy day very heavy rain and thunder
27. Made one pair shoes and loded my waggon to start to market - started and lay at mckonels stormy night snow and thunder.
28. Drove to Atlanta stay their that night - saw the cars run very brisk - clear and cold - their was eight wet days in this month and twenty clear ones employed every day in this month except one

Grubing hoe. Hoe head found in Dark Corner. Handle added. Photo and hoe made by John Bailey.

March 1847

1. Done my trading in Atlanta - started for home day on Nickagack - clear and cold.
2. Drove home - found my family well - clear and cold.
3. Mended shoes and worked on the celler - cold and very wet day.
4. Asked hands to help me to chop in my new ground - cloudy day.
5. Chopped in my new ground - had twenty -four hands to chop - a fine days work done - clear and plesent day.
6. Choped to day very tired to night - warm and plesent to day
7. Sabath day at home to day - very wet with thunder
8. Choped to day - cloudy with rain very warm.
9. Commenced spliting rails. I split 285, Alexander and Robert split 213, Anthony split 198 in all 696.
10. Split rails to day, I split 206, Alexander and Robert 180, Anthony 181 - in all 566 - hevy rain to day very worm
11. Split rails to day - I split 136, Anthony 105 in all 348 - very wet day - worked in spells - very warm day.
12. Made one bridle tremendious rains all day and thunder - rain from every corse.
13. Made rails to day - Alexander and me made 300, Anthony made 284 - in all 584 - cold day with snow in the morning
14. Sabath day - at home to day - very cold day.
15. Made rails to day - John Endsley made 402 - Alexander made 214 - Anthony made 308 - in all 924 clear and cold day
16. Made rails to day John Endsley made 214 - Anthony 206 - Alexander 200 - in all 620 - clear and cold - and windy day

Hauled wood intiie morning and went to Smiths Mill - clear and plesent day

Returned home from mill and the boyes plowed for granpap - clear and plesent.
19. Roled logs for jackson bagget and the boyes plowed for grandpap clear and plesent.
20. Wint to Smiths Mill and took 100 apple trees to Mr Deadingley and stayed all night - cloudy with rain - lay in smiths mill all night with out any supper thought it bad lodging.
21. Sabath - this day came home from Smiths Mill rained so the night before I could not come home - very cold day with snow and rain.
22. Cut grafts as S. L. Mclartys - came home and grafted - 4 rows across my garden and the boys plowed for granpap. Plowed my mule colt a little and haled one load of rails with it - clear and plesent day.
Grafted in the morning and split rails in the evening - cloudy with rain.
Grafted in the morning and split rails in the evening - finished grafting today - clear and plesent day.
commenced at the east corner
stake pound apple-winter apple
morrison apple-winter apple
virginia green winter apple
northern king-winter apple
red tuner-summer apple
town pippens-winter apple
pound pairs-fall fruit
northern gold summer apple
yellow june-summer apple
huses crabb-winter apple
horse apple summer apple
pound sweet-summer apple
haslseedling winter apple
this Grafting is done in the year 1847 in March A. N. M larty
26. worked all day on one tree with Granpap and Anthony to help me - the big white oke in the orched - cloudy and cold with snow and very high winds
27. Haled rails to day and cool - very stormy day and cold but clear.
28. Sabath day at home to day - clear and plesent
29. Halled manure to day for grandpap clear and plesent day
30. Halled manure to day for pap clear and plesent
31. Halled manure to day - clear and windy eleven wet dayes in this month employed every month day

April 1847

1. Halled ashes and dung today - clear and plesent day.
2. Rain in the morning - I went to the road to work but found no hands their and came home - bilt some fence - very worm day.
3. Wint to Wilsons to the shop - 3 plows layed and two sharped and grandpap and the boys halle dung - thunder in the morning clear in the evening and very warm.

4. Sabath day - wint to church to day - Mr. Winn preached his text was the wise virgins and the foolish - clear and plesent day.
5. Thrashed our oats and plowed some - I wint to Wilsons to the shop - thunder in the morning - clear in the evening
6. Commenced sowing our oats - broke my mule to day to tlle harrow and plow - rain at 12 oclock with thunder.
7. Plowed all day - puting in oats-clear and warm!
8. Finished sowing oats to day by hand work - very warm day - high wind
9. Roled logs for pap in the morning and rolled logs for John Endsley - clear and plesent day.
10. Worked on the road to day and the boys and grandpap roled logs and haled rails - rain to day.
11. Sabath wint to church to day - Whitley preached wint to S. H. M Larty at night - clear and warm.
12. Came home from S. H. Mlartys - commenced ridging my cotton patch - rain at 12 o clock - choped in the newground in the evening rain to day
13. Worked at different things to day - clear and warm.
14. Planted my cotton to day - warm with thunder.
15. Plowed in the morning and set out one row of apple trees - very stormy in the evening with some rain.
16. Plowed to day and Ann quilted clear
17. Plowed un well - sore eyes - clear
18. Sabath day at home-sore eyes - clear.
19. Plowed to day - clear.
20. Cliped sheap to day - clear.
21. Plowed to day - clear day.
22. Planted paps patch of corn and scatered his manure - cloudy day.
23. Commenced building new ground fence - cloudy.
24. Helped S. H. M Larty to role logs - clear - put my mair to the horse.
25. Sabath day at home to day - clear.
26. Built fence in the morning and roled logs for Mr. Entrycan. In the evening.
27. Built fence to day - very tired to night - clear.
28. Haled rails in morning and asked hands to my log roling in the evening.
29. Rolded my log to day - hands worked very brish - finished in good time - cloudy.
30. Roled logs for Mr. M Kelvy - cloudy and rain. ----fore wet days in this month and 26 dry days - a fine month for doing work.

May 1847

1. Built some fence and wint to cort - lay in the woods that night thunder and rain hurd the wolves at out camp.
2. Sabath at home to day very sore eyes cloudy.
3. Planted my sweet potatoes cloudy and very cold.
4. Built fence to day very tired to night clear
5. Built fence to day cloudy with rain.

6. Roled logs for E. Mazwell clear day.
7. Burnt some of my new ground rain.
8. Worked on my nurcery and went to Georges rain.
9. Sabath day came home from Georges cloudy.
10. Worked in my new ground burning it off - clear.
11. Burned at my new ground - clear very tired.
12. Burned at my logs in the morning and worked at my cotton in the evening - clear.
13. Plowed my orched corn clear and cool.
14. Burned at my clearing and warm.
15. Burned at my clearing warm.
16. Sabath - went to Wilson - clear rain and hail at night.
17. Commenced planting my newground - rain in the evening - Mr. Bates died to day.
18. Planted at the newground - some rain.
19. Planted to day clear and cool.
20. Burned at my newground very tired to night - clear and plesent day
21. Burned at the new ground cloudy.
22. Burned at the newground heavy rain to day.
23. Sabath day at home to day - clear
24. Planted corn to day - clear.
25. Planted corn to day went to see George in the evening rainin the evening.
26. Went to Georges to day and to the mines wet day.
27. Went to see George to day found him better rain to day.
28. Went to Smiths Mill with wheat - came home after night clear day.
29. Worked over my sweet potatoes and cotton clear day and very worm.
30. Sabath day went to church to day but (sic) not get in the house - clear and warm.
31. Plowed for grandpap clear and warm day

June 1847

1. Plowed for Granpap very warm and some rain.
2. Plowed for Granpap very warm day and clear very tired to night.
3. Plowed for granpap clear and warm.
4. Plowed for my self to day hevy rain to day.
5. Worked my apple trees to day cloudy with rain.
6. Sabath day at home to day clear and worm
7. Plowed in my new ground clear.
8. Plowed in the new ground cloudy in the morning.
9. Plowed in the new ground in the morning and some lite rain clear in the evening.
10. Plowed in the new ground - hevy rain in the evening.
11. Commenced harrowing my newground clear and plesent day.
12. Layed by my sweet potatoes clear
13. Sabath day wint to John F. Morris.
14. Wint to Campbellton to cort storm in the evening.
15. Harrowed corn to day a grate deal of thunder a grate distance off no clouds to be seen.

16. Harrowed corn to day no rain.
17. Harrowed in the morning and howed in the evening clear and very warm day.
18. Howed corn to day finished howing the new ground cloudy and warm.
19. Worked grandpaps potatoes very hevy rain to day.
20. Sabath day at home to day went in the evening to see George found him very sick plesent day.
21. Cut wheat go day Mr. Miller and Endsley cut to day plesent day.
22. Cut wheat to day Mr. Miller and Endsley cut to day plesent day.
23. Bound wheat and howed cotton clear.
24. Plowed corn to day cloudy with some rain.
25. Plowed corn to day.
26. Harrowed my apple trees hevy rain.
27. Sabath day at home hevy rain
28. Raised the Machier house and plowed some corn clear to day.

July 1847

1. Finished laying by granpaps corn and cloudy and cool day.
2. Commend laying by my new ground cloudy.
3. Plowed in my new ground.
4. Sabath day went to church to day Mr. Whitley preached from the 3rd chapter of Malachi and the 18th verse.
5. Plowed to day clear - grated some to day and have been at it for some time.
6. Plowed to day in the new ground clear day.
7. Plowed in the new ground - very dry and warm
8. Commenced thrashing wheat to day thrashed William Mequgts wheat 20 & 1/2 bushels no rain.
9. Plowed to day - their has been a grate deal of rain went round for some dayes but we are very dry.
10. Finished plowing corn to day by 12 oclock we had a fine rain this evening.
11. Sabath day at home to day rain to day.
12. Haled wheat to day and thrashed 13 bushels - a grate deal of rain went to mill in the evening.
13. Returned home from mill cut oats clear day and warm.
14. Cut oats to day - very warm.
15. Cut oats to day and thrashed John Whitleys wheat 6 bu.
16. Finished cutting oats clear.

17 Receipt to preserve cider take a pint of pulverized charcoal and put it in a barel of new cider and the cider will never ferment never contain any intoxicating quality and become more palatable the longer it is kept.

18. Sabath day pap and me wint to John Mlartys but no one at home.
19. Thrashed Entricans and MKelvys wheat 41 bushels.
20. Haled in granpaps wheat and thrashed some first rate -rain to day.
21. Cleaned up granpaps wheat he had 73 bushels no rain.
22. Thrashed my wheat 26 bushels and thrashed some for Entrycan and M Kelvy

cloudy but no rain.
23. Thrashed balance of Mr. Entrican and M Kelvys wheat 33 bushel rain to day - masured my wheat to day 39 bushels.
24. Went to Wilsons and got my mair shod stayed there all night very hevy rains today.
25. Sabath at home to day I had the headake in the forenoon very bad not much rain.
26. Worked my apple trees to day a hard dayes work cloudy
27. Halled oats to day no rain
28. Went to Smiths Mill - returned home at night.
29. Bilt some fence and thrashed some for Jackson Bagget cloudy and cold and some rain.
30. Thrashed the balance of Jackson Baggets wheat - he had 17 bushels.
31. Went to Vilarica to day left my cloath with the Mr. Patterson. Their was preaching their and (fining-pining) (sic) for burning a negro man some drinkind and some wanting to fight and some at one thing and some at another a grate deal of wickness going on.
Employed every day of month.

Drawing of Old Campbell County Courthouse
Photo: Courtesy Nancy Connell

August 1847

1. Sabath at home to day.
2. Started to Atlanta.
3. Drive in Atlanta sold flower at 2 bacon at 8 payed 30 for molasses and 10 for coffee and sugar drove out lay 5 miles from town.
4. Drove home by John Morris the worst road I ever drove.
5. At home to day haled some house logs for granpap my eyes very sore - some little rain.
6. Wint to S. W. M larty on a visit.
7. Came on to the cort ground and Mr. Carlton came home with me.
8. Sabath day at home to day.

9. Cut crib logs Robert Benson worked with me hevy rain in evening
10. Cut crib logs.
11. Robert Benson and my self made shoes for S. W. M Larty 5 pairs.
12. I wint to Villa Rica and Robert Benson and Alexander cut logs.
13. Wint to Campbellton to drill.
14. At Campbellton muster - hevy rain in evening.
15. Sabath day wint to church. Mr. Winn preached.
16. Thrashed Mr. Maqurts rye and helped McKelvy to lay the foundation of his house.
17. Helped McKelvy to rais his house.
18. Wint to Villa Rica.
19. Helped granpap to saw board timbar.
20. Wint to Georges to get his wagon.
21. Wint to David Whites.
22. Sabath day at Whites all day.
23. Came to Parkes Stricklins stayed their all night.
24. Came hoe and took Georges waggon home.
25. Helped granpap to raise his smoke house.
(rest of this month is missing)

September 1847

The first part of September is missing (The following numbers represent entries not dates)
1. Sept. 20. Wint to mill and boys puled foder.
2. Worked on the roads and the boys puled fodder.
3. Puled fodder in the forenoon and tyed fodder in the evening rain.
4. Rained all day worked with granpaps tobacco.
5. Split punchions for cribs floor and tyed some fodder.
6. Tyed fodder and puled some.
7. Sabath day wint to John Baggets.
8. Cut a board tree and maid some boards.
9. Puled fodder to day.
10. Split boards and tyed fodder.
11. Finished my fodder - I have 6800 bundles.
12. One month and two days at the fodder.

October 1847

1. Wint to Vila Rica stayed all night at S. W. Mlarty with the sick.
2. Came home and split boards and Ann and me wint to John F. Morris.
3. Sabath day - came home from Morris.
4. Wint to the general election - Carlton and White for repersentive - Carlton 38 and White 29 votes - for governer Towns 54 for Clinch 15 - Camp for senit 8
5. Layed the foundation of my crib.
6. Went to Campbell to cort cort called at 12 oclock - wint to Thomas camp at night.
7. At cort all day Mr. Camps at night.
8. At cort all day - went to Mr. Carltons at night.

9. At cort all day dismised in the evening got 45 cents for my weeks services came found my family well.
10. Sabath day went to Wilsons to day with Ann and Margaret.
11. Worked at the crib all day.
12. Worked at the crib all day.
13. Picked cotton to day picked 192 lbs.
14. Hevy frost this morning puled corn for grandpap.
15. Went to crassamere to cort of enquiry took a grist of corn to mill with me. Hevy frost in the morning commenced halling Grandpaps corn.
16. Finished puling and haling granpaps field of corn 22 loads went to William Maquirts for Anna got kicked by Jackson Baggets mair on the knee.
17. Sabath day went to John M Larty with Anne and Pap and Mom to see John found him better.
18. Went to Mr. John Carltons to send for lot no 163 came back to Thomas Bullards stayed with him all night.
19. Came home done no work to day.
20. Kiled a hog for pap in the morning and pap shucked his corn in the evening.
21. Cribed paps corn hard dayes work.
22. Went to mill.
23. Halled paps fodder and made boards.
24. Sabath day at home to day a grate dill of rain to day.
25. Split boards in the morning and then went to John Baggets corn shucking shucked until after midnight.
26. Worked at my crib in the morning then went to Endsleys corn shucking finished by 8 oclock.
27. Went to Jeames Endsleys corn shucking.
28. Went to G. W. M Lartys corn shucking.
29. Went to G. S. M Larty. And hunted some for my hogs but did not find them.
30 Hunted my hogs and found them and caried some corn to their bed.
31. At home to day Sabath day unwell to day
This has been the finest month for gathering crops I ever saw.
(Rest of this page in pencil at later date.) F. W. Mattox to Ish M. Larty stamps 10 cts imvelops 10cts.

November 1847

1. Hunted my hogs found some of them - the boys helped granpap to hall corn.
2. Made one pair of shoes for S.W. M Larty and hunted hogs some.
3. Shiled corn in the morning Alexander was very sick all day - unwell my self.
4. Caried corn to my hogs and wint to S. W. M Larty stayed all night.
5. Came home in the evening.
6. Roled the logs on my wheat land.
7. Sabath day wint to church a stranger preached a fine sermon.
8. Commenced diggin potatoes - helped to clear two hogs of S. W. M Lartys that Mr. Silman kiled by misstake one wayed 125 one 136 when clean.

9. Dug potatoes - caught one of my wile boars cut him and put him up.
10. Scraped manure wet day.
11. Hunted my hogs and wint to Williams Maqurts corn shucking.
12. Hunted my hogs to day Samuel and George Wilson and family came from North Carolina.
13. Hunted my hogs in the morning and then hilped McKelvy to raise stabbs (sic).
14. Sabath day at home to day.
15. Went to Villa Rica Baught from Sheays and Stokely
100 worth coffe.
6 yards akoaca 1.00
7 do calico 25
2 do black tambrick 10
2 dozen hookes and eyes 10
1 lb salaratas 10
1 dress shall 1.62
36 yards shirting 360
16. Hunted wolves to day.
17. Hunted to day - shot a buck and got him.
18. Dug potatoes to day.
19. Put up my potatoes and kiled a hog very cold evening.
20. Went to S. W. M Larty for seed wheat.
21. Sabath day at home.
22. Finished sowing paps wheat.
23. Went to S. W. M Larty to corn shucking came home very wet.
24. At home to day - dark and wet.
25. Went to John M Larty to see his daughter Ester married - cold snoy day - Francis Winn married her to Canidy Entrican. (Samuel Kanada).
26. Came on to Mr. Entricans to the infarm (sic) my teeth aked very bad at night.
27. Hunted my hogs all day but found none of them.
28. Sabath day at home to day - saw my hogs to day.
29. Commenced sowing my wheat sowed 4 bushels to day.
30. Finished sowing wheat and wint to Jackson Bagget to his corn shucking - my tooth aked very bad.

December 1847

1. Wednesday worked on the road very wet day and very cold.
2. Thursday worked on the road tired our old black cow had a calf to day. it had been ten months and twenty two days since she had her calf before.
3. Fryday - Worked on the road and went to mill - returned at twelve oclock.
4. Saterday - went to S. H. M Larty on a visit.
5. Sabath day went over to S. W. M Larty came home in the evening.
6. Monday Wilson and Hearvy and Green (McGuire or Alexander Green Weddington?) and Sam Wilson hilped me hunt hogs - we kiled fore that made 525 lbs. Pork.
7. Salted my meat and hunted my hogs.

8. Hunted hogs to day.
9. Made a pair of shoes for C. B. M Larty.
10. Made one pair for Mary.
11. Made one pair for Robert.
12. Sabath day at home to day.
13. Made one pair shoes for Anthony.
14. It has been very wet and warm I have had back ake very bad.
15. Commenced puling corn to day my back hurts me bad yet.
16. Haled corn to day.
17. Hunted hogs.
18. Hunted Hogs.
19. Sabath day went to S. W. M Larty.
20. Hunted hogs in the morning and went to McKelvys corn shucking.
21. Helped Maxwell to build his crib and shuck in the evening.
22. Puled at my corn.
23. Puled and haled corn.
24. Haled 15 loads of corn.
25. Christmas day John M Larty children, Margaret Ann and Martha, John and Jeames and George and John Morris Sanday and William.
26. Sabath day at home very cold day and clear.
27. Went to mill late getting home at night.
28. made one pair shoes.
29. Kiled two hogs and started to Atlanta.
30. Drove into Atlanta and traded - sold wheat at 75 cents flower at 2.50 bought coffe 11 lbs to the dollar shugar 12 lbs to the dollar sale at 2.00 per sack molasses at 35 cents.
31. Drove home after night getting home the last day in the year thus ends the year 1847. When this you se remember me and bear (*keep*) me in your mind let all the world say as they will *(may) (but)* speake of me as you find. *

**1800's poem.*

January 1848

1. January first Saturday at home
2. Sabath day at home to day plesent.
3. Monday went to the general election
4. Shucked my corn - hands worked well done in good time.
5. Put up corn today
6. Covered corn and shucks do
7. Wilson and me hunted hogs cold
8. Hunted hogs to day and made pegs for shoes
9. Sabath day wind high at home
10. Helped granpap to kill his hogs
11. Salted paps meet.
12. Made shoes - two pair for Wilson
13. Made shoes for Wilson two pair

14. Made shoes for my self
15. Done different kinds of work to day.
16. Sabath day at home very warm
17. Shiled corn and made shoes for my self wint to mill in the evening Wilsons mill.
18. Came home from mill.
19. Hunted for hogs to day - found none - put fore hogs up.
20. Helped Wright to raise his house.
21. Hunted hogs to day found my sow - commenced getting stabe logs.
22. Worked at getting stabe logs Ann and me went to Robert Bensons.
23. Sabath day came from Bensons
24. Worked at getting logs for stabe.
25. Worked at getting logs in the fore noon and roled logs for A. McKelvy in the evening.
26. Hunted hogs with Wilson
27. Went to John M Larty with (faded)
28. Made one pair shoes for Wilson.
29. Helped William Maqurt to raise his house.
30. Sabath day at home to day.
31. Getting logs to day I am 36 years old to day.

February 1848 - Missing
March 1848

Commenced grafting
Two first rowes; hall seedlings
Two second rowes; pound apple-winter
#Commenced at west end to first stone yellow june from 1st to (2nd) stone red June from 2nd to 3(rd) town pippen - from 3rd to 4 pound pairs from 4th to 5th horse apple from 5th to sixth mewes crabs - from 6th to 7th summer apple - from 7th to 8th may apple from 8th to 9th northern good from 9th to 10th morrison apple.
This grafting done in the year 1848.
#From 10th to 11th hallsendlings - from 11th to 12th red June from 12th to 13th Sewed seed from 13 to 14th town pippen from 14th to 15th pound apple winter.
This grafting done in the year 1849 - I went over the old grafting and let the old stones stand for this year.
A. N. M larty

April 1848

(Entries not as regular from this point.)
Went to cort to serve of grand jury - their five dayes.
10. Commenced plantin my orched corn.
12. Planted my pack above the stable.
Commenced braking the new ground and I wint to Winns and bought a stear to plow.
19. Mare colted to day.

May 1848

1. Sold the white cow to Wm. Maquiork commenced dresing my apple trees to day planted to day at my corn in the new field.
2. Planted to day.
3. Finished to day plant in and harrowed the orched corn.
10. Made a pair of shoes for pap and helf soled Alexanders a grate deal of rain to day.
13. Planted my sweet potatoes.
15. Commenced working my new field.
20. Very warm to day and like for rain.
21. Polly M Larty died to day S. W. M Lartys wife.
23. grate rain to day.
27. Finished plowing over my new ground hevy rain in the evening.

June 1848

1. Jeames Endsley cutt wheat for me to day.
2. Jeames Endsley cut to day - wet day.
3. Started to Atlanta with Mr. French.
5. Sold my meet for $6.30 cents per hundred wt.
8. Thrashed Samuel Wilson wheat - 12 bushels.
9. Thrashed my own 28 bushels.
10 Thrashed Willis Finchs 16 bushels Maxwell 29 bushells.
14. Thrashed John F. Morris 30 bushels.
16. Thrashed Thomas Garner - 45 bushels - some rain.
17. Some rain to day.
18. Hevy rain.
19. Plowed in the fore noon a grate deal of rain in the evening - went to Arnols mill at night.
20. Came home from mill.
21. Plowed some.
22. Plowed to day Thursday
23. Plowed in the fore noon.
24. Worked at covering granpap kitchin.
26. Finished Mr. Baggett wheat 72 1/2 bushels.
28. Finished William MacQuirk wheat 76 bushels
30. Commenced cutting oats.

July 1847

1. Finished plowing corn by 12 o clock
2. Sabath day
3. Finished cutting oats very tired thrashed a great deal this year for the public
11. I took the fever - very bad.
12.-16. Bad
17. Fever - cooled some

18. Fever about the same
19. About the same
20. About do
21. Better - set up a little
22. Better still
23. Road over to E. W. Maxwell my health is still improving.
24. I am still improving in health for whitch I desire to thank Almighty God for all his goodness to me we have all apairence of a bountiful crop - more than ever we made in one year by one half - I have had 8 bushels of wheat ground and 70 bushels yet.
25. I feel very nervious to day but I am still getting better - grate rain to day. I rested very bad last night.
26. Very nervious this morning bad cold - hevy rain in the evening - bad tooth ake at night.
27. Plesent morning - planted cucumbers to day for late ones to pickle if they are not too late.
28. Went to G. W. M Lartys and then to S. W. M Larty
29. Then to S. H. M Larty
30. Then came home - found George sick.
31. Very wet day wet all this month.

August 1848

1. Clear in the morning and cool rain in the evening.
2. Clear day went to S. H. M Lartys.
3. Clear and cool day Robert Bensons little Sam died.
4. Clear and cool in the morning - went to see Robert Benson child buried they buried at S. W. M Lartys.
5. Went to cort to day - a grate deal of drinking their some quarling - rain in the evening.
6. Sabath day at home - John Bagget and wife came to see us.
7. Very unwell all day hevy rain in the evening.
8. Unwell to day - went to Washington Hawkins to look at the level lot.
9. Unwell all day rain in the morning lite.
10. Very unwell all day getting weaker every day.
11. Very unwell Alexander went to S. W. M Larty for to get his Uncle to get Wistan bossom of Wild Chery.
12. Alexander came home with the bolsom I took of it this evening no severe cough in the evening Wilson came to see me this evening.
13. Sabath day - I had no severe cough to day - Wilson and his children stayed all day.
14. Grandpap went to Arnolds mill fodder. My cough is not bad to day but very weak the boys puled fodder.
15. Unwell to day coughed more than common toth ake at night - puled fodder.
16. I am very weak - puled fodder.
17. Some little better to day - puled.
18. I think the bolsom does me a grate deal of good - some rain to day. But it rains

every day - the boyes stil worked with fodder - commenced feeding my hogs.
19. I am a good deal better to day some rain very stormy night
20. Sabath day at home unwell - cool day - some rain in the morning.
21. Went to S. W. M Larty - clear day.
22. Returned home from S. W. M Larty - clear but it rained a grate deal at night - the boyes got a heap of fodder wet John Clinton died to day (coffin drawn in the margin).
23. Went to Jackson Baggetts and William Maquirks to day rain to day.
24. Dark day - the boyes put up some fodder.
25. The boyes puled some fodder very wet day and night.
26. The boyes trimed the grafts - Wm. Maquirk and family came to see us. He who relates falts of others to you designs to relate yours to others.
27. Sabath day at E. W. Maxwells to day - I am still getting better - no rain.
28. The boyes commenced pulling the new ground fodder - Wilson and me looked some for our hogs.
29. The boys puled fodder - very fine day - but warm and clear.
30. I wint to G. W. M Larty for papers and the children puled fodder clear day - cool in the morning.
31. I worked a little with the boyes clear and dry day - the boyes has done very well at saving fodder this month.

September 1848

I went to Arnolds mill put up some fodder.
Worked at the fodder - warm and dry.
Sabath day at home.
Went to mill and the boyes pulled fodder - like for rain.
Puled fodder - cloudy in the forenoon - some rain - very lite.
Puled fodder in the forenoon - very cloudy day.
Cliped sheep to day - very tired - like for rain.
Done no work to day - clear and cool the boyes worked some at the fodder - finished the fodder.
Commenced pulling corn - clear and cool day.
Sabath day at home.
Went to G. W. M Larty with the wagon.
Started to Atlanta.
Drove to Atlanta.
Stayed at town - rode on the cars to the store - Mounting and Back payed 50 cents.
Drove home to G. W. M Larty - rain
Came home - clear and cool
Sabath day at home to day - Margaret had her baby at night.
Went to G. W. M Larty
Started to market
Drove to Atlanta
At the Whig meeting
Started home.

(four entries scratched out)
19. At Jeames Stewerds all day.
20. Went to A. G. Weaingtons (Weddington) to see his daughter married
21. Came home from the weding.
At paps in the fore noon and gathered my apples - 28 bushels.
24. Sabath day - went to Jackson Baggets.
Kiled a beef for pap.
Went to hunt my bull.
Sowed some wheat.
30. Went to John F. Morris with Ann

October 1848

1. Sabath day cloudy
2. Went to the general election - Harlson and Willimson for congress Harleson 47 Williamson 15. Came home haled 7 loads of corn.
3. Puled corn for pap.
4. Haled corn for pap.
5. Shucked paps corn.
6. Cribed at paps corn.
7. Do Do (the Do is used as ditto)
8. Commenced gathering my corn to day.
9. Commenced gathering my corn.
10. Rain
11. Gathering corn.
12. Do Do
13. Commenced halling corn W. Maquirk shucked.
14. Went to the Shaws.
15. Sabath day.
16. Halled corn - Wilsons boyes helped me.
17. Finished halling to John Endsley shucked Mary and Archy went to scool.
18. James Endsley shucked.
19. Had my own corn shucked - my crib full and some left.
20. Cribed corn.
21. Do Do
22. Sabath day.
23. Put up shucks.
24. Went to S. W. M Lartys to make shoes.
25. Made shoes.
26. Do Do.
27. Do Do.
28. Went to Jeames Cort - sold apples.
29. Sabath day David and Selina White came last night to see us.
30. David and Selina returned home - I helped Willis Finch with his saw mill.
31. Went after my (most of this page faded)

John Endsley died this month

November 1848

1. Wednesday went to David Clinton sale.
2. Hunted my steer.
3. Hunted the steer to day.
4. Made one pair of shoes for S. W. M Larty a grate deal of rain.
5. Sabath day clear.
6. Made shoes for my self.
7. General election for presidet 16 for Talor 77 for Ca (sic).
8. Dug potatoes to day.
9. Dug potatoes and put them up payed G. W. M Larty for my paper.
10. Commenced harrowing my wheat ground.
11. Finished harrowing my wheat ground.
12. Sabath day at home - a grate deal of rain.
13. Monday went to S. W. M Larty corn shucking.
14. Got 4 plows layed came home.
15. Commenced sowing - wheat.
16. Sowed wheat to day - Ann had her baby to day.
17. Plowed some to day. Halled some wood.
18. Helped Madison Greeman to raise his house cold with snow in the evening.
19. Sabath day at home.
20. Kiled hogs to 15 head 1994 lbs.
21. Salted my meet borrowed 117 lbs salt of pap Judge Winn died to day. (paid pap is written through the 117 lbs) commenced sowing wheat again went to help make Judge Winns coffin came home found Ann very sick.
22. Sowed wheat to day - Ann sick all day a little better in the evening.
23. Sowed wheat to day very tired to night.
24. Wet day - went to mill to day.
25. Went to Jeames cort as a witness to cort decided I should not have pay for atendance then offered my pay but I would not have it Tugle was the lawyer.

26, Sabath day at home.

27. Made one pair of shoes for Antony - plowed.
28. Helped Asa Sewell to kill his hogs plowed.
29. Finished sowing wheat.
30. Helped Canidy Entrycan to work on his house then went to mill.

December 1848

1. Came home from mill went to help Canidy Entrycan to raise his house - a grate deal of rain and hevy wind
2. Made wagon frame and geed traugh.
3. Sabath day at home.
4. Started to Atlanta.
5. Traded to Atlanta.

6. Drove home after nite.
7. Haled Wilsons salt home and took a bull to him.
8. Headake all day wet day.
9. Worked at making stable dores Mr. Daniel payed my forty seven dollars to day.
10. Sabath day at home W. M. Larty and Charity and John Endsley and wife was with us all night.
11. Hung my meet and made fire for to kill paps hogs.
12. Helped pap to kill his hogs kiled six - 925 lbs of pork - cold and cloudy day.
13. Went to John Clintons sale property sold very well - I wrote to brother Alexander and John P. M Larty to day.
14. Made shoes to day - wet day.
15. Made shoes to day - wint to mill.
16. Came home from S. H. M Larty mill - very wet.
17. Sabath day at home to day.
18. Scraped manure in the fore noon made one pair of shoes for E. W. Maxwell in the evening.
19. Made two pair of shoes for E. W. Maxwell.
20. Made one pair of shoes for E. W. Maxwell. Bill for wating on me - seven dollars and twenty five cents.
21. Went to J. C. Whittleys and worked on his clock then scraped manure - very warm.
22. Went to Villarica - bought of Stokley and Sheets 50 yards shirting one handsaw - 1 file - one yard calico - gun flints - $5.50 payed cash.
23. Hunted for my hogs to day - did not find them - the boyes scraped some manure - not much.
24. Went to John F. Morris with John C. M. Larty and George and Mangum and Alexander and Robert S. H. M Larty and wife was here to day and a number of the friends children.
25. Christmas day very wet day went to granpaps a good many there all day Alexander went to Uncle Wilsons - Mary to Uncle John Morris some cooler in the evening
26. Went to help John C. Whitley to kill his hogs Bingley and John and George and Alexander, Robert Real Christmas diner done by 12 o clock then went to hunt that the call deer and meet tired enough.
27. Kiled 19 hogs to day very wet in the fore noon Bingley and John and George and Mr. Sewell and Mr. Whitley helped me 1776 pork.
28. Salted my meet thin wint to brother Wilsons.
29. Came home from S. W. M Larty rain all day.
30. Went to help Wilson to kill hogs.
31. Sabath day at home to day.

January 1849

1. Went to the election - cold day
2. Helped Jackson Baggett to kill hogs
3. Wint to John F. Morris

4. Came home from Morris
5. Wint to mill
6. Went to the election - W. M.Larty 41 votes - S. H. Watson 38 - E. W. Maxwell 35 for balifs W. M Lung 47 - W. Maquirk 41 Chafin Hartsfield 30 - cold day
7. Sabath day - fire out worked with it - commenced snowing
8. Done no work to day
9. Hunted hogs to day - went to mill
10. Helped pap to kill his hogs - cold day
11. Helped Wilson to catch his hogs - headake very bad all night
12. Wilson came and helped me to bild hog pen to catch my wild hogs
13. Went to baite my hog pen - saw nine deer - caught 3 of Wilsons hogs - all boars - cut them - went to mill
14. Sabath day - Ann and me went on a visit to Mr. Sewells
15. Started to Atlanta - lay at Jeames Stewards
16. Drove to one mile the other side of the river
17. Drove into Atlanta - traded - came out two miles - wet day - rodes very bad
18. Drove home very cold
19. Made trap doors to hog pen
20. Traped 7 hogs to day - went to the scool house - done some work on it then Wilnesday old man Winn will (sic)
21. Sabath day at home.
22. Traped two more hogs and caught one - cut 2 bores for myself one for Wilson.
23. John Baggett spayed 7 sows for me.
24. Helped Wilson to build a hog pen
25. Helped granpap to lay the foundation of his stables - split out spoke timber.
26. Helped granpap to raise his stable.
27. Went to mill - clear day - hunted hogs
28. Sabath day at granpaps all day
29. The school commenced to day - cut a road to day.
30. Went to help S. W. M Larty to hunt hogs.
31. Made shoes to day - I am 37 years old to day - headake a grate deal this month.

February 1849

1. Made one pair of shoes for Mary and mended my own - Alexander has plowed 2 days
2. Hunted hogs to day
3. Done different kinds of work to day - Ann White and Wilkeson came to se us.
4. Sabath day at home to day.
5. Done no work to day
6. Killed my pigs to day
7. Helped S. W. M Larty to kill hogs
8. Looked Wilsons hogs pen - done no work
9. Put in a bill of lumber for a house.
10. Helped S. H. M Larty to role logs

11. Sabath day - went to se Easter Entrycan.
12. Helped to rais Wm Maquirk house.
13. Made hems - went to the shop - hiaffer calfed.
14. Commenced hewing for my house.
15. Worked at hewing
16. Worked at hewing - sold one dollars worth apple trees to Umphry
17. Helped John C. Whitley too role his logs
18. Sabath day at home
19. Worked at hewing - John C. Whitley helped me to day
21. Worked at hewing - John Whitley worked to day
21. John worked today.
22. Drove to Atlanta
23. Sold bacon at 6 1/4 cents
25. Sabath day - drove home
26. Went to S. H. Watsons to day.
27. Went to mill
28. Dug my apple trees to start to market with them - the children went to school thes month - 52 days for one scollar

March 1849

1. Started with my apple tree - lay at Mr. Mmaronys
2. Drove to Parkes Stricklins
3. Drove to D. Whites
4. Sabath day at Whites all day.
5. Went to Merietta
6. Drove home found all well
7. Planted my apple trees and went to S. W. M Larty for oats and cut grafts at S. H. M Larty
8. Commenced grafting in the old grafting - the boyes commenced harrowing.
9. Grafted to day - very tired to night. Some rain to day -
10. Grafted in the fore noon - the boyes plowed in oats - hung my meet in the evening
11. Sabath day at home
12. Grafted to day 400 graftes - the boyes plowed in oats - I sowed for the boyes I am very tired - it has been a very warm day.
13. Grafted to day and the boys plowed a grate deal of rain at night
14. Grafted some in the morning
15. Very stormy
16. Made two pair shoes for S. W. M Larty the boyes plowed some hard ground.
17. Graftes three rows of trees to day - then Ann and me went to S. W. M Lartys on a visit.
18. Came home from S. W. M Larty - Sabath day.
19. Monday - finished grafting all that I think will do - the boyes plowed to day - I struck up lumber at the sawmill.
20. Made one plowstock and worked on the wheelbaro - the boyes plowed some rain.

21. The boyes plowed in the forenoon - grate storm
22. Went to mill and took S. W. M Larty - wheat home 8 bushels
23. Came home from S. W. M Larty - sowed oats - sowed onions seed - E. W. Maxwell child very sick
24. Haled my meet to the factory
25. Sabath day - drove home
26. Started to the factory with S. H. M Larty
27. Came home from the factory
28. Went to S. H. M Larty for his wagon.
29. Haled manure - 6 loads
30. Haled manure 14 loads
31. Helped Jack Baggett to role logs - the boyes haled manure.

April 1849

1. Sabath day - at home to day - S. W. Mlarty and Bingley came to se us
2. Haled manure (12 loads) and howed the gardin and beded out our sweet potatoes
3. Haled manure to day - 14 loads
4. Haled manure to day - 14 loads
5. Roled logs for Asa Sewel - the boyes haled manure - 4 loads
6. Roled logs for Canidy Entrican - the boyes went to mill
7. Roled logs for pap and myself done in good time Canidy and Esther stayed all night
8. Sabath day at home to day.
9. Commenced planting corn - planted the orched
10. Planted my pach below the house - went to S. W. M Larty - smith shop.
11. Cliped some sheep - plowed some in the nurcery - very dry
12. Worked on the scool house - Alexander cliped the sheep
13. Worked on the scool house.
14. Went to Villarica - bought two pair of shoes
15. Sabath day at home - snowing very fast - George W. M Larty came to se us to day.
16. Put my bacon in the ashes to day - 15 hams - 12 sholders - 4 midlings - the boyes plowed to day - sick to day - bones aking - vegitation very much kiled with snow.
17. Worked on my grafts - sick all day. Children started to scool.
18. Came home from S. W. M Larty - Mr. Freman was buryed to day.
20. Went with the children to S. W. M Larty and inoculated them with the cow poc. Parkes Stricklin and Mary came to se us.
21. At home - it still is very dry and cold - it looks like we would make no crop.
22. John Baggett and wife came to se us - John and me went to Mr. Baggets
23. Done different kinds of work
24. Worked on the scool house.
25. Went to mill - bought books of Mr. Wordlaw
26. helped Freeman to roled logs - $4.95 cents
27. Laying off corn ground
28. do do

29. Sabath
30. Planted corn the old field

May 1849

1. Scaterd manure
2. do do
3. Thursday went to the shop
4. Wint to the cort ground - the boyes sprouted the old field.
5. Saterday worked on our leathes. Ann went to church.
6. Sabath day at home to day - fine rain
7. Worked on my apple trees
8. Worked on my apple trees and howed corn - John C. Whitley worked to day.
9. Worked at my house lumber - Whitley
10. Hewed logs to dy with Whitley
11. Worked at getting logs
12. Planted my sweet potatoes
13. Sabath day at home
14. Monday - trimed my apple trees - sick in the evening - the boyes replanted corn
15. Made one pair shoes for Bingley and went to mill
16. Came home from mill
17. Sprouted oats to day
18. Went to S. W. M Larty - came back and started to Atlanta
19. Drove to Atlanta - traded and drove out one mile.
20. Sabath day at home
21. Plowed corn to day
22. Plowed corn and apple trees
23. Plowed corn to day Wilson and Bingley came to se us
24. Cut wheat - Mr. Endsley and Mr. Miller and Binbley and Mary helped me
25. do do
26. Went to S. W. M Larty after my chairs
27. Sabath day at home to day
28. Went to Smiths mill - sold my fodder at 50 cents per hundred wt.
29. Went to Villarica and Georges to a sowing
30. Plowed corn - clear day - Heavy had the croop very bad
31. Plowed to day

June 1849

1. Friday plowing corn - Alexander went to Parkes Stricklins
2. Went to church and then to S. W. M Larty
3. Sabath day - went to church
4. Went to John M Larty for his stears
5. Loaded my waggon and started to market - lay at Howells Fery
6. Got my wheat ground at Donehoos mill
7. Drove to Atlanta - sold my flower at 3 and 3 1/2

8. Drove to John M Larty
9. Hevy storm in the morning - drove home and cut wheat for pap in the evening
10. Sabath day at home
11. Cut wheat for pap - hevy storm at night our land washed very bad
12 Commenced halling my timber for my house a grate deal of rain to day.
13. Worked at halling lumber
14. Worked at halling lumber - John C. Whitley worked
15. Worked at haling lumber -
16. Saterday haled some to day - Ann and me went to John M Larty on a visit.
17. Sabath day at John and Robert Bensons - came home in the evening
18. Commenced laying by the old field and thrashed John Baggetts wheat - 3 bushels and James Smihs wheat 5 bushel - I was very sick all night
19. The boyes thrashed granpaps oats and wheat - 12 bushels - I was very sick all day and night.
20. Thrashed at my own wheat - I am some better to day
21. Finished thrashing my wheat - 50 bushels - I had 16 1/2 acres in wheat
22. Commenced thrashing paps wheat
23. Finished thrashing paps wheat 29 1/2 bushels
24. Sabath day - went A. McKelvys to hear Wynn preach
25. Plowed some commenced thrashing Asa Sewells wheat - very warm and dry
26. Thrashed Mr. Sewells wheat - 29 bushels and 1/2
27. Thrashed John C. Whitleys wheat 33 bushels - thrashed Mr. Meeks wheat - 16 bushels - some rain - I plowed our sweet potatoes and apple grafts
28. Plowed in the fore noon done a grate half days work and thrashed Willis Finches wheat - 14 bushels - plowed some in the evening
29. Plowed in the morning and thrashed some of John F. Morris wheat 7 1/2 bushels - plowed in the evening - hevy rain
30. Plowed some in the morning - thrashed some in the evening - finished thrashing to day - John F. Morris had 21 1/2 bushels

July 1849

1. Sabath day I went to Jackson Baggett
2. Cut oats - Robert Miller cut for me
3. Mr. Miller cut for me to day
4. Cut oats to day - Anthony and me cut to day
5. Finished cuting oats to day and thrashed Mr. Rights wheat - 6 bushels - 2 1/2 for Isac McKevy
6. Finished plowing our corn and finished tying our oats and haled in paps oats.
7. Haled in my oats - like for rain - I have 351 shocks of oats
8. Sabath day at home.
9. Haled lumber for my house - went to S. W. M Larty
10. Haled oats for S. W. Mlarty
11. Went to the mines and home - rain all day - our child very sick.
12. Stuck our lumber and cleaned our grafts.

13. Very sick in the fore noon - Mr. Wordlaw came with book - I bought $1.30 cent worth of him - our scool broke up to day.
14. Put our wheat out to sun - thrashed John Maqouirk wheat - 2 1/2 bu. I have my wheat very dry and anough to do me this year of good wheat.
15. Sabath day at home
16. Seteled with C. C. Neil for our scool - $4.50 cents and settle with Mr. Finch for my lumber - $48.31 1/2 cents
17. Went to S. H. M Larty to mill with 12 bushels of wheat
18. Went to Villarica with my flower - sold at 3 1/2 cents per lb. Came to S. W. M Larty at night.
19. Came home gathered some peaches.
20. Went to muster at Campbelton - very wit day - stayed at Thomas Bullards at night.

Photo: An old-time ferry crossing a river. www.archives.gov

21. At Campbellton - wet day - no muster to day - river very high - bad crossing the river.
22. Sabath day - the scool commenced to day - gathered peaches to day went to S. H. M Larty's with one load - stayed all night - very wet.
23. The boys fetched another load and we came home after night.
24. I was very sick all day - Mother was very sick too - it is the wetest time I ever saw this time of year.
25. Done no work
26. done no work very wet
27. Done no work.
28. Went to Smith's mill very wet

29. sabath day

Arch visited, Bullard (Henley) House - mentioned on previous page. Photo by John Bailey, 2014

30. Gather peaches to day very wet
31. Gathered peaches - it has rained nearly every day this month.
(this in pencil - Danville Ala - Gibson Ville Ala November 31st 1871)
Family record of J. R. and M. C. Farmer
Joseph R. Farmer was born April the 14, 1825 - Mary C. Farmer his wife was born March 15, 1835 - Selinah A. Farmer was born April 15, 1855 - Elizabeth L. Farmer was born April 20, 1857 - Susanah C. V. Farmer was born Jan 16, 1860 - Joseph A. D. Farmer was born June 21, 1862 - A. C. Weems was born Nov. 27, 1848 - Mary M. Weems was born Sept 17, 1874 Joseph R. Farmer departed this life Oct 14, 1863 - Susanah C. W. Farmer departed this life apr 7, 1869 - Selinah A. Farmer departed this life 19 day Aug 1876

August 1849

1. Wedsday a good deal of rain - we are still gathering peaches.
2. Very wet day - the boys haled peaches - I made a pair of shoes for my self
3. Went to the scoolhouse - grate rains to day - we have been haling peaches for some time.
4. Gathered one load of peaches and went to the cort ground
5. Sabath day at home
6. Went to S. W. M Larty to make shoes - worked at making shoes
7. made two pair of shoes
8. Made two pair of shoes - came home from S. W. M Larty
9. Commenced working on my house.
10. went to Smiths mill for joysts - but they never sawed them
11. Sowed the turnips to day and went to S. W. M Larty for his brad axe and the boys fenced the foder.
12. sabath day - clear
13. Monday worked at getting joysts - Robert Miller John Endsley - Parkes Stricklin

worked for me to day.
14. worked at the joysts the same hands worked.
15. Worked at framing to day - the same hands worked.
16. The same hands worked.
17. Worked on the house.
18. worked on the house.
19. sabath day - went to Parkes Stricklins
20. Came home - the boys pull foder.
21. Worked on house
22. do do
23. do do
24. do do
25. Worked some - heavy rain
26. sabath day at home in the fore noon - went to Parkes
27. Puled fodder for Parkes
28. do do
29. do do
30. do do
31. Went to Campbellton to muster.
Births of E. W Maxwell family
Mary Cornelia Maxwell was born Dec 24, 1833 - Mangum Calhoun Maxwell was born March 8, 1836 - Elizabeth Ann Maxwell was born May 18, 1838 - Latelia Caroline Maxwell was born Aug 9, 1840 - Margaret Ann Elisabath Maxwell was born Sep 29, 1845 - William Archibald Maxwell was born Sept 17, 1848 - David Alexander Maxwell was born April 11, 1851 - Edwin Wilson Maxwell was born Sept 12, 1855; Margaret Maxwell departed this life April 16, 1866 - Mangum C. Maxwell departed this life in Ms that is we suppose so Elizabeth Ann Maxwell departed this life Aug 27, 1839.

September 1849
1. Saturday at Parkes Stricklins
2. Sabath day came home found all well very cool day.
3. Monday - Parkes came to work to day
4. Worked on the house
5. do do
6. do do
7 do do Parkes stricklin went home - Alexander went with him - pulled some fodder.
8. Pulled fodder to day
9. Sabath day at home
10. Worked at the house
11.do do finished the fodder
12. Worked at the house
13 do do
14 Worked on the road to day Alexander and myself

15. Gathered our apples - 55 bushels and kiled a beef
16. Sabbath day at home
17. Worked at my house Parkes worked to day.
18. Worked at the house (days spent on his house are numbered in the margin)
19. do
20 do
21. do
22. Finished weather boarding my house and went to muster but their was no muster - Thomas Bullard and Wm. Maqouirk stayed with me all night.
23. Sabbath day at home
24. Helped John Whitley to raise his house.
25. Went to the shop to get the mules shod
26. Started to Atlanta
27. Drove to Atlanta - sold our apples at 87 1/2 cents
28. Drove home
29. went to muster at Cronanera the people behaved very bad
30. Sabath day

October 1849

1. General election
2. Went to the shop and to Villarica - a grate deal of rain
3. Came home from Wilson and commenced getting rock for my chimney
4. Went the shop-do-Villarica
5. Came home from the shop do
6. Worked at getting rock
7. Sold our apples 24 1/3 bushels 1.00 per bushel made a missake in the day
8. Payed Mr. C. H. Neil for my scooling - 6.90 cents
9. Worked at getting rock and commenced halling paps corn
10. Haled corn for pap
11. Frost this morning (hands drawn pointing to this entry 1st frost)
12. Shucked paps corn
13. Cribed paps corn - very tired
14. Sabath day
15. Commenced gathering my corn
16. Pulled some corn and went to John Endsley corn shucking
17. Haled some corn. I made one pair of shoes for C. B. M Larty
18. Made shoes for my own family to day
19. Made shoes to day
20. Made shoes in the fore noon - done no work in the evening
21. sabath day at home
22. Shucked my corn and raised my crib
23. Helped Willis Finch on his dam
24. Cribed my corn
25. Helped Willis Finch on his dam.

26. Put up my shucks and gathered the balance of my corn
27. Went to S. W. M Larty to a frollic
28. Came home from S. W. M Larty - John Millir and Even Flow came to se us from North Carolina.
29. Went to John Baggett corn shucking
30. Went to George M Larty corn shucking.
31. Sick to day hunted some for my hogs

November 1849

1. The boys dug potatoes - I was sick
2. Finished digging potatoes and Alexander and me went to Martins corn shucking - worked late did not finish
3. Done no work to day - very plesent day - I shot a good many squirls.
4. Sabath day - the old black cow calfed today
5. Worked at getting rock for my chimney
6. Sowed wheat
7. Sowed wheat - went to S. W. M Larty's
8. Helped Wilson with corn
9. Worked do
10. Went to Villarica - came home child very sick.
11. Sabath day at home - our child very sick all day and night.
12. done no work - Alexander went to help his uncle S. W. M larty corn
13. I went to the mill and shop.
14. Worked at getting chimney rock
15. Worked at getting rock.
16. helped Isac McKelvy to raise his house - very sick all night.
17. Done no work sick all day.
18. Sabath day went to John Baggetts
19. Went to se Winters - stayed at R. Bensons.
20. Came home from Bensons and hunted my hogs - found thim.
21. Went after my bull - brought him home.
22. Went to Prayes mill for lumber.
23. Worked at different things.
24. Hunted hogs to day.
25. Sabath day at home - very wet.
26. Hunted hogs.
27. Hunted Hogs
28. Hunted hogs
29. Hunted hogs.
30. Built hog pens to day - two pens

December 1849

1. Saterday - hunted hogs to day - caught 3 hogs
2. Sabath day at home a grate many people here to day.

3. Caught two hogs.
4. The boyes haled wood to day - I caught one hog
5. Caught one hog
6. Kiled 6 hogs to day - 531 lbs. - caught one sow and pigs-cut 3 bore pigs and marked 2 sow pigs.
7. Hunted hogs to day and salted my meet.
8. Helped Wilson to catch some of his hogs - caught 7 of his - Morgan hogs
9. Sabath day at home
10. Monday hunted hogs.
11. Hunted hogs.
12. Helped Isac McKelvy to rais his house and shuck corn at night
13. Made one pair of shoes for John M Larty
14. Hilped pap kill hogs.
15. Cut up paps meet and went to Villarica
16. Sabath day at home.
17. Caught three hogs to day - 392 lbs.
18. Started to market
19. Drove to Atlanta
20. Traded to day
21. Drove home - found all well grate storm last night
22. Hunted hogs - found one
23. Sabath day at home.
24. hunted my hogs - found one
25. Christmas day at home all day.
26. Found two of my hogs.
27. Hunted hogs - kiled one 109 lbs.
28. Went to D. Whites
29. Went to Merietta
30. Came home from D. White
31. Went to S. W. M Larty.

January 1850

1. At S. W. M Larty all day
2. Came home
3. hunted hogs to day.
4. Went to John M Larty's to help him move his house-moved it 165 yards.
5. moved the house again to day.
6. Sabath day at home
7. Went to election.
8. Made one pair of shoes for G. M. Larty
9. Made shoes to day
10. Made shoes
11. Made shoes to day for paps negroes - very tired of shoe making - Ann and me went to Jackson Baggetts

12. Came home from Jackson Baggetts-went to John M Larty to se Winter
13. sabath day at home
14. went to Campbelltown with Mr. Winn
15. Helped John C. Whitley to raise smokehouse.
16. Went after rock for chimney
17. Hunted hogs to day
18. hunted hogs to day - found some of them - sold 25 apple trees to Joshiah Kiker.
19. Went to mill to day.
20. Sabath day at home Mr. Smith preached to day at paps
21. Done no work to day - a grate deal of rain
22. Went to old Mr. Winns sale - property sold very high
23. At home - sold some apple trees
24. Caught two of my hogs and kiled one at home - 388 lbs. Pork.
25. Bated my hog pen for my tame hog
26. Caught 3 hogs at night
27. Sabath day at home
28. Sold John C. Whitley a bunch of hogs for a rifle gun and seven dollars - sold Jackson Baggett a cow and calf for ten dollars-caught one hog
29. Hunted hogs to day
30. Commenced clearing
31. Commenced building chimney-I am 38 years old to day.

February 1850

1. Worked at the chimney
2. Went to my hog pens - very wet
3. Sabath day - caught one hog
4. Very cold - done no work
5. kiled hogs to day - 11 head

6 - 9 Worked on Chimney

10. Sabath day at home
11. Mr. Winter worked to day.
12. Do do
13. Rained all day
14. snowed all day

15 Worked on chimney

16. Mr. Winter went home to day Went to Villarica to day
17. Sabath day - Mr. Smith preached at paps
18. Very wet day - went to Wm. MaQouirk for his ladder and windlass
19. worked on the Chimney

20-23 Worked on chimney

24. Sabath day at home.

25.- 28 Worked on chimney

March 1850

1. Worked on chimney
2. do do
3. sabath day at home
4. Bad of stich in my side, finished the chimney
5. done no work to day.
6. Thrashed my oats
7. Mr. Winter and me painted the chimney.
8. went to the mill - stayed at S. W. M larty.
9. Went to the shop got two scoters made came home sick
10. sabath day at home
11. Went to S. H. M Larty to sow oats
12. Commenced sowing oats
13. Sowed oats to day.
14. sowed some in the morning
15. Started to Atlanta-
16. Drove in to Atlanta - traded with Norcross - sold bacon at 6 cents
17. Drove home sabath day - after night Parkes Stricklin came to day
18. Parkes and my self pined for work
19. Commenced working on the doors
20. worked do do
21. do do
22. Parkes worked do and I worked on the road.
23. Worked on the road
24. Sabath day at home to day - I went to Parkes on the hunt of Robert and back that night
25. Monday - the boyes went to sow oats but came back John Vann (sp) died last night
26. went to help Wm Maqouirk to role logs.
27. Roled logs for my self-grate snow storm
28. Done no work today
29. Went to the saw mill for lumber
30. Went to John Endsley log roling and went to S. W. M Larty at night
31. sabath day came home from S. W. M larty

April 1850

1. Parkes commenced laying the flore
2. thru 6. finished floors
7. sabath Parkes went home - Alexander took him home.
8. The boyes plowed and I helped Maxwell to tole logs.
9. The boyes plowed and I work on the hearth stone.
10. Rain all day - layed my hearth in the chimney
11. Went to John C. Whitley's chopin frolic
12. Plowed to day and sprouted
13. Plowed to day - Alexander and Robert planted their pac of cotton

14. Sabath day at Brother John he was very sick
15. Fixed for planting cotton.
16. Commenced plantin cotton
17. Built fence in the forenoon and went to John M larty for cotton seed
18. Planted cotton
19. Planted cotton
20 Finished planting cotton to day - meeting at paps to day.
21. Sabath day - meeting at paps to day a grate meny people their
22. worked at ridging of corn ground
23. Commenced laying of corn - layed of the fresh field one way
24. layed it of the other way
25. stuck of my cotton
26. Roled logs for A. McKelvy
27. Alexander roled logs for Mr. Entrycan - I went to Villarica - bought a cote
28. Sabath day - came home from S. H. M Larty
29. Went to help S. H. M Larty to make rails
30. Commenced planting corn the fresh field

May 1850

1. Planting corn to day and cuting logs on the old field - roled the logs on the old field - finished planting the fresh field
2. The boyes braking the midle of the fresh field and I am bruning the logs on the old field
3. Went to the shop and cort ground for the make my return and the boyes plowed.
4. Went with Anne to David Whites on a visit.
5. Went to church with D. White a prespetarion preached a grate deal of rain for two days.
6. Came home from D. Whites - found all well
7. Planted our sweet potatoes and commenced working our cotton
8. Sprouted our corn
9. Roled logs for A. McKelby - Alexander choped logs for granpap
10. Commenced planting the old field
11. Finished planting the old field
12. Sabath day went to S. W. M Larty
13. Worked at our cotton
14. Roled logs for granpap a heap of hands worked slow
15. Howing in the forenoon and roled logs for J. C. Whitley and the children howed cotton
16. The boys plowed and the children and myself howed the cotton
17. Worked at the cotton and the boys plowed in the corn ground
18. Worked at the corn
19. Sabath day at the meeting at paps - a grate many people their Mr. Smith preached from Romans - Mr. Greegs preached from the Acts of the Apostals - what shal I do to be saved.

20. Plowed cotton and the boys howed
21. Rain in the morning - went to S. W. M larty to the shop - clear in the evening the boys howed.
22. Worked at the cotton very tired to night
23. Worked at the cotton lite rain in the but not enough to stop the work
24. Worked at the cotton
25. Finished working our cotton over the second time
26. Sabath day at home - crops is very backward for this time of the year - I can not se our cotton from the house
27. Plowed corn to day very tired to night
28. Started to Atlanta layed the other side of river
29. Traded in Atlanta - sold my Bacon at 6 1/2 cents - bought coffe at 8 1/2 lbs to the dollar - rice 2 1/2 sugar 13 lbs.
30. Drove home found all well
31. Went to Exekels foks (Ezekiel Polk) sale
(in pencil)
Moved the fodder - gave room to thrash oat - haled wood
in margin (Jan 9, 1872 started two letters to Georgia)

June 1850

1. Howed corn to day meeting at paps to day
2. Sabath day - meeting at paps to day Mr. Lingo preached
3. Plowed cotton Alexander and my self and the children howed cotton
4. Plowed and howed to day very tire
5. Plowed in the forenoon and commenced cutting wheat finished plowing my cotton the third time
6. Finished cutting my orleans wheat and went to mill and the shop.
7. Came home from mill - it is eighteen year this day since Anne and me was maried - their has been a great many ups and downs since that day
8. Helped granpap to move his fence round his new ground - finished working over our cotton the 4th time
9. Sabath day at home the children went to the babist meeting to day
10. Commenced plowing the old corn field
11. Finished plowing the old field the first time - we need rain very bad - dry and dusty
12. Received a gin of talor to day the boys working for granpap - sold one dollars of coffe
13. Haled in my orleans wheat and thrashed it.
14. Cleaned my orleans wheat - 16 bushels - thrashed J. F. Morris orleans 14 1/2 bushel - very sick at night
15. Thrashed J. F. Morris spring wheat 22 1/2 bushels
16. Sabath day went to meeting
17. Howed cotton all day
18. Thrashed Mr. Rains wheat 47 bushels

19. Thrashed Mr. Sewells wheat cleaned 20 bushels
20. Cleaned the balince of Mr. Sewells wheat 33 1/2 bushels - 53 1/2 in all thrashed - Lewis Maqouires wheat 16 1/2
21. Thrashed one load of Mr. Harps 5 bushels - thrashed Mr Thomassons wheat - 37 1/2 bushels
22. Thrashed J. Biggers wheat 3 1/4 bushels - tied paps wheat and thrashed some of it - rain lite
23. Sabath day at home to day - the children went to hear Winn at the new meeting house
24. Thined corn and thrashed the ballence of paps wheat 27 1/2 bushels
25. Finished thining my corn and commenced howing cotton
26. Howed cotton to day - very tired
27. Howed cotton to day
28. Thrashed John C. Whitlley wheat 17 1/2 bushels
29. thrashed Willis Finchs wheat - John Maqouirk died to day
30. Went to se John Maqouirk berried - Mr. Neace preached a smart erecetement (sp?) among the people

William Gilliam our father departed this life July 1st 1850
David Maxwell departed this life July 8, 1850
Because we do not know the day Crist bids us always watch and pray
(coffin and flowers drawn in margin)

July 1850

1. Cleaned my late wheat 10 bushels and commenced thrashing A. McKelvy wheat.
2. Finished thrashing A. McKelvy wheat 79 1/2 bushels John Shearers wheat 17 bushels
3. Howed cotton to day - Alexander plowed corn very tired to night
4. Finished howing over our cotton fifth time - went to meeting - Mr. Lingo adressed the people on Liverty both sivel and religious - commenced laying my corn
5. Plowed in the forenoon - rain at 12 o'clock - thrashed C. Wrights wheat 11 1/2 bushels.
6. Plowed in the forenoon - rain at 12 o'clock - thrashed John Endsley wheat 11 1/2 bushels the ground is very wet.
7. Sabath day - went to S. H. M Larty
8. went to S. W. M Larty for to cut oats - cut oats all day
9. cut oats to day - very tired to night.
10. cut oats to day - rain very heavy
11. Cut to day very tired and headake at night.
12. Came home from S. H. M Larty and thrashed Mr. Meeks wheat 13 1/2 bushels - thrashed one load for John Entrican 6 1/2 bu. - worked my grafts and plowed my young archet (?) - my cotton is very grasy and it is so wet I can not plow.
13. Plowed some of the ground very wet
14. Sabath day at home - a grate deal of rain - went to Wm Maqouirk at night.
15. Scraped cotton it is very dirty

16. Scraped cotton to day - very tired
17. Plowed cotton to day and children scraped cotton
18. Plowed cotton and children scraped cotton - Ann and me went to meeting - old ant Jinny M larty died to day.
19. Plowed cotton - I unwell with titeness in my head - Brother John M Larty has been sick for some time taken worse last night - heard from him to day some better
20. Plowed cotton to day - went to se brother John found him some better - received a letter Wm W. White stating that father in law had died on the first of June 1850.
21. Sabath day meeting at the cort ground - very warm day
22. Plowed cotton baught of Jacob Schoenfeld one dress for Mary one vest for Alexander. Dress 2.10 cents vest 2.00.
23. Went to hall oats haled one load John C. Whitley haled for my (?) went back stayed all night at S. W. M Larty.
24. Came home with another load a pease
25. Plowed corn in the forenoon - rain in the evening
26. Plowed corn to day
27. Finished plowing corn to day by 12 o'clock - very warm but growing weather - Anne and me went on a visit to G. W. M Larty.
28. Sabath day went to S. W. M Larty - came home in the evening
29. Howed corn in the forenoon - John Whitley and me made a table for him - the boys howing for granpap in his newground
30. Howed for granpap to day the worst howing I ever done - we have worked very hard this year in our crop and thrashing.

August 1850

1. I went to mill the boys howing for granpap - I am sick to day.
2. I went with cotton to S. W. M Larty - put posts under his gin house
3. Baught no. 159 in the 2 of Carrol from John Callton - came to meeting at the new meeting house.
4. At meeting to day a good many of the friends with us.
5. At meeting to day meeting closed to day - very litle stir among the people.
6. Thrashed John Baggets wheat 4 1/2 bushels - thrashed Wm Maqouirks wheat 7 bushels - I have been sick for several days - very sick to night
7. Better this morning but very weak
8. Washed our late wheat this morning about helf swam away and brlowed (sic) the ballence of our wheat
9. still dry
10. Went to the camp meeting
11. Sabath day at the camp meeting - came home in the evening
12. Started to the fare in Atlanta
13. Drove to Atlanta
14. At the fare more people their than I saw at one time
15. Still at the fare
16. Started home stayed at Parkes Stricklins

17. Drove home to day no rain yet
18. Sabath day went to John Carlton - great rain their to day
19. Came home from John Carlton - Parkes commenced laying my flore to day loft flore.
20. Worked at the flore to day Parkes worked to day
21. Parkes worked til midle of day and then went to the lodge
22. Parkes worked to day.
23. Parkes very unwell to day
24. Parkes worked to day very grate storm - Parkes went home to day
25. Sabath day Ann sick to day - Parkes came to day
26. Worked on the sash to day
27. thru 31. do do

Went to Mark Mucelwreath on a visit

September 1850

1. Sabath day came home from Mark Mucelwreath
2. Commenced pulling fodder
3. Puled fodder
4. Puled fodder head ake to day put up two stacks to day. 88 bundles
5. Puled fodder to day put up one stack 400 bundles I worked to day with a very sore hand
6. Went to mill and Alexander and my self worked on the mutting house - put up one stack of fodder 500 bundles.
7. Tyed fodder in the morning put up one stack 700 bundles - rain to day very plesent showers to day finished putting up my new field fodder to day 2400 bundles
8. Sabath day at home to day the children went to the Baptist meeting
9. Parkes worked at the Sash to day.
10. thru 14. do do
15. Sabath day
16. Parkes worked to day at the parteteen (sic)
17. do do
18. do do went to the lodge
19. Worked on the partetion
20. Run the stairs to day
21. Made a shuter for the room door - Parkes wint home - Ann and me went to S. W. M Larty on a visit.
22. Sabath day started home met Pap and Mam John Morris and Caroline turned back to Wilsons their all day.
23. Picked cotton I picked 101 lbs.
24. Picked in the forenoon Parkes came this evening
25. Hunted a screw pin cut it to day.
26. Worked at the screw pin
27. Parkes and Alexander went to muster Mr. Finch and Hearvy tryed to hal the pin but failed haled some tender.

28. Saterday W. H. M larty haled for me to day we haled the pin to day with hard work
29. Sabath day at home to day
30. Parkes worked today
Parkes worked for me 50 days on my house and 19 on my screw. George worked for me 15 days on the screw

October 1850

1. Parkes worked to day we worked on the screws
2. do
4. do
5. do half the day
6. sabath day at home
7. Parkes worked to day
8. thru 11. do do Parkes wint home
12. We worked on the screw do do
13. Sabath day at home.
14. Parkes worked to day
15. do
16. do
17. raised the screw
18. Parkes worked to day he went home
19. We worked on the screw
20. Sabath day pap and me went to se John he very sick
21. Worked at the Mechun house and I went to cort
22. We worked on the house picked some cotton
23. gined some
24. Packed one bag for Wilson
25. Gined to day
26. Gined to day and packed two bags
27. Sabath day very cool day
28. Gined one bag for granpap
29. Gined for Mr. Sewell to day
30. Gined and packed cotton for Mr. Sewell one bag 455 to 519
31 Gined to day packed one bag for Mr. Garm over 650 lbs

November 1850

1. Puled corn to day
2. John C. Whitley haled corn for me today we picked cotton to day
3. Sabath day at home John M Larty came to se us
4. We picked cotton to day and run the gin
5. Packed one bag for S. W. M Larty and picked cotton the finest time for gathering crops I ever saw
6. We all picked cotton - to picked 556 lbs

7. The boys gined to day and I went to muster
8. Gined cotton to day for George Allen and packed two bags
9. Gined cotton to day for Entrican
10. sabath day at home to day
11. Gined cotton for Jackson Baggett and W. H. Maqouirk one bag a peace
12. gined one bag for Mrs. Ferris
13. Gined cotton for S. W. M Larty and I went to Thomas Entriken house raising the hands worked very lazy indeed
14. Gined cotton for S. W. M Larty and packed two bags for him
15. Picked cotton to day
16. Picked cotton to day
17. Sabath day very heavy frost
18. Ann had her (erased) to day it is very cold Hearvy and Anna and Charity was here.
19. I went to Villarica and the boyes gined cotton very wet day
20. Gined to day
21. Gined to day
22. Hunted the sheap very wet day
23. Gined to day
24. Sabath day at home wint to R. Benson
25. Fined to day
26. Gined cotton to day
27. Gined to day and started to Atlanta
28. Drove near to Atlanta
29. Sold our cotton at 12 1/2 cents
30. Drove home to day very wet trip

December 1850

1. Sabath day at home
2. Gined some to day
3. Gined at my own cotton to day - wet day - gined 738 lbs from the house - started to Atlanta
4. Drove to Atlanta
5. Sold our cotton at 12 1/2 cents
6. Traded for our nusserye and
7. drove out Robert Gilliam to
8. Sabath day
9. Drove home
10. Done no work to day
11. Gined to day helped Mr. Sewel to kill hogs
12. Haled corn to day
13. Haled corn to day
14. Finished halling corn packed cotton for S. H. M larty two bales
15. Sabath day at home
16. Gined cotton to day for S. Smith and Asbery Entryken damp day

17. Gined to day cool day
18. Picked cotton out of the patch - cotton is very hard to pick clean
19. Done no worke to day the boys went to mill very wet
20. Haled wood and worked on the meeting house.
21. Hunted hogs to day found none of them Alexander went home with uncle Robert
22. Sabath day we went down to paps - John Morris and Caroline was their very wet day - the children is very bad with the hooping caugh
23. Done no work to day
24. Helped pap to kill his hogs and received some cotton into the Machien house.
25. Christmas day went to S. W. M Larty's to squirl hunt our children is very bad off with the hooping caugh
26. Went and fixed Margaret Maxwells clock sold two dollars worth apple trees to Jeames White.
27. very wet day done no work to day
28. Bingley bad off to day went to S. W. M Larty
29. Sabath day went to day to se Bingley stayed all night
30. Came home the boys gined to day
31. Dark wet day went to se Bingley - he is very bad thes ended the year 1850.

January 1851

1. Kiled Margaret Maxwell's hogs and went to the lodge - cold night
2. Snowing very fast and very cold and snowed all night
3. Clear day hunted hogs in the afternoon found some of them and kiled 5 after midnight when we got done with them
6. Went to the election payed Samuel Watson for schooling seven dollars and fifty cents - I will try and not put my name to paper after this without I expect to benifit.
7. Went to Campbellton to se Carllon the boys picked cotton.
8. We all picked cotton to day - Mary and Mangum Maxwell helped us to day
9. Hunted hogs in the forenoon and the boys gined Mr. Entrikens house cotton
10. Finished picking cotton out of the patch very pleasant day - glad we are done picking
11. Gined one bag for Mr. Sewell
12. Sabath day wrote to John P. M Larty
13. Worked on the meeting house
14. Worked on the meeting house
15. Went to the lodge and the boys worked on the house
16. Helped S. W. M Larty to catch three hogs
17. Hunted hogs found 4 of my hogs
18. Very cold - went to meeting so cold that their was no sermon preached
19. Sabath day at home
20. Kiled six hogs to day and marked six - cut two bores went to S. H. M Lartys
21. Kiled 4 hogs Wilson and Hearvey helped me to kill them
22. Salted my meet and the boys gined helped A. McKelvy to role logs - wet day
23. Packed one bale and hunted pateridges

24. Went to help S. M. M Larty to raise his mill traugh
25. Cut logs
26. Sabath day at home
27. Went after geese to Mr. Baggetts
28. Haled cotton and went to S. W. M Larty
29. Came home and kiled my hogs
30. Worked at our meet
31. Termendious cold I am 39 years old - haled wood I went with S. W. M Larty to bate hog pen

February 1851

1. Cut basket wood and salted our meet
2. Sabath day at home
3. Gined cotton to day
4. Gined to day
5. Went to Vanzants log roling
6. Packed cotton to day
7. Worked at our cotton David White and Selina and children came to se us.
8. Gined some.
9. Sabath day at home a grate many here to day - John Garman and wife came to se us.
10. David and Selina returned home - grate raines last night - I was very sick all night
11. Cool this morning the boys cut logs
12. The boys cut logs and I helped Mr. Entriken to role logs
13. Roled my logs to day and hands worked very well done by 12 o clock rain in the evening very cold.
14. Gined cotton to day
15. Grate rains last night and this morning
16. Sabath day very cold
17. We went after our bulls to Mr. Camps - plesent day one of them is the poorest cow brute alive
18. Commenced plowing to day
19. The boyes plowed and I helped Lewis Magown to role logs and Ann and me went to S. W. M Larty's
20. Went to S. W. M Larty stayed all night - grate rains at night
21. Came home
22. Made one pair of shoes for Alexander
23. Sabath day E. W. Maxwell came home from N. C. to day
24. Went to S. W. M Larty.
25. Started to Atlanta
26. Traded in Atlanta
27. Started home
28. Drove home the boyes haling manure

March 1851

1. Haled manure to day
2. Sabath day Ann and me went to John Baggett and then to W. Maqouirk
3. Commenced sowing oats
4. Payed Talors agent for his gin $80.00. Finished sowing oats to day Anne and myself went to A. McKelvy at night
5. The boyes haled at the manure and I went to Villarica to engage my meet
6. Worked at making a soap traught
7. Rained all night - all day made shoes to day for pap
8. Made shoes for Mary to day - the boyes went to mill
9. Sabath day went to E. W. Maxwells
10. The boyes went with our bacon to Villarica
11. Commenced ridgen our cotton land very tired to night
12. ridged cotton ground to day
13. Ridged cotton to day Went to meeting to day
14. Ridged cotton to day
15. Gined some and plowed some rain - Robert Gilliam came to se us
16. Sabath day Sabath scool commenced to day
17. Plowed some wind very high - cleaned out the stables
18. Plowed to day - Robert Gilliam went home to day
19. Plowed at the old field to day and yesterday
20. Commenced haling manure on the old field plesent day 13 loads
21. The whipperwill hollowed this morning - haled manure to day 14 loads
22. Very wet day in the forenoon John Baggett cut our horse and bull S. H. M Larty and W. Maqouirk and Jackson Baggett helped
23. Sabath day our scool commenced
24. Haling manure all day finished haling
25. Went to mill and to S. W. M Larty for sweet potatoes and the boys went to old Mr. Camps for our bull - set our logs afire - bedded out our sweet potatoes
26. Went to John Baggetts for paps sheep
27. Hunted sheep to day
28. Haled wood to day
29. Dark morning some rain S. W. M Larty and wife and Ann and myself went to John F. Morris on a visit
30. Sabath day went to meeting Mr. Lingo preached and wet day came home in the rain
31. Some rain - went to hunt our stears lost in the woods - commenced planting corn at twelve a clock - earlier than ever I planted at this place - it is warm and showers of rain

A. N. McLarty was born the 31st day of January A. D. 1812 Ann McLarty was born the 29th day of Sept A. D. 1814, This 19th day of April 1851

April 1851

1. Dark morning some rain last night went to hunt our stears found them rain all day

2. Planted corn to day
3. Some cooler to day planted corn to day
4. Planted corn to day finished the cotton ground by 12 a clock and commenced on the other piece
5. Rain to day the boyes went to mill and the Smith shop I made steps
6. Sabath day at Sabath scool I did not like the way it was caried on
7. Planted some corn
8. Last night a constant thunder
9. Scatered manure to day
10. The boyes scatered manure I helped Thomas Entriken to role logs.
11. Commenced planting cotton plesent day planted cotton yesterday
12. Finished planting the old field cotton I am very tired to night
13. Sabath day
14. Plowed in the cotton ground
15. Finished planting corn to day very tired to night
16. Commenced planting paps cotton field
17. Finished paps field and commenced on the patch below the house finished the patch below the house
18. Planted the orchet to day finished planting to day
19. Plesent morning Ann and me went to meeting Mr. Smith preached Norton escorted
20. Sabath day we went to meeting Mr. Greegs preached and Mr. Norton
21. Commenced working our corn - headake all day
22. Worked at the corn I went to the shop
23. Worked on the corn
24. Worked on the corn
25. Friday plowed corn in the forenoon - rain in the evening - very cold rain and disagreeable it is so cool that corn and cotton takes a poor start
26. Cotton gust commenced coming up went to meeting to day Morton preached
27. Sabath day went to meeting - Winn preached - Winn preached a very little feeling - went to night to hear Norton preach on faith
28. Fixing to start to Atlanta
29. Started to Atlanta
30. Sold my cotton for 9 cents and started home
(in pencil) a low price for cotton as it takes so much labor

May 1851

1. Drove home found all well
2. The boyes struck of cotton. I went to cort ground
3. I went to Crossamerecort the boyes worked on the meeting house
4. Sabath day at home
5. Went to G. W. M larty he made me two plows for to work cotton
6. Commenced plowing our cotton heavy frost this morning
7. Plowed cotton to day went to lodge

8. Came home plowed cotton
9. Plowed cotton to day dry weather
10. Finished working over our cotton the first time and Anne and me went to S. H. M larty on a visit
11. Sabath day came home from S. H. M larty.
12. Plowed corn to day
13. The boyes plowed - I helped E. W. Maxwell to role logs
14. Plowed corn to day - I went to S. W. MLarty and baught a cow and calf of him for 10 dollars
15. Came home from S. W. Mlarty finished working our corn over
16. Planted peas to day very dry
17. commenced working over our cotton the second time very dry weather
18. Sabath day
19. Howed cotton Parkes and me done no work
20. Pap roled logs to day very warm
21. Anna and me went to Villarica - traded some
22. Came to meeting brother Lingo preached
23. Howed cotton
24. Plowed cotton to day and children howed
25. Sabath day Parkes Stricklin came to se us last night went home this morning - he braught a carridge to pap.
26. Plowed cotton in the forenoon and thined the corn helped granpap to move fence in the evening
27. Plowed cotton to day
28. Howed cotton to day all hands eurg (sp?)
29. Howed to day
30. Howed to day
31. Went to Villarica for brother Freeman

June 1851

1. Sabath day Brother Freeman preached to day and at night
2. Went home with brother Freeman
3. Planted our sweet potatoes and sprouted our oats
4. Finished gining last years cotton
5. Plowed cotton to day
6. Plowed for granpap and howed all hands done a good dayes work
7. The children howed for granpap - Alexander and me went to the shop - It is 19 years since Anne and me was married
8. Sabath day at Sabath scool lite rain to day
9. Plowed cotton to day done a grate dayes plowen
10. Plowed cotton to day and commenced plowing corn
11. Worked on the Machien house and the boyes plowed
12. Commenced thrashing Thomas Entrikens wheat 43 bu and Kilgos wheat 12 1/2 bu
13 Thrashed Asa Sewell wheat very smuty wheat

14. Cleaned Mr. Sewells wheat 70 bushels and thrashed granpaps 22 bushels
15. Sabath day at home
16. Plowed corn to day
17. Plowed to day
18. Thrashed some of John F. Morris wheat
19. Thrashed some for John F. Morris - Sewell 17 bu
20. Finished thrashing for John F. Morris 72 1/2 bushel - shined apple tree to day - Alex Baggett 14 1/4 bushel
21. Willie Clinton wheat to day 37 1/2 bushel - John C. Whitleys 9 1/2 bushels skined a tree
22. Sabath day went to meeting
23. Thrashed 12 bushels for Wiley Clinton - skined a tree to day thrashed 11 bu for Wiley Clinton thrashed 45 for Wm Thompson
24. Thrashed 23 bushels for Thompson and 17 1/2 for Lewis Maqouirk
25. Thrashed Mr. Meeks wheat 10 1/2 bu - Mr. Meeks 6 1/2 do Thrashed E. W. Maxwell wheat 35 bu
26. Plowed in the forenoon and commenced thrashing A. McKelvy wheat in the evening very tired tonight
27. Finished thrashing A. M. Kelvy wheat - cleaned A. McKelvy wheat 76 bushels thrashed C. Wright 8 1/2 bushels
28. Thrashed David Entriken wheat 38 1/2 bushels do John Entriken do 39 bushels
29. sabath day we went to meeting Mr. Lawton preached in the morning and in the evening
30. Commenced cuting oats - the boys plowing cotton thrashed Wm. Maqouirks wheat 13 1/2 lite rain to day done a grate deal of work in this month entirely two much business.

July 1851

Finished cuting oats the boyes plowing cotton tied up our oats and haled them in dry to day - we are sufering for rain very bad.
2. Commenced enocalating my nurcery the boy plowing cotton the children howing corn cotton blossoms a plenty
3. Howing cotton very dry corn looks very bad - my cotton in durty and hard to how
4. went with children to Villarica to the exabition - stayed at S. W. Mlarty all night
5. Came home from S. W. Mlarty howe cotton very dry the crop is failing fast
6. Sabath day
7. Monday howed cotton
8. Howed cotton
9. Finished howing our cotton field by 12 a clock thrashed Canady Entriken wheat 6 1/2 bu - plowed some in the evening
10. Enoculating some to day the boys howing cotton
11. Started to mill at sweet watter
12. Lat at mill all day
13. Sabath day came home from mill

14. The boyes plowed cotton I went after sheap to Jackson Baggetts
15. Done no work to day - cloudy day - the boys howed cotton Ann and me went to S. W. Mlarty
16. Came from S. W. Mlarty the boyes howed cotton
17. went to David Whites
18. Went to Exibition
19. Went to Marietta
20. sabath day came to Parkes Stricklin
21. Came home we had some rain while we were gone
22. Worked at our cotton
23. Worked at our cotton
24. Worked do
25. Worked do
26. Went to Jeames Cort it is dry
27. Sabath day went to meeting
28. The boyes went after the stear to Camp
29. It looks like every thing will burn up for want of rain
30. done no work to day - made a wash traugh
31. Done no work to day - it lookes like the crop would dry up

August 1851

1. Dug a soap traugh to day
2. Cloudy day no rain to day
3. Sabath day G. W. M Larty and wife with us last night and to day - some rain - Sinda married last night a good many negroes at paps
4. Cloudy and like for rain - nice rain in evening
5. Rain
6. Went to the lodge
7. Stayed at S. Mlartys and Charles Polk - Anna and me
8. Came home we went to the sing the teacher and lady came home with us
9. Went to the sing to day
10. Sabath
11. Went to S. W. Mlarty to work on thrasher
13. Sick to day
14. Started to Atlanta - Ann and Alexander and my self drove into Atlanta
15. Traded at Norcross store
16. Drove home found all well
17. Sabath day at home to day
18. Done no work to day - Alexander very sick - we have had a good rain
19. Dark day
20. Dark day and rain
21. rain to day
22. Very little rain to day
23. Finished paps buggy house

24. Sabath day at home
25. Commenced puling foder
26. do do
27. rain
28. Worked at the foder
29. do do
30. Sabath day at the scool

September 1851
1. Puled foder to day
2. do
3. do
4. do do finished puling foder
5. Tied foder and marked some cotton blossoms

dry all this month
(The entries are incomplete and scatered from this point. Pages are missing especially of the Civil War years.)

March
8. Commenced grafting south side of the garden - the first row pound apple - 2 yellow

June - 3 Red June - 4 Hallseeding - 5 Morrison apple - 6 Touwn pippen.
The weather is very wet - no plowing can be done very hevy rains about every other day - we are very backward with our plowing

26. Commenced sowing oats

October 1851
We have picked a good deal of cotton
4. Went to camp meeting in Cobb

Missing entries

very dry weather
18 picked cotton - rain at night
19 Sabath day (in pencil)

January 1st 1852
1.Cloudy to like for rain
February
Cloudy in the evening (months of year written in margin)
April 3 clear & cool
Dates are for January 1852
May 4 nice day

June 5 wet and cold some snow
July 6 Cold windy day
August 7 windy day
Sept 8 cool morning
October 9 Plesent day
Jesse Mcellareath commenced working for me the 16th day of February, 1852
March 8th 1852
Grafting for 1852 - commenced at NW corner to first stone Hallseedlings to second stone pound apple - to 3rd stone toun pippen - to 4 stone Sewell seedlings - to 5 stone red June - to 6 stone Morrisons apple
R. M. Pitman near Nelsons fery want trees
Mr. Umpheyr wants 12 late and 8 early trees

February 1852

Very plesent for this month but very cold - sowed our oats in this month

March 1852

Commenced clearing our new ground planted some corn in this month - very dry and windy in this month very good new ground corn

April 1852

Fine growing month
May fine growing month
June started to Texas but went no farther than Mississippi glad to get home some day weather
July fine growing month
August a plenty of rain
Wilsons wife died on the 25th - grate rains on the 26 and 27th
31 very plesent day the fodder is tere up very day - tained my apple trees to day

January 1853

Father departed this life on 21st of this month aged 77 and 28 days

April

5. Commenced planting corn 2 finished the 6 acre patch
15. commenced sowing oats
18. planted to day
19. planted to day
20. finished to day 11 o'clock planted 33 acres this year
22. roled my new ground logs hard days work
23. Helped Mr. Freeman to role
25. Commenced working our corn in the last years new ground

Lines that plese me
I live for those that love me
for those I know are true
for the heaven that smiles above me
and awaits my spirit too
for all human ties that bind me
for that task by God assigned me
for the bright hopes left behind me
and the good that I can do
I live to learn their story
who've suffered for my sake
to emulate their glory
and follow in their wake
bards martyrs patriots sages
the noble of all ages
whose deeds crowd history's pages
and times grate volume make
I live to hale that season
be gifted minds foretold
when men shall live by reason
and not alone by gold
when man to man united and every wrong thing righted
the whole world shall be lighted
as eden of old
I live to hold communion
with all that is devine
to feel there is a union
twiset nature's hart and mine
to profit by affiction
reap truthes from fields of fiction
grow wiser from conviction
and fulfil each grate design
I live for those who love me
for those who know me true
for the heaven that smiles above me
and awaits my spirit too
for the wrong that needs resistance
for the cause that lacks assistance
for the future in the distance
and the good that I can do
A. N. Mlarty March 27, 1853

May 1853

Very dry throughout this month

June 1853
still very dry no rain

July 1853
Very dry the corn is nerely cut off that is old corn the worst apairence of a crop I ever saw - cotton is very small and white with bloom - a fine rain to day
4. Showery to day
5. A good rain to day - Started to Atlanta - very warm
6. In Atlanta - traded to day
7. Drove home
8. Plowing corn laying by
9. Layed by our sweet potatoes and planted a patch of corn
10. Sabath day lite showers
11. Hevy rain to day in the evening - commenced plowing our cotton
12. Rain to day the ground is wet
13. Plowed at our cotton
14. plowed do do
15. Finished plowing over the cotton
16. Rain today
17. sabath day rain
18. Howed cotton
19. Howed cotton
20. Plowed corn in the new ground rain to day
21. Rain to day worked some
22. Worked at the corn no rain
23. Worked at the corn planting peas
24. sabath day at meeting
25. Worked our newground - I am planting peas yet
26. Worked mothers cotton and commenced plowing my cotton and sprouting my new ground
27. do do
28. Finished laying by our crop-dark wet day
29. A grate deal of rain to day
30. No entry

August 1853
Rain a plenty this month went to the fair in Atlanta, but never went in the fair
9. Barbacue on the 9th
10. Started to the fare in Atlanta
12. Drove home - commenced getting our rock for our chimney
20. Dry and cool nights
26. Went to Pumpkion town to the nomination - nominated Bery Watts for the senit and S. W. Hartsfield for the reprasenitiv - Bevors, Cochram Gibson and some others we will try to Miord them for their frienship and some of the delagats

September 1853

3. Fathers property apraysed at $1800
5. Commenced gathering cotton
14. Campmeeting commenced a very warm meeting
15. Old Mrs. Smith died to day
26. Picked cotton to day it is very hard to pick
27. do do

Journal for 1854

Finished planting corn the last of March
Finished planting cotton the 26 of April
Planted our sweet potatoes the 27 of April
June - done a grate deal of work in this month at cort in February and in March again as Grand Juryman

August 1854

1. Very dry the first of this month
18 Rain to day a good rain - I have been worse with pains for some time than ever I was - my cotton is titer this year than ever I had in this country or any other - but we are blessed more than we deserve for if we was to get only what (we) deserve we would be pore indeed.
Property that A. N. M Larty give to his daughter Mary on the 13th day of Dec 1854 two beds and cover 50.00 one burrow $15 - 1 glass and drawer 1.50 - 3 chairs 1.87 1/2 - 1 side saddle 14.00 - 1 bed stead 5.00 - 1 clock 3.50 1 cow 10.00 1 sow and pigs 6.00 - ovin and lid 1.05 - one little pot .40 - one kittle 1.00 - one big pot 2.00.

February 27th 1855

Ann had her child to day - very cold this month
March 9th commenced grafting
commened at the north east corner 9 first rows Hallseedling - the next 8 rows Morrison apple - 2 Sewells seedling - 1 row town pippen - 3 rows red June - 2 horse apple - 2 Northern good - 1 pound apple - 1 yallow June

March 1st 1855

dr to Young Vansant
1 day washing of his negro woman
do to weaving twenty five yards
do to working one day in shop
dr to Young Vansant 40 cents for interest

November 14, 1855

My wife Anne departed this life ***(11/10/1855)*** - she was sick for some months but she never repined - she allways said the will for the Lord be done - the night before she departed she said she never felt so easy in she sayed the happy spirts were all around her bed and in truth Jesus can make a dieing bed a soft as downy pillows are - She wanted all her friends and children to come and pell for them selves how easey Jesus can make a dieing bed - she said she was going to leve us but if we would put our trust in the Lord Jesus Christ our parting would not be long A. N. M larty March 25th 1856.

Artifacts found, on the site of Dark Corner Settlement, near LLs 221 & 222 by John Bailey, photo by John Bailey.

Entries listed here are from a store ledger:

A. N. McLarty must have operated a general store type of business in addition to his farming. The use of "dr" means debtor. Some entries are not in chronological order. Most of the accounts are scratched through and listed as paid or settled.

Money received for peaches in 1854
Jacob Vanzant dr to 933 lbs foder at 75 cents per hundred 7.00

February 17, 1854

Maguorick dr to 16 apple trees	1.60	
G. W. Laminack dr to 56 trees		5.60
credit to	5.00	
	.60	
Divid Entrikin dr to 10 trees	1.00	
do to White dr 10 trees	1.00	
April 20th 1854		
received of Reubin Vanzant	$20.00	

Account with Young Vansant
May 23. Young Vansant dr to A. N. McLarty to 75 cents for tithe loned money
July 31, 1855 do to @.50 for manual cote paid to Herring .50
September 7th do to 30 cents in settlement 30

March 20th 1856 do to two dollars worth shugar 2100
August 11 Young Vansant to 65 cents 60 for slate and book
Oct 30th to one lb soda 10
1856 do to 1.00 worth coffe 1.00
1 bolt shirting 2.66
cloke stuff 1.17
Feb 10th to 23 lbs from 5 3/4 1.32
13.47
.50
13.97

Young Vanzant dr to
two pair of shoes 2.50
to 2 lb shot .20
to do lead .20
to percushion caps .37 1/2
to two spools thread .10
to 10 gallon mollasses 3.35
to paid for gun 9.00
five plugs tobaco .50
received 10.00 dollars
16.21 1/2
10.00
6.20 1/2
Young Vanzant dr to settlement 2.66
June 16th borrowed 15 dollars from S. W. McLarty - A. N. Mclarty

H. B. Elder Barnesville Pike Co. Ga

June 7th 1853
Jessie McElwreath to 1.00
August 11th do to $12.00
September 9th 1853
Joel Rice dr to 6 pair of shoes at $1.12 1/2 per pair $6.75
Thomas Hennon to cash 2.95
Thomas Hennon for tabaco .25
Dur Mam 2.25

Jesse Mcelwreath to $15.00
do for shirting 1.00
do for tabaco .50
do for hat 2.00
do for trunk 2.00
29 do to 40.00
June

January 7th 1854 Joseph R. Farmer
dr to A. N. McLarty one coat 12.00
March 1854 Thomas Hennon dr to 5.00 loans
May 1854 Joseph R. Farmer dr to one vest 4.00
Joseph R. Farmer to 50 cents for tan
May 9th 1854 Thomas Hennon dr to one dollar worth coffe 1.00
June 31st 1854 George Kelly dr to lbs bacon at 8 cents per lb 4.00 received of Samuel Hollman $4.00

1856 received of Thomas Hennon 54 bushels cotton seed at 10 cents a bushel

December 16th 1851
Mr. Harp dr to 25 apple tree
Martin McElwreath dr to 25 apple trees by Mr. Harp 2.90

January 9th 1852
Mr. Pain dr to 82 lbs pork 5 cents per lb $4.10
January 30th 1852
Thomas Entriken dr to two dollar worth apple trees 2.00
Jan 30th Margaret Maxwell dr to apple trees at 8 cents per tree $2.16

February 9th 1852 John Entrykin dr to one dollars worth apple trees
April 15th 1852 John C. Whitley dr to 60 lbs bacon at 8 cents per lb $4.80
June 15th 1852
1 thrashed C. W. (?) wheat to day 31 bushels
2 David Enterkins wheat 47 bushels
3 Louis Maquire wheat
4. Asa Sewells 74 bushels
5. John McLarty 40 bushels
6. James Smith 22 bushels
7. John Entirkins 32
8. C. W. Maxwell 69 bushels
bought S. W. McLarty 73 lbs flower at one time 81 lbs another time 154 lbs settled in full
(One day after dathe we or either of us - William Mclarty his name - remember me when I am gone) (this in pencil)

August 20th 1851
G. W. McLarty to
1 sack salt 1.90
3 1/2 lbs tobaco 1.22
40 lbs coffe 5.00
1 sacred harp .75

pap to 1/2 doz glass tumblers 1.00
to one hat 1.50
do one lb soda .10
do one lb tea 1.25

October 31st 1851
dr to G. W. McLarty
for sundery articles mistake of $2.80 Which makes the account $14.19
Borrowed of S. W. Mlarty for the pay David $3.00
do to 1.00 and 78 cents for tax

March 1856
Jeames Smith dr to one side of lather price not named
Jeames Smith to $ (?) dollar
April loaned money
9th Rabern dr to 50 trees $5.00
Hodge Rabern dr to 50 trees $5.00
Andrew McBear dr to 20 trees - $2.00
29th Margaret Maxwell dr. to 22 apple trees 10 cents per tree - 2.00

April 1856
1st H. Oxner to 15 apple trees 1.50
Young Vansant dr to one side of lather loaned to him
29th Joel Rice to 81 lbs sole lather 25 cents per lb $2.00
do to ten dollars loned money 1.00

September - 1856 (?)
Mr. Jones to 53 lbs bacon 6.62
Nov 19th do to 17 lbs 80 2.12
W. A. McLaty dr to A. N. McLarty settlement $ 55.00
Feb 10th W. A. McLarty to one dollars worth shugar 1.06
1lb soda
April 19 dr to W. A. McLarty $15.20
May 16th dr to W. A. McLarty 1.45
William A. McLarty
received of the money that he let me have at one time
$20.00
another time 2.00
another time 5.00
do to 2.00 dolars worth nalies ` 2.00
rope .75
soda and ginger .25
do to 40 cents for tax .40
do to to dollar for coffe 1.00

September 1856

24th rec of Ezekel Polk $5.00

November 1856

4th*
10th George Loweng to settlement 93 cents
15th Margaret Maxwell dr to 28 apple trees 10 2.80
20th Henry Oxner dr to 1 side sole lather 1.50
30th (in pencil) Henry Oxner picked cotton for J. R. Farmer 7.61
do do 9.55
17.16
Martha Vansant 2.00 John Vansant 1.36 Paid to Henry Orener (Oxner) 2.96

Dec 21, 1856

Rec of Yong Vansant 64.31 misstak
for Sarah Mlarty cotton
bought for Henry Oscer (Oxner) one bunch thread 1.00 cents due on it
Yong Vansant 60 trees
C. Bowen 50 trees
Wm Maqouirk 155 trees
Nathen Lipcomb 60 trees
John Hewey 48 trees
C. Wheeler 50 trees
D. Butler 60 trees
John Ergle 18 trees
Henry Ohner (Oxner) 40 trees
Henry Ohner to $6.67 for sale
Jeams Greegs 25 trees
Wilks Vansant 50 trees
Caroline Rice 25 trees
E. Whitley 300 trees (rec of Whitley 20 dollars)
F. (E.) W. Maxwell dr to $2.00 for Madison
do to 20 apple trees $6.00
do to Brandy 1.00
payed to Mary C. Farmer $2.50
do to
Mrs. Danforth to 30 trees 3.00
Mary C. Farmer to 7.75
Young Vansant to powder .75
do to Shott
500.00

April 4th 1857

paid Mr. Pain 42.00 for shingles
dr to S. W. Mlarty 7 lbs tobacco 30 2.00
dr to J. R. Farmer to 70 lbs bacon
Sarah Mlarty to 200 trees
to seven dollars and forth five 7.45
do to 5.00 due A N. Mlarty $8.85
list of cotton sold
600 at 30 cents $180
1 bag at .30
2 bags at $140
1 do at $ 27
Sarah Mlarty to one half bushel peas
received of Sarah M larty 4.00

April 11 commenced planting cotton - sowed the seed and did not cover them I think it a bad plan-planted 60-

May

Worked very hard all this month - to time lost only waiting on mother - she is worse with pains than ever saw any body

June

still hard at work - Mother --(illegible)
17th Sabath day mother very ----the season very good rain a -----(page missing)

October 1857

8. Joel Rice to $4.50 cents loned money
Recvd of Joel Rice $15.00

November 4th 1857

Due to W. A. M Larty in settlement
paid W. A. Mlarty $202.14
due A. H. M larty $79.57
received of W. A. Mlarty $186.24
in notes for collection $15.49
received a recipt on Thomas A. Lathem for notes on E. W. Maxwell
amount 250.00
7.48

list of notes
1 on John Bright and M. Freman $71.49
1 on John M. Johnson and Endsley 48.00
1 on John Ergle and Samuel Hallman $7.42 (marked paid)
1 on Samuel Hallman $9.13 (maked paid)
1 on John P. McKelvy and Isaac W. McKlvy
1 on G. W M Larty $73.10

1 on M. C. Maxwell and E. J. Mattock $21.25
1 on A. G. Endsley and Wm P. Clinton $5.50
1 on William Hallman 12.00
1 on Francis Wilson and Isaac Bentley 20.00
1 on Madison Freeman and W. S. Wisley 21.00
1 on A. N. Stone James D. Stone 8.87
1 on Thomas Wickes 4.07
this is W. A. Mlarty notes that I have for collection - A. N. McLarty

list of notes belonging to Joseph R. Farmer one on Jacob Vansant 24.26
1 on Lindsey Freeman John Ergle 8.00
1 on A. G. Endsley Wm P. Clinton 8.25

April 19th 1858
21st commenced planting cotton 22-23-24
24th hevy frost this morning
28 finished planting cotton
29th plowing corn
30 plowing corn

May 1858
I finished plowing our corn -nise time to work Leuisa sick for several days

August 4th 1858
received 1.50 cents - due 50

1859 made 18 bales cotton

1860
January done a good deal of work
February plowed all this month
March - Plowing this month
23 commenced planting corn

January 17, 1861
At home our regment is now at Griswoldvill - I want my children to know that the Griswold family is the best friends that the soldiers has met with and the Causeys and Brantleys and Williams - if our country had all such men we could conquer the world - A. Mlarty
(about 21 pages cut from book at this point)
the remaining pages lists debts and receipts)
Joseph R. Farmer cotton 1 bale 320 1 to 364 at 11 cents 75.24
baggen and roping 6 3.00

	72.24
Mothers part	18.37
balance due Farmer	54.18
paid to Wallis	18.37
due J. R. Farmer	35.81

1865
Thomas Hicks dr to A. N. Mclarty
1 sow and pigs
cotton

1866
to one bushel of peas 1.50
Dederick Laminack to one bushel peas 1.50
Jeames Linsey to 1/2 bushel peas

November 1866
3rd Young Vansant dr to 5.00 dollars by settlement
Sold 80 lbs for confederate money

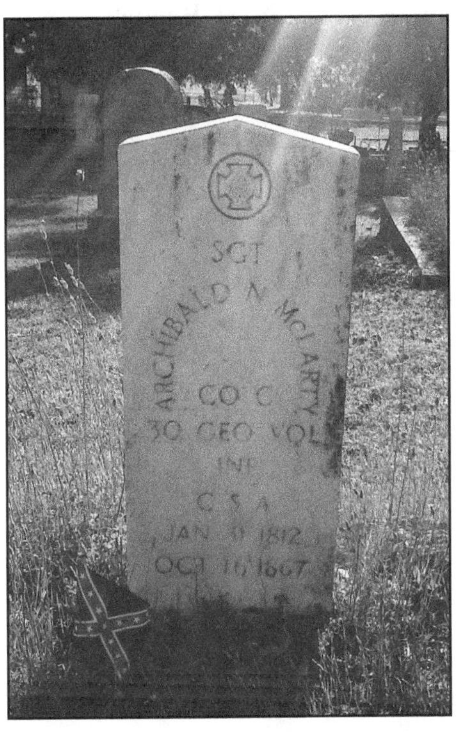

Sergeant Archibald Newton McLarty, Company C, 30th Georgia Volunteer Infantry was born January 31, 1812, died October 16, 1867 in Wood County Texas. He is buried at Winnsboro City Cemetery.

Appendix A:

Cemeteries in the Dark Corner

The marker was found adjacent to the former Douglas County landfill on Cedar Mountain Road, inside of and to the right of the landfill entrance. Elizabeth Benson, July 16, 1793 - 1833.

Baggett Family Cemetery

Location: 3180 E. Baggett Road, Douglasville, GA 30134;

33°43'05.00"N 84°48'34.43"W

Baggett, Emma Adella 10/25/1869 - 11/24/1903

Baggett B. J. 2/15/1865 - 4/4/1943

Baggett, Nannie E. 9/23/1844 - 6/2/1919

Bell, Infant 10/20/1884 - 10/20/1884 daughter of Mr. & Mrs. W. F. Bell

Baggett, John 12/27/1817 - 1/9/1893

Baggett R. S. 12/1/1825 - 2/24/1881 wife of John Baggett

Baggett, L. V. 2/1/1858 - 12/8/1875 daughter of J. A. & R. S. Baggett

Baggett, Annie R. 10/2/1877 - 2/17/1880 daughter of S. T. & N. C. Baggett

Baggett, Stephen 12/29/1784 - 2/19/1877

Baggett, Sarah 2/10/1791 - 10/9/1881

S. J. 7/12/1835 - 7/11/1883

Mary 4/6/1820 - 12/17/1902

Susan 2/21/1829 - 11/11/1903

14 inscribed stones - 7 unscribed

Inactive Cemetery, Oldest grave 1/9/1863, Last burial 4/4/1943

Benson Cemetery

Location: The marker was found adjacent to the former Douglas County landfill on Cedar Mountain Road, inside of and to the right of the landfill entrance.

7196 Cedar Mountain Road, Douglasville, GA 30134;

33°45'27.49"N 84°48'41.01"W

Elizabeth Benson, July 16, 1793 - 1833.

Note: Elizabeth Kemp was the first wife of Reuben Benson, born May 27, 1786, in Greenville District, SC.

Reuben Benson died June 16, 1864, and is also buried here in the family cemetery a mile north of the old Winston railroad station about five miles northwest of Douglasville. In 1931 his marker was located, reading: Reuben Benson, departed this life June 16, 1864, age 78 years, 19 days.

Enterkin Cemetery

Located: Close to the intersection of Bright Star Road and Douglas Bouvelard.

Name: **Dates:**

John Enterkin 1815-1873; John was the brother of Samuel Kanady Enterkin.

Mary McElreath Enterkin 1820-1882; wife of John Enterkin.

John and Mary Enterkin are the parents of Ludie S. Enterkin 1854-1927.

Enterkin-Winn Cemetery

Location: 2809 Mann Road, Winston, Douglas County, Georgia

Name **Birth** **Death** **Comments**

Row 1:

1. Sarah E. Winn, 1834-1925 (Wife of James Henry Winn and daughter of Ezekiel Polk, pioneer settler of present Winston area.)
2. J. H. Winn, 1828 - 1896 (James Henry Winn, first postmaster and merchant at Winn, whose name was changed to Winston; original county commissioner of Douglas County; son of Rev. Francis Winn.)
3. Charles Wesley Winn, 1858- 1921 (Son of James Henry Winn.)
4. Easter E. Winn Hill, 8/25/1911 - 11/18/1987
5. Mary Virginia Winn, 1872-1947 (Wife of Henry Oscar Winn, daughter of Samuel Kanady Enterkin, 1825-1888, and wife Ester Virginia McLarty, both buried McLarty-Benson Cemetery.)
6. Henry Oscar Winn, 1864-1930 (Son of James Henry Winn; Henry Oscar's sons Joseph Wilford "Joe" Winn and Theodore Winn operated Winn's Store on Mann Road
7. William Henry Winn, 9/4/1907-12/24/1990

Row 2:

8. Infant daughter of Lot and Myrtle Sayer, born - died 1902 (Myrtle was the daughter of George W. Enterkin, 1857-1911, Son of Samuel Kanady Enterkin.)

Row 3:

10. Myrtle E. Sayer, 1880-1923 (Daughter of George W. Enterkin.)

11. Jennie D., wife of George W. Enterkin, 1861-1892 (Jennie Druscilla, daughter of James Henry Winn.)

12. G. W. Enterkin, 1857-1911 (Son of Samuel Kanady Enterkin; George W. was the railroad and express agent at Winn in the 1880s.)

13. Jessie D. Enterkin, 11/9/1891- 7/19/1982

14. Theodore Winn, 3/13/1906-4/25/1983

15. William Murphy Enterkin, 1866-1949 (Son of Samuel Kanady Enterkin.)

16. John David Enterkin, 1860-1940 (Son of Samuel Kanady Enterkin)

17. Joseph Wilford Winn, 1914-1949 (Son of Henry Oscar Winn)

Row 4:

18. Annie Mae Enterkin, 1902-1925

19. Samuel W. Lee, 1874-1955 (Son of John Taylor Lee and Millie Sewell Lee.)

20. Wife Annie Pearl Lee, 1884-1914 (Daughter of Ludie S. Enterkin, 1854-1927, noted below, and Mary Winn Enterkin.)

Row 5:

21. Ludie Stephens Enterkin, October 9, 1854 - February 7, 1927 (Son of John and Mary McElreath Enterkin.

22. Wife Mary Ann Enterkin, 1854-1945 (Daughter of James Henry Winn.)

Row 6:

23. Sarah Elizabeth Enterkin, 1870-1938 (Daughter of Jay G. Rice; wife of Charles Olin Enterkin, 1864-1906, buried McLarty-Benson Cemetery; Charles Oin was a son of Samuel Kanady Enterkin noted above.)

24. Clarence Aubrey Enterkin, Pvt. US Army, WWI, 1/12/1892-5/2/1961

25. Myrtle Black Enterkin, 4/9/1902-10/9/1952

Hildebrand Family Cemetery

Location: This family cemetery is way back in the woods off Brewer Road in the northwest part of Douglas County.
About 15 - 20 graves but only three known burials:

John Hildebrand
October 31, 1798
August 8, 1866

Anna Hildebrand (nee Anna Van Horn)
w/o John Hildebrand
May 17, 1812

August 24, 1877

Isaac Newton Hildebrand (Co. C 30th GA Infantry)
s/o John and Anna Hildebrand
March 19, 1840
July 20, 1864 (killed in the Atlanta Campaign)
There is also a memorial marker for Isaac's brother who died in the siege of Vicksburg and whose burial place is therefore unknown:

Alfred Green Hildebrand (56 GA Infantry)
October 1, 1842
July 3, 1863 (killed in action, Vicksburg, Mississippi)

Kennedy-Brittain Cemetery

Location: This family cemetery is in Winston, two miles north of Bankhead Highway on Mann Road. It is on the right side of the road and has an iron gate flanked by brick columns. The cemetery is rectangular in shape with five rows of graves and a total of 30-35 graves. There is a dirt roadbed that encircles it, and there are additional fieldstone marked graves that lie in the woods beyond that roadbed.

Row 1 (west most row):
Cecil Brittain Culpepper
11 Jun 1903 - 30 Jul 1990

Frank Kennedy Hamby
22 Nov 1918 - 10 May 1981
Killed Eilat, Israel

Bernard H. Brittain
19 Dec 1894 - 20 May 1953
Ga Pvt. 12th Inf. 9th Divn WWI

Alfred Tyre Brittain
15 Oct 1865 - 20 Nov 1942

Mary F. Kennedy
26 Jan 1873 - 27 Jan 1953

John Ralph Brittain
1920 - 1993

Aulton K. Brittain
27 Feb 1893 - 6 Nov 1918 (war casualty)
GA Pvt. 307th Inf. 77th Divn. WWI

J. J. Kennedy
27 Sept 1835 - 25 Apr 1905
Co. F., Cobb's Legion, CSA

H. A. (Hester Ann) Kennedy (nee Dorris)
w/o J. J. Kennedy
25 Nov 1845 - 2 July 1895

Next are five fieldstone-marked graves, two of which are apparently children. One of these is likely the grave of William Haralson Kennedy, son of J. J. and Hester who was born 15 Apr 1865 and died 27 Feb 1870.

Nancy Kennedy Kirby
1870 - 1943

James H. Kirby
25 Jan 1912 - 30 Sept 1944
Ga PFC., 168 Inf, WWII

Row 2
Samuel Leathers
2 May 1846 - 22 Sep 1855

M. I. Leathers
7 Jun 1852 - 4 Dec 1852

Byron Kirby
9 Jun 1893 - 29 Jun 1969

Leta Kirby
24 Oct 1896 - 29 Jan 1983

One fieldstone-marker grave (child).

Row 3:
Allen Ray Brittain
2 Nov 1947 - 19 Jun 1997
SP4, U. S. Army, Vietnam

Double marker for infant twins
Jeromy Ralph Brittain Jeffery John Brittain
11 Aug 1974 - 12 Aug 1974 11 Aug 1974 - 13 Aug 1974

William W. Winn
24 Oct 1883 - 28 Jun 1976

Nellie M. Winn
16 July 1887 - 30 May 1964

Elizabeth Winn, 1862 - 1951

J. M. (James M.) Alexander
2 Nov 1840 - 24 May 1915
Co. C, 30th Georgia Inf, CSA

C. E. Alexander
(w/o J. M. Alexander)
9 Oct 1837 - 26 Apr 1929

A. J. Hassell
(d/o G. A. Hassell)
3 July 1858 - 15 June 1862

M. J. Hassell
(d/o G. A. Hassell)
25 Apr 1854 - 29 May 1854

A grave completely surrounded by fieldstones but open on top, no information.

Row 4:
Enclosed box tomb with no information.

John Kennedy
Apr 1791 - 28 Oct 1848

Elizabeth Kennedy
(w/o John Kennedy)
3 Jan 1796 - 2 Jan 1874

Row 5:
Kennedy
Mar 1846 - Aug 1847 (This is the grave of a slave, a little girl named Tebia.)

Two other slave names are known: a woman named Looky who was born circa 1789, and another young woman known as Matilda who was born circa 1826. It is not known if they are buried in the cemetery or perhaps in the graves outside the perimeter road.

Leathers Cemetery

Location: This cemetery is on High Point Road, just west of where the power lines intersect the road. The house next to it is 9026 High Point Road. It is clearly visible from the road since two of the graves are inside a large above ground vault.

Peter Leathers (h/o Polly Ann Leathers) June 16, 1816 - April 4, 1901

Polly Ann Leathers (w/o Peter Leathers) January 4, 1821 - August 23, 1887

Peter and Polly are buried in the vault. The only other marker grave is that of their daughter.

Polly Ann Entryken November 20 1843 - March 19, 1862

There are about 10 more graves that are not marked even with fieldstones.

The 1850 census of Carroll County (11th Division) shows the following about this family:

Peter Leathers 35 farmer, born in SC; Mary "Polly" 26 GA; Franklin 9 GA; Amanda 7 GA; Mary "Polly" 5 GA; Samuel 3 GA.

McLarty Family Cemetery

Location: Brittain Road off Cedar Mountain. R.

Carnes, Peter James (infant) 11/17/1882 - 11/17/1882

Carnes, Peter d. 8/30/1920 Age 87 yrs. (h/o Sophia Carnes)

Carnes Sophia (no dates) (w/o Peter Carnes)

Connell M. C. died 3/8/1926

H. F. died 8/10/1926

Hart, Margie (Mrs. Taylor) born 5/17/1910, died 1/20/1944 Age 33

Hawkins, Amanda L., died 1/12/1888

Hawkins, George W. 5/27/1871 - 8/20/1944

Hawkins, William Harris 11/26/1889 - 3/7/1923 (WWI Vet)

Hollomon, Fannie Hawkins 4/24/1879 - 11/3/1945 (m/o Thad Holloman)

Hollomon, Thad 8/04/1893 - 1/1/1919 Co. B 516 Eng. Stev. Bn.

McClarty, Clark born ca. 1830 - died 6/23/1906

Mclarin, Nrcy 1858 - 1912

Polk, Sally, died 1862

Scales, W. H. 9/16/1891 - 2/27/1896

Scales, Walter 4/03/1890 - 6/22/1891
Shelton, C. Mrs., died - 1/00
Sutton, W. M. 6/17/1903 - 10/18/1925 daughter of Mrs. Studders
Anderson, J(ames) W. 6/14/1838 - 6/28/1881 Co. C., 30th Ga Inf
Benson, Harriet C(aroline) McLarty 1/31/1826 - 4/07/1896 w/o James LaFayette Benson
Benson, James LaFayette 4/15/1822 - 5/9/1902
Brown, Mary C. McLarty 10/31/1846 - 4/30/1885 (w/o Posey Newton Brown)
Brown, Posey Newton 6/13/1849 - 7/17/1896 (h/o Mary C. McLarty Brown
Dorris, Martha E. (Benson) Anderson 1/7/1849 - 2/2/1926 (m. 1st J. W. Anderson, then J. Dorris)
Enterkin, Charles O. 4/24/1864 - 4/2/1906
Enterkin, E(sther) V(irginia) (McLarty) 5/09/1830 -7/26/1906 (wife of S. K. Enterkin)
Enterkin, P(olly) V(irginia (McLarty) 12/19/1838 - 12/15/1912 (w/o David Fletcher Enterkin)
Enterkin, S(amuel) K(anada) 8/13/1825 - 4/13/1888
McElreath, C(arson) S. 3/27/1842 - 11/13/1881 (Co. A, 56th Ga Inf.
McElreath, Jane (McLarty) 6/01/1823 - 5/22/1878 (w/o Mark McElreath)
McElreath, Mark 1811 - 2/21/1858
McElreath, Martha (Vansant) born 1845 w/o Carson McElreath
McElreath Our Baby c/o Carson & Martha McElreath
McLarty, John, Jr. 3/07/1802 - 3/14/1856
McLarty, John Sr. 12/25/1775 - 1/21/1853
McLarty, Martha (White) 11/11/1801 - 11/11/1842 1st w/o John McLarty Junior

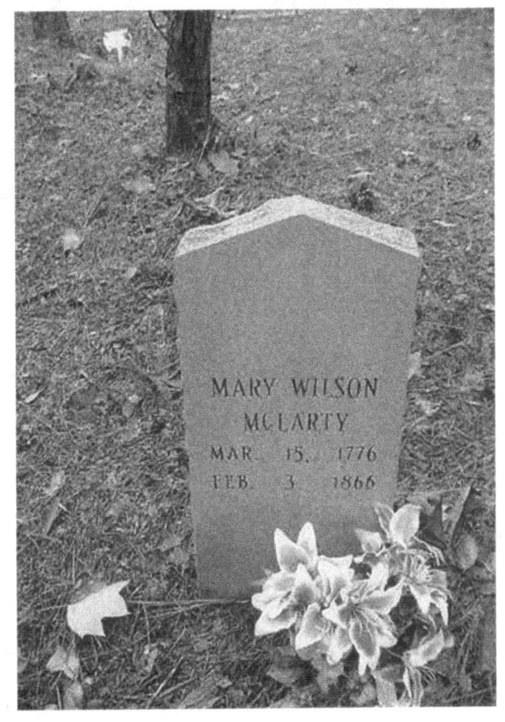

McLarty, Mary (Wilson) March 15, 1776 - February 03, 1866 w/o John McLarty, Sr. Ten of her grandsons, and five of her granddaughter's husbands were killed in the Civil War.

McLarty, Mary 1/20/1832 - 11/12/1842 d/o John & Martha McLarty
McLarty, Mary "Polly" (Polk) 8/13/1810 - 5/21/1848 1st w/o S. W. McLarty
McLarty, S(amuel) W(ilson) 8/28/1799 - 7/11/1863
McLarty, Sarah E(leanor) (Anderson) 7/27/1814 - 3/04/1881,
2nd w/o John McLarty, Jr.
Morris, J(ames) C(olumbus) 9/08/1934 - 6/19/1903 Co., C 30th Ga Infantry
Morris, S(arah) E. (Polk) 4/16/1843 -10/22/1909 w/o J. C. Morris
Polk, C(harles) S(helby) 5/29/1814 - 7/10/1879
Polk, Catherine (McLarty) 1/16/1821 - 3/26/1907 w/o C. S. Polk
Polk, Charles Thomas 11/23/1860 - 8/12/1916
Polk, J(ames) E. 12/09/1845 - 11/07/1888
Polk, M(argaret) A(nn) Freeman 3/17/1855 - 3/18/1907 w/o C. T. Polk
Polk, Mattie J. 2/13/1882 - 9/04/1884 d/o C.T. & M. A. Polk
Polk, Trannie C. 1/16/1884 - 5/15/1905 d/o C.T. & M. A. Polk

Farmer, Joseph R., Pvt. (grandson of J. McLarty) Memorial marker 30th Ga.
Hartsfield, George W., Pvt. (grandson of J. McLarty) Memorial marker 56th Ga.
Maxwell, Mangum Calhoun, Pvt. (grandson of J. McLarty)

Memorial markers for the McLarty grandsons and granddaughter's husbands.

Memorial marker 41st Ga died in hosp. Oxford, Mississippi.
McLarty, Alexander W., Lt (grandson of J. McLarty) Memorial marker 31st Mississippi. KIA Franklin, Tn.)

McLarty, Archibald DeKalb, Pvt. (grandson of J. McLarty) Memorial marker 56 Ga.

McLarty, James K., Corporal (grandson of J. McLarty) Memorial marker 29th Mississippi. KIA, Murfreesboro, Tn

McLarty, Samuel Manon, Sgt. (grandson of J. McLarty) Memorial marker 30th Ga.

McLarty, William Alexander, (grandson of J. McLarty) Memorial marker 56th Ga.

McLarty, William L. Pvt., (grandson of J. McLarty) Memorial marker 4th Mississippi.

McLarty, William Wallace, Pvt. (grandson of J. McLarty) Memorial marker 41st Ga. KIA Perryville, Ky.)

McLarty, Wilson Lafayette (grandson of J. McLarty) Memorial marker 4th Miss.

Polk Cemetery

This family cemetery is in the woods on the NW side of the intersection of Conners Road and Richardson Road, in the backyard of what was once the Polk plantation house (which faced what is today Richardson Road). There are only two graves:
Charles Marion Polk
Co. A 56th GA Infantry
1836 - 1865

An un-inscribed field stone
The latter is probably a Polk child that died during the War Between the States. It is definitely not the grave of his wife, Mittie Carnes, who went on to collect a Confederate pension years later.

The Stewart Cemetery

This cemetery was visited by Joe Baggett in July 1979. In poor condition at the time, it is located in the woods near the intersection of Walton Store Road and Cave Spring Road, off Ga. Highway 92 north of Douglasville.

In memory of S. A., wife of J. H. McLarty, born August 9, 1836, died December 3, 1858, 22 yrs., 3 mos. & 24 days. (Note: Sarah Ann, daughter of James and Nancy Stewart, married John Harvey McLarty, son of Stephen H. McLarty.)

Francis M. Winn, Co. E, 9th Georgia, Lieutenant Artillery CSA
(Note: Francis Milton Winn, born Oct. 29, 1836, died April 1924, married Nancy Jane, daughter of James and Nancy Stewart)

In memory of F. M. Stewart, born May 23, 1832, died Dec. 16, 1871
(Note: married Martha Elizabeth, daughter of Alexander G. Weddington)

Martha E., wife of F. M. Stewart, born Sept. 30 1834, died Sept. 11, 1886.

Infant daughter of Mr. and Mrs. A. H. Winn, born Sept. 23, 1868, died Jan 20, 1871.

Winn - Watson Cemetery

Location: North Flat Rock Road off Cedar Mountain Road in woods behind the home at 1471 North Flat Rock Road northwest of Douglasville.

Francis Winn, born 1801, died March 1862
"Mark the perfect man, And beneath the upright For the end of that. . . " (broken; the last line is "Man is peace").
(Note: Rev. Francis Winn, formerly of Gwinnett County, Ga., established the Methodist Episcopal Church South at Flat Rock in what was then Campbell, now Douglas County, 1860. His widow Drucilla was living as late as the 1870 census of Campbell County.

Samuel H. Watson, born 1812 died 1855 (broken).

In memory of Hannah Polk Weddington, born Sept. 1, 1812, died Aug. 27 1874.
(Note: Hannah Polk married Alexander G. Weddington in Cabarrus County, N. C., in 1825. Her husband, Oct 30, 1806 - Sept. 2, 1893, is said to be buried here.)

J. W. H., son of N. A. and M. E. Hamby, March 25, 1883 - April 22, 1883 (broken).
(Note: Parents Newton A. and Margaret Plunkett Hamby are buried at Ephesus Baptist Church, Douglas County, GA.)

Isabella Trapp, Sept. 10, 1840 - May 10, 1896
(Note: Daughter of Irish immigrants George and Mary Allen, below)

Mary Allen, May 15, 1803 - Feb 28. 1877 (broken)
George Allen, Nov. 20 1800 - June 9, 1872

John Allen, April 13, 1835 - May 13, 1862

S. C. Black, died July 7, 1873
(Note: Sarah Catherine Weddington, daughter of William C. Weddington and wife of William G. Black; they married Dec. 5, 1835, Cabarrus County, N. C.

A. G. W. Black (hand carved) (Note: Alexander Green Weddington Black, son of William G. and Sarah C. Weddington Black died 1860.)

Many graves marked only by fieldstones or broken beyond recognition.

Appendix B: Huey Letters

Bowden Collegiate Institute

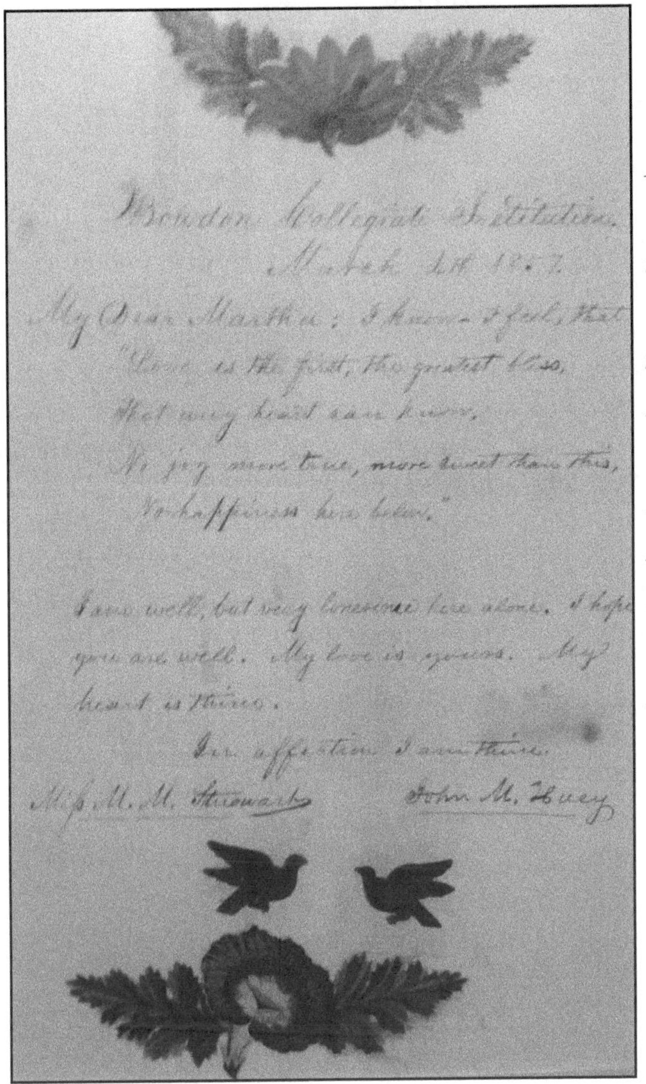

Bowden Collegiate Institution.
March 7th 1857.
My Dear Martha: I know - I feel, that
"Love is the first, the greatest bliss,
That any heart can know,
No joy more true, more sweet than this,
No happiness here below."

I am well, but very lonesome here alone. I hope
you are well. My love is yours. My
heart is thine.
In affection I am thine.
Miss M. M. Stewart John M. Huey

March 7th 1857

My Dear Martha:

"I know - I feel, that Love is the first, the greatest bliss, That any heart can know. No joy more true, more sweet than this, no happiness here below."

I am well, but very lonesome here alone. I hope you are well. My love is yours. My heart is thine.

In affection I am thine.

Miss M. M. Stewart

John M. Huey

(Martha Melinda Stewart was the daughter of Nancy and James Stewart; ***she*** was attending the Bowden Collegiate Institute.)

Letter: Courtesy Robert Nix, Huey's great-grandson.

Huey—A Prisoner of War

On back of folded letter - used as an envelope:

Mrs. M. M. Huey
Dark Corner
Campbell County, Georgia

Via Flag of Truce
Fortress Monroe
In Care Col. Mulford
Ast. Ex. Agent

Fort Delaware Jan 28th 1865

My dear Wife: Again with great affection I write to you. Thanks God, I am still in the best of health, and in good spirits. I have suffered untold uneasiness about you and our three precious little children. Yesterday I recv'd a letter from Mother dated Dec. 21st stating you were all well. Oh, what consolation it gave me! Your letters of May 5th, and Sept 24th, came to hand. Do not be uneasy about my welfare. I am well treated. Kind friends supply all my actual wants. With profound sorrow I learn that Dock, and John L. Humphrey are no more. You can write all private family news that you please to me. Where are all the Boys, white and black? Is uncle Allen still with you? How is Mam and her family? I hope there may soon be an Exchange of Prisoners, or what would suite me better, an honorable peace restored, and a return of prosperity to our whole land. May we look to God for patience in adversity and for relief in due time. Back your letters as I sign mine. I send you a stamp. Write soon. I am thine till death. Accept my love and esteem.

John M. Huey

Mrs. M. M. Huey
Dark Corner
Campbell County
Georgia

Private Co. A. 56th Ga. Regt.
Prisoner of War - 8. Division
Fort Delaware, Del.

(Proof for application for pension?) Huey wounded

Talledega, Ala
August 13, 1899

Mr. Jessey M. Huey:

Dear Sir: - Yours of 7th inst. making inquiries concerning the wounding of your father, was sent out to our camp a day or two ago - I was a Lieutenant in Co. A 56th Ga. Regt. and was only a few paces from your father when he was wounded at Missionary Ridge. I asked him if he was badly wounded - His reply was - "I don't know, Lieutenant" I then placed my finger in the place where the ball struck him - and I thought at the time the ball had gone into his head - I made out a list of casualties and sent to the Newspaper in Atlanta. In that list was your father reported severely wounded in head - A few days after the battle I received a letter from your mother asking me to give her an honest opinion as to the true condition of her husband. I submitted her letter to Dr. Peddy our Surgeon, and he gave it as his opinion that Huey would die, and I think I so wrote your mother. Many of our old Co. have passed over the river - and those who survive are scattered. I will give you a list of some of the Co. who I think are still living. D. F. Brewster, J. P. Brewster and D. B. Woodruff all at Newnan, Ga. D. F. Brewster was in the milieu when your father was wounded - W. A. Tanner is at Rivertown, Ga. Tom Carnes was also in that battle - I think Tom is a preacher and lives near Villa Rica, Ga - You ought to find a member of the old Co. around Villa Rica and Douglasville - Geo. Souter the McLartys, the Vansants - Jim Wheeler - Jack Morris, Henry Morris, Jim Morris - Lum Clinton, Bolin Thomas, Will Cleckler - and others were from that section - no trouble to find plenty of comrades to make proof of your fathers being wounded.

I will take pleasure in serving you in any way I can, if it will in any way benefit John M. Huey's wife and children - for he was my friend in places where friendship was put to a crucial test. A truer man, a braver soldier, than your father was not to (be) found in Confederate ranks. He was always the same quiet, calm, moral - John M. Huey - in camp, on the March, as well as in battle. Now if you need further assistance, all you have to do is to command my service. With kindest regards to all, I am yours truly.

J. T. Loveless.

John Mason Huey (Hughey) did survive this war injury and returned home to his family. He was born May 31, 1928 and died November 16, 1891, the son of John Huey, born 1798 in South Carolina and Elizabeth Shearly, 1798-1868. He married Martha Stewart, daughter of James and Nancy **Stewart** in 1858, in Campbell County. She was born June 13, 1834 and died August 16, 1911. Both are buried at the County Line Baptist Church in Lithia Springs, Georgia. John M. Huey was the teacher in Dark Corner School in 1854 and 1855; he was the first surveyor of Douglas County and later a tax collector, and active in the Baptist Church and Clerk of the Tallapoosa Association. He enlisted as Private on April 25, 1862 in Co. A, 56th Georgia Regiment Volunteer Infantry from Campbell County. He was captured at Missionary Ridge, Tennessee on November 25, 1863, paroled at Point Lookout, Maryland on February 1865, received at Boulware & Cox's Wharves, James River, Virginia for exchange on March 10-12, 1865 and paroled in Atlanta, Georgia on May 18, 1865.

He and Martha had nine children: 1) Elizabeth who married Will Alley; 2) Jesse James Huey, 1861-1888, married in 1885 to Sallie E. Causey; 3) Marion Huey, born 1866, married Mandy Hutcheson; 4) William Elijah, 1871-1933; 5) Ethel Mae, born 1878, married John R. White; 6) Lavinia, 1862-1930, single; 7) Henry LaFayette, born 1969, married Bertie James; 8) Martha Emma, 1875-1950, married John W. Hendrix; 9) Joseph Alonzo, 1867-1926, married Abbie L. Baggett, 1868-1953.

CREDITS

Chapter 1—Early Roads Led to Dark Corner
Map of MD #730: Campbell County Courthouse; Map: **Georgia Early Roads & Trails. Circa 1730—1850,** Dr. John H. Goff, Georgia Department of Archives; Seven Springs Museum, Powder Springs Georgia. Map: 1991-92 Hemperley, Marion R., **The Alabama Roads**, Part III, North Georgia Journal, Winter. Vol. 6, Issue 2, page 57, The Middle Alabama Road, Revised.

Chapter 2—Why the name Dark Corner?
Map: 1959 Douglas County Soil Survey No. 1, U. S. Dept. of Agriculture, Soil Conservation Service, Issued November 1961; Douglas County Public Library, Fannie Mae Davis Special Collections Room. 1975, Krakow, Kenneth, Georgia Place Names, Macon, Georgia, Winship Press. 1987, Fannie Mae Davis, **Douglas County, Georgia Indian Trails to Interstate 20**, W. H. Wolf Associates, Roswell, Georgia. Interview with Donald and Billie Brittain.

Chapter 3—The First Pioneers
Kennedy: Photo: The Kennedy House built about 1905. Permission Sam Henley, taken by John Bailey 2014. Oral history written as Kennedy Family Genealogy and Documents, courtesy of Sam Henley. Joe Baggett's **Who Was Who in Douglas County,** Volume I, page 149, Douglas County Public Library, Fannie Mae Davis Special Collection Room. ibid Davis, **Douglas County, Georgia Indian Trails,** p. 514.
Keaton: Photo and Keaton Family History, courtesy Herman "Billy" Keaton, 2003, <ancestry.com> Federal Census Records; Keaton Family Cemetery Listings. Georgia, Property Tax Digest. Find-A-Grave - Keaton. ibid Baggett, **Who Was Who,** Vol. I page 148.
Clinton: Fold3, Historical Military Program; ibid Baggett **Who's Who** Volume I, page 64. <ancestry.com> Public Member Trees; 1830, 1840, 1850 & 1860 Campbell County Federal Census Records; Georgia, Property Tax Digest - 1855; Campbell County Military Indian War 1838 Volunteers list. Genealogy of John P. Clinton, Barbara Ann Koon Ferguson, <home.earthlink.net>; Revolutionary War Pension Application Abstract - William Clinton, USGenweb Archives by Mary Lu Johnson. 1960, Compiled for the State of Georgia by Lillian Henderson, **Roster of the Confederate**

Soldiers of Georgia 1861-1865, Longino & Porter, Inc. Vol. 5; page 839. **Find A Grave.** Research by Greg Dansby.
Carnes: Photo: taken by John Bailey, 2014. Will of Thomas Carnes, December 8, 1860/Carroll County. <ancestry.com>, U. S. Federal Census Records, Fold 3 Military Program, ibid Baggett **Who's Who in Douglas County**; ibid Davis, **Douglas County Indian Trails,** pages 483-484. Ritha Carnes affidavit for a pension; Research by Greg Dansby.

Chapter 4—Early Land Lots Acquired
Photo: 1847 Map of the State of Georgia. Compiled under the direction of His Excellency, George W. Crawford. 1993, Gladys Palmer Hobgood Camp and Judge Thomas Lee Camp, **Old Campbell, Georgia Land Records 1828-1854, Deed Books A, C, D, E.**, Wolf, Associates. Westmoreland, Joan Turbyfield, Roswell, Georgia

Chapter 5—1830 & 1840 Census Photo: The Civil War House, taken by John Bailey 2014, permission Harold Parr. <ancestry.com> Information taken from the Campbell County, 1830 & 1840 U. S. Federal Census Records.

Chapter 6—The Dark Corner Settlement
Photos; 1848 William Conner Letter. U. S. Postal Records. Photo of Dark Corner School; 1974, Adelaide McLarty, **McLarty Family of Kintyre, Scotland Mecklenburg County, N. C. and their Descendants,** Crabtree Press, Inc. found at the Douglas County Public Library, Fannie Mae Davis Special Collections Room.
Photo; Benson Store: Taken by John Bailey. Photo of M. B. Watson & Lillie; ibid, Davis, **Indian Trails,** p. 18. Photo; Bates family: ibid **Who Was Who,** Vol 1, p. 335. Photo; Campbell County 1870, U. S. Federal Census. Text: www.archives.gov Post Office Records. U. S. Postal History, National Archives Microfilm Publication, M1126 Reel 102 & 103, Post Office Department of Records of Site Locations 1837-1950, Campbellton County, Georgia. National Archives Microfilm Publications M-841, Record of Appointments of Postmasters, 1832 - Sept. 30 1971, Campbellton County, Georgia. <www.archives.gov/research/post-offices/> Records of Postmaster Appointment <www.connerprarie.org> Interactive History Park: The Early Postal System. Richard Argo, North Georgia Journal of History, Volume 6 Issue 2, page 63 - 65, ***Shedding A Little Light On A Dark Corner In Douglas County.***

Anderson; King - ibid Baggett; **Who Was Who**, Vol. 1, p. 11-12, Federal Census Records <ancestry.com>

McLarty - ibid **McLarty Family of Kintyre,** <ancestry.com> public member trees; Federal Census Records. McLarty Family History, courtesy Sandy Whittington.

Bates ibid **McLarty Family of Kintyre**; pages 85. <ancestry.com> Federal Census Records, Douglas County, Georgia; ibid Davis, **Indian Trails,** page 301,

Watson - ibid Baggett, **Who Was Who,** Vol. II pages 292-294; <ancestry.com> Federal Census Records. ibid **McLarty Family of Kintyre,** p. 107-108.

Dark Corner School - ibid North Georgia Journal; 1854 & 1855 Dark Corner School Class Roll photocopied from a copy found at the Douglas County Public Library, Fannie Mae Davis Special Collection Room.

The Brush Arbor - *The History of Douglasville First United Methodist Church,* Douglas County Public Library Fannie Mae Davis Special Collection Room. ibid Davis, **Indian Trails to I-20**; ibid Camp, **Old Campbell County, Georgia, Land Records 1828-1854**. Book E, page 498. 1987, Argo, Richard, An Historical Paper, **Dark Corner Days**; University of West Georgia, Special Collection Room, Folder # 28.

Chapter 7—Property Tax Digest - 1855 GMD #730

Georgia, Property Tax Digest, Campbell County, Georgia, Militia District #730, Section 2, District 5, Dark Corner, 1855, <ancestry.com>

Chapter 8—From The Cornfield to the Battlefield

Caption: **Haisten's Trunk, Letters Written from Civil War Encampments,** Robbie Stephens Rogers, Dianne R. Byrd. Photo: Private Young, courtesy Ed Thompson. Photo: Two Hildebrand Brothers: Taken by John Bailey, permission, Johnny Camp. 1977, Compiled by Cleo Twilley Willoughby, **The Willoughbys,** White Wing Publishing House, Cleveland, Tennessee, p. 330. 1912, A. P. Adamson, **Brief History of the Thirtieth Georgia Regiment**, pages 79-85, The Mills Publishing Company, Griffin, Georgia. The 1866 Georgia Property Tax Digest for Campbell County. 1891, ***The War of the Rebellion: A Compilation of the Official Records of the Union and Confederate Armies***, GPO Washington, D. C. Davis, Major George B., Mr. Leslie J. Perry and Mr. Joseph W. Kirkley, Board of Publication; This is in seven parts of a 170 volumes of the official papers of both armies.

Chapter 9—The Civil War Comes to Dark Corner

to: Civil War Troops/Ferry www.archives.gov. Photo: Iverson, http://en.wikipedia. 'widi/alfred_Iverson,_jr.; Photo: Adams, http://en.wikipedia.org/wiki/silas_Ad- ;; Photo: Wolford http://en,wikipedia.org/wiki/Frank_Lane_Wolfod. Photo: Union :ampment in Atlanta: freepages.genealogy.rootsweb.ancestry.com, Yankee Occu- ion of Atlanta, Sept - Nov 1864. The Library of Congress. Three Fannie Hardgrove son photos and a letter to her, from David Clopton: University of West Georgia, ram Library, Special Collections Room, Ann Belle Weaver Collection, Bright :dgrove Family Papers, Folder # 28 Dark Corner, Folder # 17, Photographs. Photo: ion Army - Rootsweb, Atlanta during the Civil War Photographs. ibid 1891, ***The r of the Rebellion: A Compilation of the Official Records of the Union and nfederate Armies***, Research on Official Records of Cobb County and Dark Cor- , courtesy Jeff Jerkins; Seven Springs Museum, Powder Springs, Georgia. 2013 nderson, Ray, ***The 100 Day War,*** Lillium Press, Douglasville, Ga. 1971, E. B. Long :h Barbara Long, ***The Civil War Day by Day Almanac, 1861-65***, Doubleday & mpany Inc. New York. 1998, Hartley, Chris, article in ***Civil War Magazine***. <an- stry.com> 1864 ***Census for Re-Organizing the Georgia Militia, Campbell County,*** 30th Militia District, compiled by Nancy J. Connell. ibid ***North Georgia Journal***, ges 76 & 77. 1986, Shelby Foote, ***The Civil War A Narrative Red River to Appo- ıttox,*** Vintage Books, A Division of Random House, New York, page 40. 1994, ***The vil War Book of Lists***, Compiled by editors of Combined Books, Conshohocken, nnsylvania. Civil War Documents found at the Seven Springs Museum, Powder rings, Georgia.

hapter 10—Freedmen

ıoto: O. O. Howard, http://en.wikipedia.org/wiki/Oliver_O._Howard. by Matthew :ady. Georgia Property Tax Digest, Campbell County for years 1866, 1867, 1868, 369, and 1870.

hapter 11—Voters & Reconstruction Oath

ancestry.com> Georgia, Returns of Qualified Voters & Reconstruction Oath Books, 367 - 1869, pages 19 - 22; Fold3 Historical Military Records.

hapter 12—Southern Claims Commission - Fold3 Historical Military Records: ampbell County, Carroll County and Douglas County, March 1871.

Chapter 13—Pioneer Families

Photo: Corncrib, taken by John Bailey, 2014. Enterkin Photo: courtesy Billie Lee and Alyce Dodson King. Photo: McLarty daughter/granddaughter, courtesy Sandy Whittington. Photo: McLarty/Vansant, courtesy, Sandy Whittington. Photo: James A. McLarty family, courtesy Dianne McLarty. Photo: G. W. McLarty home, ibid: **McLarty Family of Kintyre.** Photo: Ezekiel Polk from original, courtesy Elaine Steere. Photo: Winn family, Douglas County Public Library, Fannie Mae Davis Special Collections Room.

Baggett: ibid Baggett, **Who Was Who,** Volume I, p. 19-21; <ancestry.com> Public Member Trees, Federal Census Records; ibid, Fold3; **Roster of the Confederate Soldier, 1861-65**, Vol. C, page 535; Georgia Marriages to 1850. Find A Grave.

Benson: ibid Baggett, **Who Was Who**, Vol I p. 24; <ancestry.com> Public Member Trees and Census Records. Benson Family Genealogy, courtesy Jim & Alma Benson.

Endsley: ibid Baggett, **Who Was Who,** Vol 1, p. 91**:** ancestry.com; Federal Census Records; Public Member Trees; Endsley Family. ibid **Roster of the Confederate Soldiers,** Vol. 3 p. 537; Vol 5: p 840. 1855 Georgia Property Tax Digest.

Enterkin: ibid Baggett, **Who Was Who**, Vol I, p 92-94; ancestry.com; Enterkin family history.

Hartsfield: ancestry.com, public member trees, U. S. Federal Census Records, 1855, Georgia Property Tax Digest. The Hartsfield family genealogy.

Maxwell: 2003, Douglas County Genealogical Society, Inc. and County Heritage, Inc. **The Heritage of Douglas County Georgia 1870 - 2002,** p. 156, submitted by Neil McKelvey, permission to use, The Douglas County Genealogical Society. ibid Baggett, **Who Was Who**, Vol. II page 199. <ancestry.com>; <familytreemaker.com> 1850 & 1860 U. S. Federal Census, Campbell County, Family of Dr. E. W. Maxwell.

McGouirk: <ancestry.com> family member trees; U. S. Federal Census Records; . Family genealogy courtesy, Tommy Brookshire.

McKelvey: <ancestry.com> Federal Census Records; ibid Baggett **Who Was Who**, Vol. I, page 187. Georgia Property Tax Digest.

McLarty: ibid **McLarty Family of Kintyre**; McLarty Family History, courtesy Sandy Whittington

Morris: 2001**,** Morris Family Compiled by Joe Baggett, Douglasville, GA. 1974, ibid **McLarty Family of Kintyre**; www.rootsweb.ancestry.com.

Polk: Find A Grave, ancestry.com, Public Member Trees; U. S. Federal Census Re-

ords. ibid Davis, **Indian Trails,** Genealogy.com; Fold3, Historical Military Records.
itha Carnes affidavit for a pension. Research by Greg Dansby.
ewell: ancestry.com; Federal Census Records; Sewell Family Data Collections.
outhern Claims Commission, 1871. 1859 letter from George Lowery
tewart: ibid Baggett, **Who Was Who,** Vol II pages 260-261; ancestry.com; Census ecords; Stewart Family Genealogy. ibid **Roster of the Confederate Soldiers. The eritage of Douglas County Georgia 1870 - 2002,** p. 156, submitted by Neil McK-lvey, permission to use, The Douglas County Genealogical Society
trickland: ibid Baggett, **Who Was Who,** Vol II pages 265 & 267.
Winn: Descendants of John Wynn/Winn; <http://genforum.genealogy.com/ga/camp-ell/messages/137.html> posted by Joe Baggett; June 12, 2001. **Roster of the Con-federate Soldiers, Book 3, pages 542-543.**

Chapter 14—More Pioneer Families
Photo, Brown, courtesy Sandy Lewis Whittington; Photo, Camp, courtesy, John Camp; Photo, Darnell, courtesy Darnell family; Photo Dorris, courtesy Marclyn Martin; Photo, Hawkins, courtesy Greg Dansby; Photo, Tobe McLarty, courtesy Fred Sparks, Photoshop restoration, Elaine Bailey; Photo, Hildebrand, courtesy Sandy Lewis Whittington; Photo, McElreath, courtesy McElreath family; Photo, Miles family, courtesy Alyce Dodson King; photo Rice/Enterkin, courtesy Mildred Thompson; Photo, Roach, courtesy Debra Munn; Photo Murdoc/McLarty, courtesy Nancy Huckeba (Engling); Photo, Thompson, courtesy, Ed Thompson; Photo, Wal-drop, courtesy, Allen Waldrop; Photos, Moses and Jane White, courtesy Debra Mann; Photo, Weddington, courtesy Debra Munn; Photos, Willoughby, from **The Willough-bys;** Photo, vial of Mercury, courtesy Ed Thompson.
Brittain: ibid **The Willoughbys,** p. 330; Brittain Family Genealogy, in possession of Alyce Dodson King; <ancestry.com> U. S. Federal Census Records, Social Security Death Records.
Brown: Brown Genealogy, Sandy Lewis Whittington, ancestry.com, Public Member Trees, U. S. Federal Census Records. ibid **Roster of Confederate Soldiers,** 5:904.
Camp: Camp family history, courtesy, Johnny, Doug, and Tommy Camp.
Carnes: 2003, Douglas County Genealogical Society, Inc and County Heritage, Inc. **The Heritage of Douglas County Georgia 1870-2002,** page 56, article #140, by Dr. Donald Carnes, Submitted by Diane Carnes Connally. Peter Carnes Family History,

courtesy, Greg Dansby, great-great-grandson of Peter Carnes.

Darnell: <ancestry.com> Tape recording by Roy Black, Interview with Francis Williams. ancestry.com - Public Member Trees.

Dorris: Dorris family Genealogy in possession of Alyce Dodson King, <ancestry.com: U. S. Federal Census Records, Find-A-Grave.

Hawkins: Hawkins Family Genealogy, courtesy Greg Dansby; ibid **Roster of the Confederate Soldiers,** book 1:54, book 4:701; Federal Census Records.

Hightower: ibid **McLarty Family of Kintyre,** p. 829-830; <ancestry.com> 1850 & 1860 Federal Census Records. **Roster of the Confederate,** book 4:388.

Hildebrand: <ancestry.com> 1860 Federal Census, Georgia, Property Tax Digests - 1847; Baggett, **Who Was Who**, Vol I page 129; **The Hildebrand Family of Douglas County,** Sandra Lewis Whittington. **Hildebrand Family Genealogy,** courtesy, Linda Willoughby Leatherman. ibid **Roster of the Confederate Soldiers** Books: 3:538; 5:903.

Keaton: ibid Baggett, **Who Was Who,** Vol 1, page 148-149; Keaton Family Genealogy courtesy, Herman"Billy" Keaton.

Kennedy: Kennedy Family History, courtesy Sam Henley. ibid **The Willoughbys,** p. 331. ibid Baggett, **Who Was Who**, Vol I, pages 149-150.

Mann: 1850 & 1860 Federal Census Records; Carroll County marriage Book C1, Page 11; Mann family genealogy courtesy Linda Willoughby Leatherman. ibid **Roster of the Confederate Soldiers,** Book 5:903.

McElreath: ibid Baggett, **Who Was Who,** Vol I pages 181-182; ancestry.com, Public Member Trees, Federal Census Records; Find-a-Grave; Fold 3, ibid **Roster of the Confederate Soldiers,** Vol 5:841.

Miles: ibid, Baggett, **Who was Who,** Vol. I, page 201; <ancestry.com> U. S. Federal Census Records; Enterkin Family Genealogy, Miles Family Genealogy courtesy Alyce Dodson King.

Nalley: <ancestry.com> U. S. Federal Census Records. Baggett, ibid **Who Was Who**, page 217.

Polk, Peter: ibid Davis, **Indian Trails**, page 540-541. Polk Family History, research of Greg Dansby.

Rice: Rice Family Genealogy, Ed Thompson, Mildred Thompson;

Roach: ibid Baggett, **Who Was Who,** Vol II, page 242, Debra Munn Adopted Family

Genealogy. ancestry.com, Family Member Trees, U. S. Census Records.
Stanley: Murdoc/Stanley Family genealogy, Nancy Huckeba. U. S. Federal Census Records.
Thompson: Thompson Family Genealogy; Ed Thompson, Mildred Thompson U. S. Federal Census Records, Fold 3 military program. .
Waldrop: ibid Baggett, **Who Was Who,** pages 286-287; **Roster of Confederate Soldiers**; 2:759; ancestry.com, Public Member Trees; U. S. Federal Census Records. 2003, Douglas County Genealogical Society, Inc. and County Heritage, Inc. ***The Heritage of Douglas County Georgia 1870 - 2002,*** page 230 by Allen Taylor Waldrop. Waldrop family History, courtesy, Allen Waldrop.
Weddington: Baggett **Who Was Who**, Vol II page ; <ancestry.com> Family Member Trees and Federal Census Records. Find A Grave, Research by Greg Dansby.
Willoughby:1977, ibid **The Willoughbys**, pages 369-417. Family genealogy, courtesy Linda Willoughby Leatherman.
Young: Young Family Genealogy, courtesy Ed Thompson and Mildred Thompson. ibid Baggett, **Who Was Who**, Vol. II, p. 318; Census Records; Fold 3; Find A Grave.

Chapter 15—Dark Corner Fades into History
Map: Dark Corner 1928 school, Douglas County Surveyor's Department, Courtesy, Carl Lewis. Photo, Francis Williams, courtesy Mrs. Williams. Photo, Bertie Lee, taken by John Bailey. Photo, Railroad Crew, courtesy, Mildred Thompson.
2001, July 10, <genforum.genealogy.com/ga/douglas/messages/101.html> Douglas County History, posted by Joe Baggett. ibid; Davis, **Indian Trails**, page 301.

Chapter 16 - Journal of A. N. McLarty
Photo of A. N. McLarty's home: ibid **The McLarty Family of Kintyre.** Photo: artifacts, found at the site of the Dark Corner Settlement by John Bailey while metal-detecting. Photo: The Bullard-Henley-Sprayberry House, taken in 2014 by John Bailey. Photo: Grubbing Hoe, head of hoe found while metal detecting in the settlement site of Dark Corner, handle added. Hoe and photo by John Bailey. Photo: Ferry crossing, www.archives.gov. Photo: Drawing of the Old Courthouse in Campbellton, found at the Campbell County Courthouse in Fairburn, courtesy Nancy Connell. Text: www.rootsweb.ancestry.com/~gaCampb2/People.htm
The U. S. GenWeb Project GaGenWeb Campbell County, Con-

tributed by Sandy Whittington.

Appendix A—Cemeteries in the Dark Corner Area

Photo: Tombstone of Mary Wilson McLarty, mother of Archibald Newton McLarty, courtesy of Sandy Lewis Whittington. Campbell County GAGenWeb

Ephesus Church Cemetery and Douglasville City Cemetery - Find-A-Grave.

The Georgia Project of US GenWeb Campbell County Cemeteries:

Benson Cemetery: Surveyed by Joe Baggett in 1982.

Baggett Cemetery: <http://www.rootsweb.ancestry.com/~gacampb2/Cemeteries/Baggett.htm> Submitted by B. Roger Smith.

Enterkin Cemetery: Submitted by Sandy Whittington.

Enterkin-Winn Cemetery: ibid Campbell County; Surveyed by Joe Baggett in 1977 and cleaned and re-surveyed by Douglas County Cemetery Preservation Commission in 2001.

Hildebrand Cemetery: Surveyed by Sandy Whittington.

Kennedy-Brittain Cemetery: ibid Rootsweb: Submitted by Sandy Whittington.

Leathers Cemetery: ibid Rootsweb.

McLarty Cemetery: ibid: Surveyed by Sandy Whittington.

Polk Cemetery: ibid Rootsweb: Submitted by Sandy Whittington.

Winn-Watson Cemetery: ibid Rootsweb: Submitted by Sandy Whittington.

Appendix B —Huey Civil War Letters, Robert Nix, Huey Family Collection.

Interviews with:

Earl Albertson, Richard Argo, Carolyn Bell, Billie and Donald Brittain, John Camp, Lisa Cooper, Nancy Connell, Martha Elizabeth Cole, Charlie Dodson, Greg Dansby; Johnny Fernander, E. F. Griggs, Harry Hay, Sam Henley, Nancy Huckeba (Engling), Alyce Dodson King, Bertie Enterkin Lee, Billie Lee, Harold Parr, Suzanne Sammons, Fred Sparks, Elaine Steere, Ed Thompson, Mildred Thompson, Pat Usry, Myra Wade, Tommy and Allen Waldrop, Sandy Whittington, Francis Williams, and Linda Willoughby Leatherman.

Index

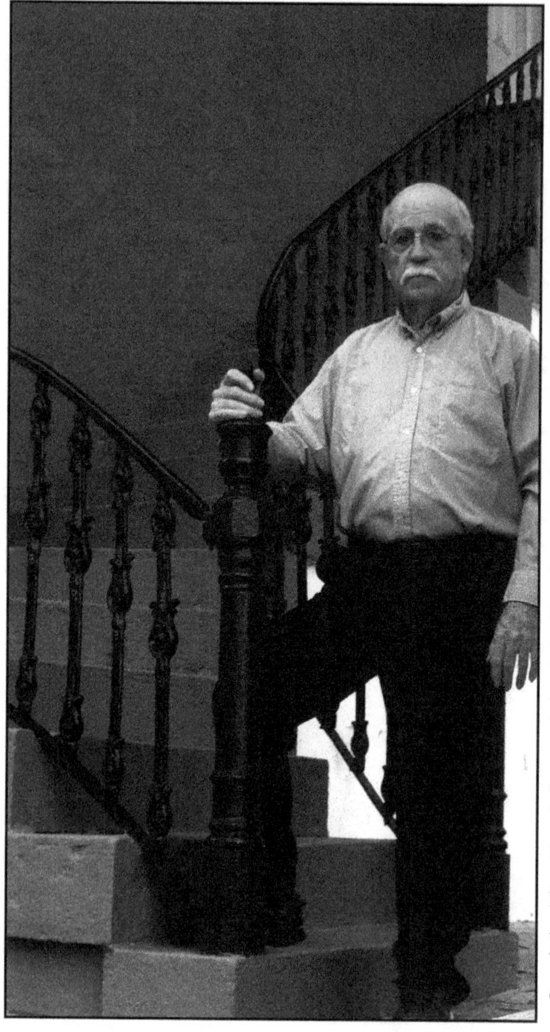

Author at the Campbell County Courthouse In Fairburn, Georgia.

John Bailey was born in Charleston, South Carolina, moved to Georgia when he was twelve, graduated from Villa Rica High School and attended West Georgia College. He is married to Elaine, has two children, a son-in-law, and two grandchildren.

John has been published in ***The Civil War Times, The Virginia Country Magazine*** and ***Military Images***. He was the Historical Editor of ***Looking Good Douglas County,*** magazine. John has spoken to groups on the Civil War and Native American History for over thirty years.

He volunteers at the Villa Rica Gold Mine Museum, giving tours and demonstrating gold panning. He demonstrates flint napping at festivals and events. His hobbies are making arrowheads, metal detecting and reading Civil War History.

Printed in the USA
CPSIA information can be obtained
at www.ICGtesting.com
LVHW080719300424
778807LV00013B/206

9 780692 240564